From Society to Nature

A Study of Doris Lessing's
Children of Violence

BY

INGRID HOLMQUIST

Inaugural dissertation by due permission of
the Philological Section of the Arts Faculty
of Göteborg University to be publically examined
in English at the Department of English,
Lundgrensgatan 7, Room 237, on May 31st, 1980, at 10 a.m.,
for the degree Doctor of Philosophy

For an Abstract of the thesis, see overleaf.

Minab, Surte 1980

Abstract

Holmquist, I. 1980. From Society to Nature: A Study of Doris Lessing's *Children of Violence*. *Gothenburg Studies in English 47.* 219 pp. ISBN 91-7346-083-4.

This study deals with shifts of consciousness in Doris Lessing's *Children of Violence.* Two ideological positions can be noticed in particular: schematically, *Martha Quest* through *A Ripple from the Storm* are characterized by a socialistically oriented criticism of society, whereas *Landlocked*, and more clearly *The Four-Gated City,* are marked by a form of mysticism, which presents an expansion or evolution of the human psyche as a solution to social and cultural problems.

This work demonstrates that the ideological change, which at first sight seems quite abrupt, is prepared for by certain ambiguities or tensions which pervade the earlier volumes of the series. Because of the Bildungsroman character of the series, the analysis follows the heroine, Martha, in her search for identity and shows that her relationship to reality is filtered through two different forms of consciousness, one called social or sociological, and another termed nature versus culture.

In the first three books the social thinking in terms of roles, class, and institutions conflicts with the nature-culture approach which emphasizes instinctive, unconscious, and elemental forces. There are also different evaluations of feeling and intellect, intuitive and analytical approaches to experience. These tensions are largely dissolved in the last two novels which are distinguished by a general biological or metaphysical view of mankind with priority given to irrational modes of perception.

The female perspective which informs the two modes of consciousness is explored. The tensions within the earlier novels are particularly apparent in the ambiguous image of Martha's identity as a woman. What has been called the social female consciousness appears in Martha's struggle against the family. The family generates a passive, potentially masochistic womanhood which must be overcome in order for Martha to develop an authentic identity. The perspective of biological female consciousness, on the other hand, considers femininity to be the central and creative part of Martha's self: womanhood represents a life-giving principle in opposition to destructive, male-dominated culture.

The thesis argues that the latter perspective provides a starting-point for the mysticism of *Children of Violence.* The tensions within the earlier novels can, however, also be related to Lessing's intellectual background, to a conflict between Marxism and depth psychology. For the fully developed mysticism of *The Four-Gated City,* the Sufi mysticism of Idries Shah appears to be the major source of inspiration. Lessing's final transition from social radicalism to mysticism is intimately connected with the political climate of the late 1950's.

The first three chapters treat *Children of Violence* as a self-contained unit, whereas in the final chapter an attempt is made to give an overview of the female and general social concerns in Lessing's work. A Survey of Research, mainly devoted to unprinted dissertations, is also included.

Key words: Doris Lessing, *Children of Violence,* female perspective.

ACTA UNIVERSITATIS GOTHOBURGENSIS
Box 5096
S–402 22 Göteborg 5
Sweden

ACTA UNIVERSITATIS GOTHOBURGENSIS

GOTHENBURG STUDIES IN ENGLISH 47

From Society to Nature
A Study of Doris Lessing's
Children of Violence

BY
INGRID HOLMQUIST

ACTA UNIVERSITATIS GOTHOBURGENSIS
GÖTEBORG SWEDEN

ISBN 91-7346-083-4
ISSN 0072-503X

Distributors:
ACTA UNIVERSITATIS GOTHOBURGENSIS
Box 5096
S–402 22 Göteborg 5

Printed in Sweden by Minab, Surte 1980

Acknowledgments

I wish to thank my supervisor, Docent Monica Lauritzen,
for the expert advice and personal support I have enjoyed
during the writing of this work.

My thanks are also due to Professor Erik Frykman
for his careful reading of my manuscript, and to my fellow
students, Ronald Paul and Ms. Jan Ring, who both read the
whole thesis, revised its language and helped me in
innumerable ways.

Outside the English Department I am especially
indebted to Docent Mats Furberg of the Philosophy Department, who has given me invaluable critical guidance and
kind, untiring encouragement throughout my work.

This study is dedicated to my mother, Britt Holmquist,
whose courage, generosity and sensitivity have provided me
with a source of inspiration in all my efforts.

February 1980, Ingrid Holmquist.

Abstract

Holmquist, I. 1980. From Society to Nature: A Study of Doris Lessing's *Children of Violence. Gothenburg Studies in English 47.* 219 pp. ISBN 91-7346-083-4.

This study deals with shifts of consciousness in Doris Lessing's *Children of Violence.*Two ideological positions can be noticed in particular: schematically, *Martha Quest* through *A Ripple from the Storm* are characterized by a socialistically oriented criticism of society, whereas *Landlocked,* and more clearly *The Four-Gated City,* are marked by a form of mysticism, which presents an expansion or evolution of the human psyche as a solution to social and cultural problems.

This work demonstrates that the ideological change, which at first sight seems quite abrupt, is prepared for by certain ambiguities or tensions which pervade the earlier volumes of the series. Because of the Bildungsroman character of the series, the analysis follows the heroine, Martha, in her search for identity and shows that her relationship to reality is filtered through two different forms of consciousness, one called social or sociological, and another termed nature versus culture.

In the first three books the social thinking in terms of roles, class, and institutions conflicts with the nature-culture approach which emphasizes instinctive, unconscious, and elemental forces. There are also different evaluations of feeling and intellect, intuitive and analytical approaches to experience. These tensions are largely dissolved in the last two novels which are distinguished by a general biological or metaphysical view of mankind with priority given to irrational modes of perception.

The female perspective which informs the two modes of consciousness is explored. The tensions within the earlier novels are particularly apparent in the ambiguous image of Martha's identity as a woman. What has been called the social female consciousness appears in Martha's struggle against the family. The family generates a passive, potentially masochistic womanhood which must be overcome in order for Martha to develop an authentic identity. The perspective of biological female consciousness, on the other hand, considers femininity to be the central and creative part of Martha's self: womanhood represents a life-giving principle in opposition to destructive, male-dominated culture.

The thesis argues that the latter perspective provides a starting-point for the mysticism of *Children of Violence.*The tensions within the earlier novels can, however, also be related to Lessing's intellectual background, to a conflict between Marxism and depth psychology. For the fully developed mysticism of *The Four-Gated City,* the Sufi mysticism of Idries Shah appears to be the major source of inspiration. Lessing's final transition from social radicalism to mysticism is intimately connected with the political climate of the late 1950's.

The first three chapters treat *Children of Violence* as a self-contained unit, whereas in the final chapter an attempt is made to give an overview of the female and general social concerns in Lessing's work. A Survey of Research, mainly devoted to unprinted dissertations, is also included.

Key words: Doris Lessing, *Children of Violence,* female perspective.

ACTA UNIVERSITATIS GOTHOBURGENSIS
Box 5096
S–402 22 Göteborg 5
Sweden

Table of Contents

Abbreviations Used

MQ	*Martha Quest*
PM	*A Proper Marriage*
RS	*A Ripple from the Storm*
LL	*Landlocked*
FGC	*The Four-Gated City*
GH	*Going Home*
GN	*The Golden Notebook*
Briefing	*Briefing for a Descent into Hell*
Summer	*The Summer Before the Dark*
Memoirs	*The Memoirs of a Survivor*

Introduction

Doris Lessing's *Children of Violence* is a "Bildungsroman"[1]
in five volumes,[2] which centres on a woman, Martha Quest,
and her relationship to reality. The first four books take
place during the 30's and 40's and describe Martha's life
in a colonial African society which Doris Lessing calls
Zambesia. In the initial volume, *Martha Quest*, Martha is a
rebellious teenager, living first with her parents on their
farm, and later alone in the country's capital city where
she works in an office, and where she enjoys the attentions
of the city's young men. In *A Proper Marriage*, she is a
dissatisfied young woman, living in a traditional middle
class marriage, wife to a colonial civil servant, Douglas
Knowell, and mother of their daughter Caroline. Towards the
end of the book the marriage breaks up and Martha leaves her
husband and daughter and involves herself in a left-wing
political group in order to fight racism and find an alternative life style. Her life with "the group," as a political
activist and as wife to the communist Anton Hesse, is described in *A Ripple from the Storm*. This life ends with her
becoming politically disillusioned, and once more disappoint-
ed in marriage. In *Landlocked* Martha prepares herself for
taking leave of her life in Africa, at the same time as she
is immersed in a love affair with a political refugee,
Thomas Stern.

The final volume, *The Four-Gated City*, takes place in
post-war England. Martha at this point has ensconced herself
as a general help-mate in an English upper class family, the
Coldridge family. She functions as mother of the children in
the family, as secretary/adviser and lover of the male head
of the family, Mark, and as soul-mate to Mark's schizophrenic
wife, Lynda. Her existence with the Coldridges involves
Martha's reappraisal of her life as a woman. She also

continues the process of political re-orientation which she
began in *Landlocked*. From having been concerned with external
social change she becomes increasingly interested in inner
solutions to social and cultural problems. Particularly in
connection with Lynda she develops a form of mysticism,
concentrating on reaching an inner, all-encompassing and
total consciousness. This consciousness is presented as an
alternative to the external, partial and fragmenting consciousness which dominates social existence, and which has
destructive and violent consequences. *The Four-Gated City*
ends in a vision of the demise of the Western world, some-
time in the 1980's. The catastrophe, vaguely defined, is
caused by radioactivity or chemical warfare. It is related
in an appendix which moves the novel into the future, to
about the year 2000. In the appendix the reader discovers
an aged Martha, who has survived the catastrophe and lives
on an island off the coast of Scotland. Her life is taken
up with some children who have been born with the sort of
consciousness that she and Lynda struggled for. These
children are presented as a promise for mankind's ability
to develop and survive.

Many of Martha's experiences in the first three books
in the series have parallels in Doris Lessing's own life:
they could be read as covert autobiography. *Children of
Violence*'s autobiographical aspects will not be treated in
this dissertation; nevertheless a brief outline of Lessing's
life may serve as a point of reference for the reader.

Doris Lessing was born in Persia in 1919. Her parents
were British and her father worked in a bank. When she was
two years old the family moved to Rhodesia and supported
themselves by farming. Like her heroine, Doris Lessing was
brought up in the country and later supported herself through
various jobs in Salisbury until she moved to England in 1949.
Like Martha, Doris Lessing had been married twice and, also
like Märtha, her marriages seem to have been tied up with
definite phases of her life. Doris Lessing's first marriage
seems to have been a traditional one within a colonial
mileu, while her second, with Gottfried Lessing, was bound

up with her life as a communist in Africa. Doris Lessing
also had children: a girl and a boy in the first marriage,
whom she left upon divorcing their father; and a son from
the second marriage, whom she took with her to England.[3]

When Doris Lessing came to England she quickly
established herself as a writer, and with that the obvious
similarities between her life and Martha's come to an end.
In 1950 Lessing published her first novel, *The Grass Is
Singing*, and began an extensive and successful career as
a writer. Besides *Children of Violence* she has written
seven novels, several collections of short stories, a few
plays, two biographical narratives, a book on cats and a
book of poems. The works that have attracted most attention,
besides *Children of Violence*, are the novels *The Golden
Notebook* and *The Summer Before the Dark*.[4]

Children of Violence was written over a long period
of time: *Martha Quest* was published in 1952 and *The Four-
Gated City* in 1969. The series exhibits both formal and
ideological changes. There are shifts from book to book,
but two different ideological and literary positions can
be seen in particular: an "early" one, represented by
Martha Quest through *A Ripple from the Storm*, and a "late"
one, which is in evidence in *Landlocked* and *The Four-Gated
City*. My interest in the changes within *Children of Violence*
stems from my first reading of the series. *The Four-Gated
City* seemed to me not to agree with or correspond to the
other books. My impression had been that I had been reading
a realistic, socially engaged work about a woman who had
revolted against a bourgeois view of women and society.
I became confused and disturbed when in the last novel
I was confronted with a text charged with metaphysics and
symbolism, in which mysticism was offered as a solution to
social problems, and in which the main character had
adapted to those demands on her as a woman which she had
earlier tried to overcome. Conversations with others who
had read *Children of Violence* showed that my reactions
were not unique. This made me even more anxious to try to
discover what was actually involved in the series.

Closer study, partly of *Children of Violence* and partly
of Doris Lessing's life, gave certain leads in the perplex-
ing development of the work. I learned that Doris Lessing
had been an active communist during the 40's and 50's, had
left the Communist Party shortly after the Soviet intervention in Hungary in 1956,[5] and had subsequently developed an
interest in psychiatry and various esoteric studies, particularly in Islamic Sufi mysticism,[6] as propounded by
Idries Shah in several books published in the 60's and
early 70's.[7] The late 50's seem to have been a critical
time in Lessing's life from which she emerged with a sense
of an all-pervasive violence in human life and with a vision
of the future as cataclysmic. The solution to this plight
she no longer sees in socialism or in ordinary political
activity, but in a revolution of consciousness: like Martha
in *The Four-Gated City* Lessing has on several occasions
argued that in order to survive, human beings must overcome
the "compartmentalised" condition of their minds and develop
a new unified consciousness.[8]

Lessing's own development throws light on *Children of
Violence*, but gives neither a nuanced nor an exhaustive
image of the changes that occur in the series. The text
itself upon closer scrutiny turned out to be at once more
clarifying and complex. While Doris Lessing's personal
life confirmed my feelings about an abrupt ideological
break, the text refuted them. The movement towards
mysticism seemed to occur already in the earlier books as
an undercurrent. At the same time my experience of a de-
finitive re-orientation remained, which I would now locate
in *Landlocked*, not *The Four-Gated City*. A new "inward turning" attitude is clearly dominant in *Landlocked*, albeit
more developed philosophically in *The Four-Gated City* -
which is why at first glance one tends to connect the
change with the last novel. The chronology of the books also
makes it reasonable to see the first three novels as one
block and the two later as another. *Martha Quest*, *A Proper
Marriage*, and *A Ripple from the Storm* were published in
1952, 1954 and 1958 respectively. The series was then

discontinued until 1965 when *Landlocked* appeared, followed
by *The Four-Gated City* in 1969. Closer examination of the
texts also showed that this ideological development could
be associated with other problem areas than those suggested
above. Principally, the treatment of women showed itself to
be essential to the understanding of the texts.

In my study I will attempt to analyse the development
within *Children of Violence* by showing that Martha's relationship to reality is characterized through two different
outlooks which can be seen as expressions of two forms of
consciousness. Tensions between these modes of consciousness lead to a change from one outlook to another.

My analysis follows the portrayal of Martha's growth
and development, what I have called her search for identity
(see Ch. I, Sec. 1). The subject issues from the "Bildungsroman" character of the series and has been treated by
other researchers; it has also been recommended by Doris
Lessing herself: in one of her statements about *Children of
Violence* she remarks that the series deals with relations
between the individual and the collective.[9] Both Lessing
and her critics see the collective as society. For reasons
which are given in the first chapter I would delimit the
social collective to refer primarily to the family. Further,
I work with another collective concept, that of nature, for
nature as well as the family contains norms. Both the
family and nature make demands upon Martha, which are
collective in that they do not recognize her experience
of herself as an individual but emphasize her function as a
social and natural or biological entity.

My basic method is thematic; I trace the development
of consciousness in *Children of Violence* through the treatment of certain themes or thematic structures. The family
and nature can be called thematic structures since they
appear throughout the whole series and have a shifting
significance. To these main themes I connect others, for
example relations between mother and daughter, man and
woman, and relations between feelings and intellect, intuition and reflection, rationality and irrationality,

consciousness and unconsciousness. This thematic analysis
proceeds from Chapter I through Chapter III. In the fourth
and final chapter of the dissertation I interpret consciousness in *Children of Violence*, partly through comprehensive
text analysis and partly through relating that analysis to
various external phenomena: to other works of Doris Lessing
and her statements, to theories about women and society and
to various issues in politics and society.

In its main aspects my work is related to women's
studies. A major concern in my analysis of *Children of
Violence* is to trace its female perspective. This I do by
following Martha's development as a woman which I consider
central to the series. The tensions between the two forms
of consciousness which I have referred to above appear most
clearly in the presentation of Martha's female identity.
This is particularly true of the earlier novels; in them
interesting problems of women are articulated which for
various reasons take on a more abstract and generalized
character in the later books. What happens to the female
themes in *Landlocked* and *The Four-Gated City* is for me an
important part of delineating the development of consciousness in *Children of Violence*. My personal sympathy with the
point of view conveyed in the early books has perhaps
limited my perception of the later books. I have tried to
repair this by giving at the end of Chapter IV a "contemporary" reading of them, which to some extent revises my
earlier interpretations.

Finally, a few words about what I do not treat in the
dissertation. I do not give a formal analysis of *Children of
Violence* but examine its consciousness and its ideological
implications. The formal changes which accompany the development of consciousness in the texts have already been
thoroughly analysed by another critic, and consequently I
mention them only when relevant to my purpose. Neither is
my dissertation a study of *Children of Violence* as a
"Bildungsroman," even though mapping Martha's female
identity and the female perspective of the series could
be of interest for a study of a "female Bildungsroman."

There is also an explanation why I do not include *The Golden Notebook*. Doris Lessing wrote it during the long interim period between books of *Children of Violence* - it was published in 1962, between *A Ripple from the Storm* and *Landlocked*. *The Golden Notebook* contains the first signs of Lessing's ideological change, and in that sense it is relevant to my analysis. However, I have chosen to give only a summary examination of it (see Ch. IV, Sec. 2), because even if it demonstrates the transition from the early to the later attitudes in Doris Lessing's work, it does not reveal anything new about the development of consciousness in *Children of Violence*. *The Golden Notebook* also includes various themes not directly relevant to *Children of Violence*, such as the situation of art and artists, and it lacks themes which are very relevant, like the family. Also, *The Golden Notebook* is Doris Lessing's most discussed work; there is extensive material dealing with it, which is sufficient for my purpose.

Survey of Research

Doris Lessing is internationally known and the object of a
great deal of interest throughout the world. A complete
survey of the research carried out about her works is therefore beyond the scope of the present study. I have limited
myself to those dissertations which are available through
University Microfilms International, and to English and
American material as regards books and articles.

In 1974, when I began working with Doris Lessing's
works, a handful of dissertations about her had appeared.
In June, 1979, there were no less than 28. Two of these
have been published in book form and there is also a brief
presentation of Lessing by Dorothy Brewster in Twayne's
English Authors Series. In addition, there are numerous
articles on various aspects of her work. A special issue
on Lessing in *Contemporary Literature* in 1973 has been re-
issued in book form.

In this survey I shall concentrate on dissertations.
Articles, and books which treat Lessing together with
other writers, will only be brought up if they add important
aspects to her work. I have left out those dissertations
which exclusively examine formal matters and those which
do not bring up *Children of Violence*.

The most relevant dissertations for me are those that
discuss changes in Lessing's development, those that treat
her consciousness of women and those that focus their analysis on *Children of Violence*. None of these subject areas
are particularly prominent in Doris Lessing research.
Most critics cover large parts of her work but evidence most
interest in *The Golden Notebook*. They tend to see her
fiction as a unified whole, and they often slight the
female concerns in her writing.

Only three dissertations and a few articles concentrate

on *Children of Violence*. Of these I consider Dorothy Bergquist Wells's "The Unity of Doris Lessing's *Children of
Violence*," 1976, the most important since, despite its
title, the thesis takes as its point of departure the lack
of unity in *Children of Violence*. Wells underlines that
the novel series shows both formal and ideological changes.
Formally, the novels from *Martha Quest* through *A Ripple from
the Storm* can be characterized by a "straightforward
realism of surface" and by an "old-fashioned omniscient
point of view," while *Landlocked* and *The Four-Gated City*
reveal an experimental technique. Ideologically Doris
Lessing progresses from "rationalism" and "communism" to
"mysticism" and "psychology."[1] Furthermore, Wells points to
the break made by Doris Lessing in her creation of *Children
of Violence* and argues that *The Golden Notebook* anticipates
new directions within her work.

After Wells has presented the above arguments, she
makes a volte-face and declares that the aim of her study
is to show that *Children of Violence* has a basic "unifying
design,"[2] which is contained in the consistent thematic
concern with the relations between the individual and the
collective. Doris Lessing's view of mankind's social conditions changes during the writing of *Children of Violence*,
but her interest in the subject continues and functions as
an organizing principle in her work, which compensates for
the lack of continuity.

This assertion seems self-evident to me and hardly
deserves the major part of a dissertation to prove. That
Wells sees the relations between the individual and the
collective as nullifying the set of problems she earmarked
for herself can perhaps be explained by the fact that her
interest in *Children of Violence* seems to be primarily
formal. It is the aesthetic break in the novel series that
really bothers her, even though she notices the thematic
break. In my opinion the strength of Wells's dissertation
lies not in what she considers her main argument but in
her thorough analysis of the formal developments in *Children
of Violence*. These developments are striking and have been

noticed by critics before, e.g. Florence Howe,[3] but Wells
is the first to make these developments the subject of an
exhaustive analysis.

There is one other dissertation which concentrates on
ideological and formal shifts in Doris Lessing's writing:[4]
Karen A. Kildahl's "The Political and Apocalyptical Novels
of Doris Lessing: A Critical Study of *Children of Violence*,
The Golden Notebook, *Briefing for a Descent into Hell*,"
1974. This dissertation is more concerned with thematic
than formal elements but resembles Wells's in its evalua-
tion of the development of Lessing's work. Formally Kildahl divides the novels into "conventional" (*Children of
Violence*, I-IV), "experimental" (*The Golden Notebook*),
and "apocalyptic" (*The Four-Gated City*, *Briefing for a
Descent into Hell*).[5] She claims that philosophically "these
novels reflect an odyssey of thought that is of significance
for our times: broadly from a belief in the liberal, rational
assumption that a progressive and just society can be
achieved, to a vision of a nightmarish and disintegrating
society whose irrational members cannot avoid destruction.
More specifically, they document a journey from a hopeful
Marxist ethic to a vision of a supra-rational world."[6]

Although I agree with the general outline of Doris
Lessing's ideological development given by Wells and Kildahl, I find their analyses too sweeping and imprecise.
Kildahl seems to interpret Lessing's development from
vaguely modernist criteria: to her Lessing typifies modern
man/woman's loss of ideology and is loosely compared with
Dostoyevski, Hesse, Huxley and Koestler. Still, this shows
her ambition to set Lessing's work in a larger context, an
aim which is missing in Wells.

In Kildahl's as well as Wells's analysis of *Children
of Violence* the novel series falls too simply into two
parts without any overlap. Both critics recognize strains
of mysticism in the earlier books, without allowing it to
influence their analyses of them. Moreover, Kildahl makes
the mistake of seeing the first four books as a unity.

The two other dissertations which treat *Children of*

Violence exclusively represent the predominant trends within Lessing research which give little weight to changes in her work and treat her writing as a consistent whole. In "A Thematic Study of Doris Lessing's *Children of Violence*," 1971, Diane E. Sherwood Smith states, like Wells, that the fundamental thematic intention of the series is to demonstrate the individual's relationship to the collective. Smith's aim is to investigate how "plot, character, imagery and style" relate to that theme.[7] Smith's study was the first to deal with *Children of Violence* and offers many valuable insights into the series. The overall result, however, seems too clear-cut and schematic. In her examination of the plot, for instance, Smith discovers that Martha is dominated by group attitudes in the first four books but overcomes that domination in *The Four-Gated City*. According to Smith, in *Martha Quest* and *A Proper Marriage* the collective can clearly be defined as capitalism, and in *A Ripple from the Storm* and *Landlocked* as socialism. Martha's relationship to her parents and her first marriage represent her dependence on capitalism, while her second marriage represents her being bound to socialism.

This interpretation disregards Martha's adjustment to the collective in *The Four-Gated City*. Also, Smith's definition of the collective in terms of capitalism and socialism is problematic since in her analysis they are not given very substantial treatment. From her study it is unclear how Martha's family experiences connect with capitalism or socialism; Martha's relationship with her mother and her search for identity as a woman - thematic elements which are immediately connected with her experience of the family - for example fall outside Smith's analysis for the most part.

The schematic aspect of Smith's paper seems to stem from her having gained her pattern of analysis from Doris Lessing's essay, "The Small Personal Voice" rather than from direct study of the texts. In the introduction to her dissertation Smith cites a passage from the essay where Lessing rejects big finance and socialistic bureaucracy, affirming powers of individual responsibility and critical

thinking. Thus Smith discovers a model to characterize the
whole of *Children of Violence*. For Smith Doris Lessing's
critically thinking individual is Martha in *The Four-Gated
City*, liberated from the chains of capitalism and dreams
of socialism. This interpretation is based on an unhistor-
ical reading of both "The Small Personal Voice" and *Children
of Violence*. "The Small Personal Voice" was written in 1957;
it is a document of the time which is representative of the
earlier books in the series, but whose relationship to the
ideology which dominates the later books is problematic
(cf. Ch. IV, Sec. 6).

Schematic treatment of another kind occurs in Ellen
Cronan Rose's study "Doris Lessing's *Children of Violence*
as a Bildungsroman: An Eriksonian Analysis," 1974. As the
title suggests her study issues from Doris Lessing's
description of the novel series as a "Bildungsroman."
Cronan Rose claims that the theories of the psychologist
Erik H. Erikson are valid for an understanding of this
unconventional "Bildungsroman," where the heroine is
followed all the way through to her middle age. However,
Rose's dissertation is not primarily a study of genre,
but more of an analysis of the "case of Martha," i.e.
an exclusively psychological analysis, which, despite
interesting observations about Martha's character, contains
certain basic problems.

The connections between Erikson's and Lessing's view
of the relationship between the individual and society
are scarcely examined by Rose, which makes it unclear in
what ways his theories are relevant to *Children of
Violence*. Rose's dependence on Erikson leads her to
psychoanalyse Martha's personality in a more circum-
stantial way than the novels can support. Rose postulates
a basic psychological conflict in Martha, the origins of
which are attributed to her early childhood even though
it is not described in *Children of Violence*. According to
Rose, because of unsatisfactory primary contact with her
mother, Martha develops a schizoid personality type,
characterized by "ontological" insecurity and a passive,

adaptive "oral" relationship to reality.[8]

In her use of Erikson and her pronounced psychological interests, Rose stands somewhat outside the mainstream
of critics. Before I come to its chief representatives, I
find it appropriate to mention the first dissertations to
have been written on Doris Lessing:[9] Father Alfred A.
Carey's "Doris Lessing: The Search for Reality. A Study
of the Major Themes in her Novels," 1965, and Paul
Schlueter's "A Study of the Major Novels of Doris Lessing,"
1968. These theses were written before it was possible
to obtain a clear overview of the different phases of
Doris Lessing's work; Carey encompasses the novels up to
and including *The Golden Notebook*, Schlueter also includes
Landlocked. In 1973 Schlueter's thesis was published as a
book called *The Novels of Doris Lessing*. The book extends
his analysis to *The Four-Gated City* and *Briefing for a
Descent into Hell*, but it adds little to his former treatment of Lessing's work. Schlueter and Carey both establish
certain basic themes of Lessing, e.g. racial problems,
communism, relations between men and women; Carey also
deals with the conflict between generations and the situation of the writer. However, while Schlueter for the most
part relates the contents of the novels, Carey conducts a
detailed thematic analysis, which leads to an assertion
about Doris Lessing's world view. According to Carey,
Lessing dissociates herself from ideological systems
because she considers them defence mechanisms, and she
recommends instead an intuitive and instinctive relationship to the world.

After Schlueter and Carey the studies of Doris Lessing
become more synthetically orientated. The critics often
choose a theme or motifs which they deem fundamental and
which they trace through her writing. Examples of such
dissertations include Ellen W. Brooks, "Fragmentation and
Integration: A Study of Doris Lessing's Fiction," 1971;
Lois A. Marchino, "The Search for Self in the Novels of
Doris Lessing," 1972; Velma Fudge Grant, "The Quest for
Wholeness in Novels by Doris Lessing," 1974; Patricia Ann

Young Halliday, "The Pursuit of Wholeness in the Works of
Doris Lessing: Dualities, Multiplicities and the Resolu-
tion of Patterns in Illumination," 1973; and Mary Ann
Singleton, "The City and the Veld: A Study of the Fiction
of Doris Lessing," 1973. Slightly changed Singleton's
thesis was published as a book called *The City and the
Veld: The Fiction of Doris Lessing*, 1977.

These dissertations resemble each other a good deal.
They are all general in scope and survey the greater portion
of Doris Lessing's production. They emphasize a conflict
between fragmentation and wholeness, and they all understand Doris Lessing's work as an expression of an
integrated philosophy of life - which I think they make
easy for themselves by concentrating on her later works,
from *The Golden Notebook* onwards. The most illuminating
of all these works seem to me to be those of Brooks and
Singleton. Brooks was the first to especially examine
Lessing's contacts with depth psychology and Laing's
psychiatry; she has convincingly demonstrated Lessing's
dependence upon Jung, particularly in *The Golden Notebook*.
She was also the first to investigate Lessing's portrayal
of female consciousness, but mainly in *The Golden Notebook*.

Singleton treats Doris Lessing's work in relation
to two motifs which she calls the "city" and the "veld."
The "city" stands for a split, fragmented perception,
informed by reason and logic but lacking in "mythic"
consciousness. The "veld" represents the unity of nature,
but one in which the "individual counts for nothing."
The price of this unity is to be caught up in the "cease-
less round of natural repetition, all instinct with no
reason." According to Singleton, Lessing strives for a
synthesis of these motifs which Singleton calls the "ideal
City" or the "City in the veld." It symbolizes a unified
form of conciousness that contains "intuition along with
reason, both myth and logic, . . . a man-made harmony -
part of nature, yet at the same time separate from it.
. . ."[10] To underline her argument Singleton, like Brooks,
applies Jung's and Laing's theories to Lessing's work and

also shows influences of mysticism, notably of the Sufi mystics.

I find Singleton's approach enlightening; it confirms my own opinion that the relations between nature and culture, the conscious and the unconscious, the rational and the irrational are central to *Children of Violence*. However, I strongly disagree with Singleton's claim that Lessing's late novels demonstrate a synthetic and harmonious treatment of these themes.

Another dissertation which touches on questions similar to those dealt with by Brooks and Singleton is "The Irrational Element in Doris Lessing's Fiction," 1978, by Tamara Mitchell. Like Brooks, Mitchell focuses upon the continuous presence of mental breakdown, dreams and visions in Lessing's writing, and, like Singleton, she argues for Lessing's synthesis between rationality and irrationality. She sees Lessing's deepening interest in the irrational as an "accretion of levels and perspectives." According to Mitchell, Lessing "adds" a new "spiritual note" to the social and and psychological dimensions of her work.[11]

The inclination to see Doris Lessing's work as an expression of an integrated world view is also present in several dissertations which compare Doris Lessing's aesthetics and ethics with their fictional equivalents in her work. In "Vision and Nightmare: A Study of Doris Lessing's Novels," 1971, Noeline Elizabeth Alcorn asserts - from her reading of "The Small Personal Voice" - that Doris Lessing's literary credo can be characterized by "commitment," which is not bound to any ideological system but consists of a belief in humanity balanced between "vision" and "nightmare."[12] *Children of Violence* and *The Golden Notebook* contain the most synonymous transcriptions of that belief according to Alcorn. Alcorn, however, seems to me guilty of the same type of schematizing as Smith.

A more sophisticated attitude is shown by Sally Hickerson Johnson in her study "Form and Philosophy in the Novels of Doris Lessing," 1976. Like Alcorn, she begins

with Doris Lessing's "affirmative vision" in "The Small
Personal Voice,"[13] which she perceives as a result of
Lessing's contact with Marxism and as compatible with her
later interest in Sufism. Johnson touches upon the question
of an ideological change in Lessing, but then abandons it,
judging it relatively unimportant. Johnson views Doris
Lessing's Marxism as an expression of a "religious
impulse,"[14] hence the connections with Sufism. What she
in fact considers the central problem in Doris Lessing's
work is the tension between a belief in "essential goodness" and "fidelity to political realities," a tension
which can also be formulated as a conflict between a
"realist method" and "romantic content."[15] According to
Johnson, this tension exists in the Marxist aesthetic, but
in Doris Lessing it is reinforced by her propounding the
utopian mentality existing in Sufism. Johnson argues that
the central conflict can be traced in the "symbolic reso-
lution of conflicts" in *The Golden Notebook* and *The Summer
Before the Dark*, in the "ambiguous ending" of *The Four-Gated
City* and *The Memoirs of a Survivor*, and in "thematic
deflations" in *A Briefing for a Descent into Hell*.[16]

In "A Reconciliation of Opposites: A Study of the
Works of Doris Lessing," 1970, Selma Burkom finds that
Lessing's work reveals a similar conflict. Burkom maintains
that Lessing's technique can be described as realistic, but
her philosophy remains romantic and idealistic. Closer
examination of her texts shows that realism is modified
by symbolistic and archetypal aspects that annul the
conflict, which can thus be said to be superficial.

There are also two theses that concentrate on the
issue of determinism. In "Stages of Consciousness in Doris
Lessing's Fiction," 1977, Mary Elizabeth Draine claims that
the conflict between "fatalism" and "freedom" is the
organizing vision behind Doris Lessing's fictional world,[17]
and in "Repetition and Evolution: An Examination of Themes
and Structures in the Novels of Doris Lessing," 1978,
Susan K. Swan Sims asserts that Lessing's novels support
a view of reality as a "cyclical process."[18] Draine sees

the solution to Lessing's major dilemma in her characters'
consciousness of the conditions that have determined them.
She points to an evolutionary force in *Children of Violence*
which Martha cannot escape but which she can become
conscious of and act upon. Sims argues that Lessing's
novels reflect her growing assertion that human beings
can only avoid the imprisonment of the cyclical process
by examining and cultivating their interior lives. Like
Sims and Draine and other critics who have touched on the
question of determinism in Lessing's work, I consider it
to be a vital concern, which I discuss in Chapters III and
IV.

All of the dissertations examining Lessing's production
as a unified whole have, in various ways, increased the
understanding of her later works, especially those studies
which relate her texts to psychiatry, depth psychology and
romantic and idealist philosophy. These references are
also present in several articles which tend to confine
themselves to more limited aspects of her writing, e.g.
"Doris Lessing and Romanticism" by Michael L. Magie;
"Doris Lessing and R.D. Laing: Psychopolitics and Prophesy"
by Marion Vlastos; "The Sufi Teaching Story and Doris
Lessing" and "Doris Lessing and the Sufi Way" by Nancy S.
Hardin; and "The Sufi Quest" by Dee Seligman. Seligman's
article parallels a discussion of Doris Lessing's Sufism
in her dissertation "The Autobiographical Novels of Doris
Lessing," 1975, which generally has a biographical direc-
tion I find less constructive.

The drawback of the general trend of criticism lies
mainly in its emphasis on the "eternal" to the detriment
of the temporal. Lessing's metaphysical and religious
interests are stressed and the social depreciated, so
that her fiction loses its concreteness, its connections
with society, and seems too abstract and general. Burkom
gives perhaps the best example of a critic who totally
ignores what is not idealistic and romantic in Doris
Lessing, with the result that in her analysis Lessing
becomes far too unified and harmonious. As I have

indicated earlier this can also be said about Singleton and
Mitchell. The tendency to underline the religious aspect of
Doris Lessing is also present in Johnson's work. But she
also discusses the presence of other features in the texts
and captures their sense of tension and contradiction.

   With the exception of Ellen Brooks, the writers of the
dissertations mentioned above have not paid much attention
to Doris Lessing's representation of women. This subject is
studied in a number of works which highlight woman's consciousness as their main area of analysis. The earliest of
these is Agate N. Krouse's thesis "The Feminism of Doris
Lessing," 1972, which discusses whether Doris Lessing can
be considered feminist and if so what sort of feminism she
represents. Krouse differentiates between "explicit" and
"implicit" feminism[19] and concludes that Lessing's contribution to literary feminism must be placed within the
latter category. According to Krouse, Lessing shows little
interest in the discrimination of women in work, education
and politics, but she does give thorough analyses particularly of the destructive influence of the traditional
marriage on the female psyche.

   Krouse's main strength lies in this more precise definition of Doris Lessing's feminism, which is often taken for
granted by critics without close scrutiny. The weakness in
Krouse's paper seems to me to be that her method forces her
to devote too much attention to what she calls "explicit"
feminism, only to be able to prove that it is less interesting. Such categorization leads to a certain limitation; her
contribution consists of detailed examinations which prove
to be unintegrated with Lessing's overall views of the
world. Krouse disregards her ideological development, which
I believe is intimately connected with her consciousness of
what it is to be a woman. Because of this Krouse is unable
to understand her representation of women in the late works
and exposes her confusion about Martha's character in
The Four-Gated City.

   Another thesis dealing exclusively with Lessing's consciousness of women is "Twentieth-Century Woman in the Early

Novels of Doris Lessing," 1978, by Donna Joanne Walter. Walter is not interested in the question of Lessing's feminism and instead defines as her purpose to analyse Lessing's female perspective "by looking at the crucial physical and psychological components of female development and at the life priorities established by Doris Lessing's heroines." She also wants to identify "major philosophical and psychological influences on Lessing's developing representation of woman's consciousness."[20]

Walter sees the overriding problem of Lessing's heroines as a conflict between "Victorian norms" and "twentieth-century chaos." In *The Grass Is Singing* through *A Ripple from the Storm* women react to it in a psychologically "adolescent" manner, whereas in *The Golden Notebook* and *Landlocked* their attitude is "adult."[21] Walter's definition of the female dilemma seems to me quite vague and I disagree with her strictly psychological interpretation of Martha's development in terms of youth and adulthood. Through not dealing with *The Four-Gated City* Walter, like Krouse, misses vital aspects of Martha's female identity. Walter's reason for limiting herself to what she calls the early novels is that the later ones indicate new directions within Lessing's thought. Since Lessing's reorientation is first expressed in *The Golden Notebook* and *Landlocked*, works termed "early" by Walter, her division of Lessing's production seems quite arbitrary and undercuts her own argument for not dealing with the later novels. Walter finds Freud, Jung, Simone de Beauvoir and Marxist theory to be the shaping influences on Doris Lessing's creation of women. Although I agree with her choice of influences I am critical of her treatment of them as will be shown later.

Other critics who have written on Lessing's image of women have included her with other writers, mainly female. Sidney Janet Kaplan, in the book *Feminine Consciousness in the Modern British Novel*, 1975, investigates the ways in which the consciousness of women is structured in the novels of Dorothy Richardson, May Sinclair, Virginia Woolf

and Doris Lessing; Michele Wender Zak in her dissertation
"Feminism and the New Novel," 1973, relates influences from
a "feminine principle" on the work of George Eliot, Henry
James, Virginia Woolf and Doris Lessing;[22] and Lynn Sukenick,
in her dissertation "Sense and Sensibility in Women's
Fiction," 1974, analyses the theme her title suggests in
novels by George Eliot, Virginia Woolf, Anaïs Nin and Doris
Lessing. Suckenick's chapter on Lessing has been published
as an article in *Contemporary Literature*, 14 (1973). Finally,
there are the theses "Madness and Sexual Politics in the
Feminist Novel: Studies of Charlotte Brontë, Virginia
Woolf and Doris Lessing," 1977, and "From Sex-Role Identification Toward Androgyny: A Study of Major Works of
Simone de Beauvoir, Doris Lessing, and Christa Wolf,"
1978, the former by Barbara Hill Rigney and the latter
by Brigitte Wichmann.

The comparative approach of these theses is of less
interest to me, but the actual analyses of Doris Lessing
offer significant insights. This is especially true of the
theme feelings/intellect and intuitive/rational understanding. Through focusing on themes that I consider
important to the ideological development in *Children of
Violence* these studies are more pertinent to my major
concern than Krouse's and Walter's. Their broad approach,
however, makes them rather sketchy and leaves a great deal
to cover. Questions concerning the significance of the
family, such as the mother-daughter relationship, are not
investigated by these critics in any detail.

There are also a few less comprehensive studies of
Doris Lessing's consciousness of women which deserve mention.
Elayne A. Rapping in "Unfree Women: Feminism in Doris
Lessing's Novels," makes a productive analysis of *The Four-
Gated City*, and Alice Bradley Markow offers interesting
observations about "The Pathology of Feminine Failure in
the Fiction of Doris Lessing." The idea of feminine failure
in Lessing's work is also suggested by Patricia Meyer
Spacks who briefly discusses Lessing in *The Female
Imagination*.

Chapter I   The Background of Martha's Quest

1 Introduction

This chapter introduces thematic elements that are brought
out in Martha's quest for identity. It analyses her relationship to her parents, her early sense of self and her
first means of orientation towards reality. I use the term
identity to cover Martha's search for a personally and
socially satisfying sense of self.

My analysis concentrates on *Martha Quest*, although
material from later books, especially *A Proper Marriage*,
is also considered. However, my discussion of Martha's
parents attempts to give a general picture of them based
on information given throughout the series, since certain
aspects of their influence on Martha are better understood in that way.

Although my main interest is thematic, there is one
narrative element that ought to be mentioned. In *Martha
Quest* through *A Ripple from the Storm* there is an omniscient narrator whose main function appears to be to provide
a corrective to Martha's own perspective. This device is no
longer present in *Landlocked* and *The Four-Gated City* where
a correspondence seems to exist between the narrative
voice and Martha's.[1]

As I try to bring out the tensions and conflicts involved in Martha's search for identity, the corrective
function of the early narrator might be assumed to be of
great interest in the sense of being a potential guide to
"correct" interpretation. I have not found this to be the
case, however; instead the narrating voice itself seems to
be involved in the formulation of the conflicts. For this
reason I will not pay special attention to this voice
but simply refer to its narrative function.

2 *Children of 'Violence'*

The title *Children of Violence* suggests that violence is a
central influence on Martha's identity. However, what is
meant by violence is ambiguous. On the one hand it means
war. Martha is a child of World War I; she is born during
the war and both of her parents have experienced it, Mr.
Quest as a soldier and Mrs. Quest as a nurse. But violence
also refers to oppressive social conditions, both of the
society in which Martha grows up and that which is communicated to her through her parents, in particular her mother.
The pressures of society are primarily represented by the
institution of the family. Furthermore, as Martha lives in
a colonial society she is exposed to the effects of racism.
Children of Violence indicates certain correspondences
between racial and family relationships which make it
possible to see the racist system as a parallel to that
of the family (see Ch. II, Sec. 2.5). Still, as a direct
influence on Martha, racism appears to have less importance than the family.

I see Martha's confrontation with the family as her
crucial experience of violence in *Children of Violence*,
1-3, whereas war seems to be a fairly abstract entity
with regard to her development in these novels. In the
late books war is a major concern and there it is also
said to have been *the* formative influence on Martha (see
LL, p. 222). To my mind this presentation of her has
little foundation in the early part of the series.

3 Violence as Social Pressure

3.1 The Family

> She |Martha| could see a sequence of events, unalter-
> able, behind her, and stretching into the future.
> She saw her mother, a prim-faced Edwardian school-
> girl, confronting, - but in this case it was the
> Victorian father, the patriarchal father - with

> rebellion. She saw herself sitting where her mother
> now sat, a woman horribly metamorphosed, entirely
> dependent on her children for any interest in life,
> resented by them, and resenting them; opposite her
> a young woman of whom she could distinguish nothing
> clearly but a set, obstinate face. And beside these
> women, a series of shadowy dependent men, broken-
> willed and sick with compelled diseases. This the
> nightmare, this the nightmare of a class and genera-
> tion: repetition (PM, p. 124).

In this quotation the main social structures which influence the formation of Martha's identity are indicated.
Her parental family brings her in touch with bourgeois
demands on women[2] and with conflict-ridden, asymmetrical
relationships between parents and children and women and
men. These social structures are upheld through the institution of the family. Their reproduction is expressed by
the theme of the "nightmare" of "repetition" in the early
novels of *Children of Violence* (cf. MQ, p. 39; PM, p. 102;
RS, p. 66).

Martha's mother is the primary socializing agent
within her family. This is hinted at in the quotation above
which also suggests that within the family the woman can
reach a position of power vis-à-vis men and children. In
Children of Violence the mother is often presented as
destructive, something which can be explained through the
central role accorded to the woman as a socializing influence within the family. In spite of the fact that the
society depicted is patriarchal (see Ch. II, Secs. 2.2,
2.5), the mother rather than the father is presented as
the real threat to the children.[3]

3.2 The Mother

Mrs. Quest is presented as largely conditioned by her
middle class family background, by its social conventions
and pretensions, its bourgeois view of women as wives and
mothers only and its sexual puritanism. We are told that
Mrs. Quest had tried to rebel against her family by

acquiring a profession as a nurse. Her attempt at inde-
pendence had been ineffectual, however, and in *Martha
Quest* we meet her as a frustrated middle-aged woman living
a traditional married life, attempting to compensate for
her disappointments by domineering her family and especially her daughter Martha.

Mrs. Quest's dependence on her past is brought out
step by step throughout the novel series. In *Martha Quest*
we are made aware of the social pretensions of her class
background; for example, we are told that she was laughed
at when she first arrived in Africa because of her piano,
her expensive rugs, and her visiting cards (see MQ, p. 27).
In *A Proper Marriage* we learn about her rebellion as a
woman, how she had quarrelled with her patriarchal father,
"lived her own life" as a nurse and not married until
very late (PM, p. 125). Her fight with her father and her
decision to be a nurse instead of a "Victorian young lady"
are retold in *Landlocked* (LL, p. 76).

The early novels of the series implicitly explain
Mrs. Quest's unsuccessful rebellion against her family by
presenting a society within which the bourgeois notion of
woman's social function is dominant. In Mrs. Quest's as
well as in Martha's generation women are shown to be
bound by their functions as wives and mothers (see Ch. II,
Sec. 2.2). In this context Mrs. Quest's attempt to revolt
by becoming a nurse appears ironic in the sense that the
caring function which this job implies only seems to be
an extension of the demands put upon women in the family.
This aspect of her fate is more explicitly articulated in
the late novels: "her life had gone - nursing. She had
got her way, had fought her father who would not speak to
her for months, had won her battles. She had nursed - as
a young woman, then through the war, and then her husband.
. . . But never had she known 'beauty' " (LL, p. 77).

"Nursing" is here contrasted with "beauty" and these
two phenomena are presented as contrary aspects of womanhood: "nursing" is associated with the caring and nurturing qualities of woman's function as mother whereas

"beauty" is related to sexuality and to woman's role as lover. This contrast is also stressed in *The Four-Gated City*, where Mrs. Quest is presented as "Plain Jane" who had only one choice, namely who to marry, "before she became a mother, and a nurse and had no choice but to sacrifice herself" (FGC, pp. 282-283). Throughout the novels Mrs. Quest's sexual puritanism is presented as an important ingredient in her frustrated womanhood. Fear of sexuality is looked upon as a general characteristic of "the English puritan tradition" (MQ, p. 306). This tradition was communicated to Mrs. Quest through the norms of her family "whose chief virtue had been respectability, described as 'a sense of proportion', as 'healthy'" (LL, p. 76).

The conflict between "beauty" and "nursing" which is formulated in *Landlocked* can be said to characterize Mrs. Quest throughout the novels. In the last two novels this conflict is viewed as a primarily psychological problem rather than a social one, however. In the early books Mrs. Quest's female identity appears to be the result of the bourgeois education of women which was begun by her patriarchal father, whereas in *Landlocked* it seems to be caused by lack of love from her mother. This lack appears to make Mrs. Quest mentally fit for nursing only, a disposition strengthened by her surrounding world which defines her as "plain Jane" and a "good sort" and which expects her to fulfill traditional motherly functions (FGC, p. 280). Mrs. Quest's relationship to her mother is presented symbolically in her dream about her dead mother who gives her three red roses from "heaven" which in Mrs. Quest's hands turn into medicine bottles: "Medicine bottles, yes; that was her life, given her by a cruel and mocking mother" (LL, p. 77).[4]

In the first three novels Mrs. Quest on the surface seems to be a typical representative of her background with a harmonious rather than frustrated relationship to its attitudes in matters of class, race, sex and womanhood. For example, she wants to turn Martha into a nice

middle class girl and rid her of "silly ideas" about
politics (MQ, p. 82). She also wants Martha "properly"
married (MQ, p. 318) - that is, safely settled as wife
and mother in a respectable marriage. With regard to
Martha's roles as a woman, Mrs. Quest seems somewhat ambivalent. On the one hand she wants Martha to have a traditional married life, on the other, she expects her to
become a professional woman, to have a "career" (MQ, p.
14). This contradiction is only apparent, however, since
both aspirations spring from her middle class ambition of
respectability and social success: "Mrs. Quest used the
word 'career' not in terms of something that Martha might
actually do, such as doctoring, or the law, but as a kind
of stick to beat the world with . . ." (MQ, p. 14).

Nevertheless, Mrs. Quest's attitudes to her past and
present social reality are shown to be quite complex
already at this stage. We are made aware of a strong element of compensation in her adherence to middle class norms.
She tries to follow the traditions of her past almost to an
extreme: for example, she dreams of Martha as an English
debutante, although "her family had not by many degrees
reached that stage of *niceness* necessary to coming out
. . ." (MQ, p. 29). Mrs. Quest's compensatory attitude can
be viewed as a response to the social degradation which
she experiences as a farmer's wife in a colonial country,
but it can also be interpreted as an overly anxious and
guilty adjustment to norms she had once opposed. The
adherence to "niceness" which characterizes her aspirations
for Martha is one of the things she had rebelled against by
becoming a nurse, which "no real lady was, in spite of
Florence Nightingale" (LL, p. 76).

Mrs. Quest's overall attitude to the world appears to
be marked by a fundamental evasion of reality which on the
one hand is expressed through compensatory social ambitions
and on the other manifests itself in a stereotyped and
ritualized relationship to experience. Her thoughts and
feelings are expressed through clichés and set phrases;
she relates to her experiences in an "official" fashion

(FGC, p. 300). The connection between her "official" attitude and her relationship to the past is indicated in her
clashes with Martha and in her habitually aggressive attitudes towards what she sees as the freedom of the younger
generation. Her reactions to her daughter's resistance to
her ideas are so violent that they point to a struggle
against her former self: "Thoughts of Martha always filled
her with such violent and supplicating and angry emotions,
that she could not sustain them . . ." (MQ, p. 82).

The general characterization of Mrs. Quest indicates
that she has internalized the rigid social norms of her
background in an attempt to rationalize her unsuccessful
rebellion and to create a meaningful existence for herself.
Through adoption of the values of her oppressive past Mrs.
Quest acquires a more or less coherent view of life but at
the expense of a deep sense of guilt and alienation from
her authentic responses to her surroundings, which are
transmuted into authoritarianism. Guilt and authoritarianism
and stereotyped role patterns are important elements in the
treatment of the family in *Children of Violence*. They play
a vital part in the relationship between Mrs. Quest and
Martha as well as in other relationships between the generations in the novel sequence.

3.3 The Mother/Daughter Relationship

Through her relationship with her mother Martha acquires
certain patterns of reaction which determine to a large
extent her communication with other characters in the
novels. This psychological aspect of the mother-daughter
relationship is my focus of attention here, while its
social implications are less emphasized. The social ideals
which Mrs. Quest represents have already been dealt with
in the previous section and will be further discussed in
the next chapter. Still, it is important to remember that
the overall presentation of the relationship between
mother and daughter indicates that an oppressive and

hierarchical society is passed on from generation to generation through the institution of the family.

In her relationship with Martha, Mrs. Quest appears
to reproduce her own family situation. She had once submitted to the authority of her family and now her energies
become directed towards Martha's submission to her own
authority. Martha resists her, and their relationship
turns into a relentless struggle for power within which
their personal interaction takes on a twisted and perverted form. While Martha is still living on the farm
two incidents occur which are significant in this context,
namely the "pink eye" episode and the "battle of the
clothes."

When Martha is about to graduate from secondary
school in order to go to the university, she is afflicted
with a pink eye infection. Her eyesight is temporarily
affected and she is afraid of going blind, a fear which
she communicates to her mother by letter. Mrs. Quest
arrives at Martha's school in town and takes her daughter
to two oculists. One of them finds nothing wrong with
Martha's eyes, while the other is "patient" and "ironical"
and agrees with Mrs. Quest's idea that Martha's eyes are
damaged (MQ, p. 37). The narrator comments: "Curious that
Mrs. Quest, whose will for years had been directed towards
Martha distinguishing herself - curious that she should
accept those damaged eyes so easily, even insist that they
were permanently injured when Martha began to vacillate"
(MQ, p. 37). The outcome of this incident is that Martha
never graduates; instead of going to university she goes
back to her parents' farm where she is supposed to "rest
her eyes"; but she reads more than ever (MQ, p. 37).

Mrs. Quest's behaviour during the pink eye event seems
contradictory in the sense that she, rather than Martha, is
presented as actively promoting Martha's university studies.
However, since her real need is social and psychological
control of her daughter, her irrational behaviour is only
apparent. Mrs. Quest's actual choice of action during the
event may be explained by the interaction that takes place

between her and Martha. Martha's letters to her can be
interpreted as appeals, as admittance of emotional dependence. In the struggle between mother and daughter this
kind of plea is a sign of weakness, an acceptance of a submissive role, which puts the other party in a position of
power. Mrs. Quest's actions, then, can be viewed as spontaneous responses to Martha's submissive attitude, which
makes her take on the role of power and authority and give
up her long-term plans for Martha's career in favour of
the more immediate possibility of control over her.

Martha's reactions cannot be interpreted as clearly
submissive, however. They form an ambivalent pattern which
contains both rebellious and submissive elements. On the
one hand, she tries to avoid her mother's plans for her
career which involve going to a "snob school," a university,
which is very much a part of the society that she opposes
(MQ, p. 42); on the other, she responds to what she instinctively feels to be her mother's basic need - her wish to
domineer and control.

The Four-Gated City confirms the interpretation of the
pink eye incident as a confused act of rebellion. Describing
Francis Coldridge's decision not to pass his A-levels and go
to university, the narrator comments: "Long ago Martha had
made the same decision, had fought with cunning, ruthless-
ness, desperation, hardly knowing what it was she was doing,
except that she was saying, no, no, I won't" (FGC, pp.
416-417). The paradoxical outcome of Martha's strategy -
her ending up on the farm, more exposed to Mrs. Quest than
ever, can be explained as a result of the dead-locked situation in which she had been put by her mother's various
demands. Thus when she tries to avoid having a "career" on
her mother's terms, she falls into the trap of her mother's
need to control her in another, more direct form.

Still, Martha's protest is characterized by an inherent
weakness and can also be interpreted as an unconscious wish
to submit herself to her mother's influence. An ambivalent
longing to become the victim of a destructive force is demonstrated in her experience of Mrs. Quest as the "eternal

mother, holding sleep and death in her twin hands like a
sweet and poisonous cloud of forgetfulness . . ." (MQ, p.
39, my italics).[5] Martha's adopting the role of victim
parallels her father's attitude, a question which will be
brought up again in section 4.

The other crisis which takes place between young
Martha and her mother is the "battle of the clothes" (MQ,
p. 33). On the surface this battle concerns social conventions. Mrs. Quest forces the 16-year old Martha to wear
children's clothes since this is the fashion of a girl in
a "nice family" who has not yet reached the age of 18 and
"come out" (MQ, p. 29). On a deeper level the issue of the
clothes is related to Martha's sexuality which Mrs. Quest
fears and Martha instinctively nurtures. Mrs. Quest tries
unconsciously to undermine Martha's sense of identity as a
woman by joking about her clumsiness, an effort which
Martha attempts to counter by spending much time examining
herself in the mirror, murmuring "like a lover: Beautiful,
you are so beautiful" (MQ, p. 29).

The struggle ends when Martha makes herself a white
evening dress for the dance at the Van Rensbergs. When
Martha shows herself in "triumph" to her mother in her
new dress, thinking "you can't do anything about it now,
can you?" (MQ, p. 94), she has taken the first step towards
establishing her sexual identity. Thereby she has won the
battle of the clothes which, like the pink eye episode, is
a question of who is in power, who has control.

Martha's sexuality is revealed as a central factor in
the development of her identity. The scene in which she
presents herself to her parents in her evening dress is
given archetypal overtones. It is a symbolic presentation
of the end of childhood and the beginning of adulthood in
which she fulfills a "rôle" which is "timeless" (MQ, p. 95).
Martha's open assertion of her sexuality releases her from
the "spell" (MQ, p. 38) which she has felt herself to live
under since the pink eye affair and gives her sufficient
energy to leave her parents for a life of her own in the
city.

The two incidents suggest certain ways of human interaction which appear to be typical of the overall contact
between Martha and her mother. Most importantly, Mrs. Quest's
attempts at controlling Martha and Martha's resistance make
their personal interaction function according to a pattern
of oppression and submission. The roles of oppressor and
oppressed change according to who is momentarily the strong-
est, but no equal and spontaneous communication appears to
be possible. To my mind this power struggle between mother
and daughter is shown to have definite sado-masochistic
connotations - not in a sexual sense, but in the psychological sense of enjoyment in the exertion of one's strength
and power at the expense of another's weakness on the one
hand, and on the other, in the attraction of a submissive
position of being controlled by a superior power.[6]

Martha is said to feel "triumph" when she finds her
mother's weak spots, as for example in the battle over the
clothes (MQ, pp. 94, 311), but she is also presented as
drawn to the role of victim, subordinated to her mother's
control as in the pink eye episode. Mrs. Quest's need to
master her daughter we have seen demonstrated above and it
continues throughout the series; she is also occasionally
shown to indulge in dreams where Martha is subjected to
humiliation and to be "triumphant" at signs of weakness
from Martha (FGC, pp. 305-306; LL, p. 89). Mrs. Quest also
demonstrates a masochistic leaning in that her quarrelsome
and critical attitudes to Martha are so provocative that
they can be interpreted as ways of asking for punishment.
On one of these occasions Martha reacts with the anger
which Mrs. Quest seems to ask for. Martha's violent reaction
has the effect of reducing Mrs. Quest to a little girl:

> She looked astounded at her mother, at this extra-
> ordinary phenomenon which she had after all seen so
> often before. Mrs. Quest, that handsome matron with
> her broad downright face, had collapsed into a small
> girl. Yes, a pathetic frightened little girl sat there,
> looking at Martha with small sad blue eyes which
> slowly filled with tears (PM, p. 332).

This conflict shows the reversal of Mrs. Quest's authoritarian parental attitude to Martha. Mrs. Quest's change

from matron to little girl when submitted to authority suggests an unintegrated personality which either needs to be in power or is reduced to the helplessness of a small child.

This incident also demonstrates the complex emotional interaction which is involved in the relationship between mother and daughter. At the sight of the change in Mrs. Quest, Martha feels that she has been cruel and becomes filled with pity at the thought of her mother's "hard and disappointing life" (PM, p. 333). She embraces her mother only to feel her gather strength by this show of emotion: "Horror filled Martha. She realised that by this one moment of pity she had completely undone what she might have achieved: pity itself was contaminated, then?" (PM, p. 333).

The quality of pity is important in the relationship between the two women in that it expresses emotional concern and dependence. In the interaction between mother and daughter emotional concern is interpreted as a sign of weakness which puts one of them (usually Mrs. Quest) in a position of power. Martha's show of pity strengthens Mrs. Quest's position, just as Martha's appeal to Mrs. Quest during the pink eye incident makes Mrs. Quest adopt the role of oppressor. This pattern is further confirmed in *The Four-Gated City*. Martha prepares herself for her mother's visit by going to a psychoanalyst in order to get back her pity for her mother without being destroyed by it:

> Pity, a long time ago, had been an enemy. Pity could have destroyed.
> What Dr Lamb must do for her was to give her back pity, the strength to hold it and not be destroyed by it. She must be able, when her mother came, to pity her, to love her, to cherish her, and not be destroyed (FGC, p. 261).

Pity in this context is closely related to guilt, another binding emotion which the power struggle awakens in Martha. She is sensitive to the implicit and explicit accusations of ingratitude which are part of her mother's psychological

blackmailing. She has to reason with herself to repress her
guilt when Mrs. Quest reminds her of some service not asked
for. A typical example of this is Martha's reaction when she
has moved into town and her mother comes and volunteers to
look after her, because she is "such a helpless creature":
"Martha, as usual, . . . pointed out to herself that her
sudden guilt was irrational, since she had not asked them
to leave the farm and come in after her" (MQ, p. 122).

In her relationship with her mother Martha experiences
that love can be used in a struggle for power. She learns
that emotions can fill the functions of traps which bind one
and limit one's freedom.[7] As a result she develops a mechanism of uninvolvement which reappears in other relationships,
especially with men, and which functions as a defence mechanism against social and psychological pressures.

During the crisis of the pink eye episode Martha is
capable of little emotional distance to her mother - she
experiences her as a "baneful figure," a "witch" (MQ, p.
39). But little by little she disassociates herself emotionally. This she does through the expansion of her reflective
awareness.[8] The development of Martha's consciousness is
dealt with in section 5.2; here I want to point to the split
between intellect and emotions which appears to be the outcome of her attempt at emotional detachment and intellectual
awareness. Her lack of an integrated personality is most
clearly expressed in a passage from *A Proper Marriage* which
describes her in one of her clashes with her mother:

> Martha scarcely listened |to her mother|. She was
> engaged in examining and repairing those intellectual's
> bastions of defence behind which she sheltered; that
> building whose shape had first been sketched so far
> back in her childhood she could no longer remember how
> it then looked. With every year it had become more
> complicated, more ramified; it was as if she, Martha,
> were a variety of soft shell-less creature, whose
> survival lay in the strength of those walls. Reaching
> out in all directions from behind it, she clutched at
> the bricks of arguments, the stones of words, discarding
> any that might not fit into the building (PM, p. 123).

In this quotation we are made aware of certain complications
in Martha's intellectual and emotional life. The defensive,

outward quality of her intellectual awareness is strongly
underlined and so is her emotional vulnerability. Her rebellion against her mother is shown to make her quite lonely
and insecure. It makes her think of herself as "exiled,"
in search of an alternative home (MQ, p. 106), a new social
context where she can be emotionally acknowledged and where
her values are shared. This longing is contained in her
vision of an ideal city and in her dreams of various
"brotherhoods" (see MQ, pp. 22-23, 157, 282), an issue
which will be brought up again in section 5.

As an adult Martha will display a tendency to get caught
in negative social and emotional situations; this is mainly
presented as due to social pressure, but it can also be understood as a result of the psychological handicap which she
acquires in her relationship with her mother (see Ch. II, Sec.
2.6). Martha's analytical capacity will be her main defence
against outside pressure, but it will be combined with
passivity and evasiveness (see Ch. II, Sec. 2.7). Her illnesses as a reaction to external demands keep recurring
throughout the series. In *A Ripple from the Storm* she is
seriously ill, not primarily psychosomatically, but nevertheless as a reaction to the strain of her political
activity. In *The Four-Gated City* Martha takes to her bed
at the news of her mother's arrival, suffering from a mental
breakdown which manifests itself in physical immobility.[9]

The vicissitudes of Martha's early relationship with
her mother appear to be of vital importance to an understanding of her development. Within the novel series this
relationship is explicitly discussed only in *The Four-Gated
City*, and then in a fashion which deviates from the picture
of it given in the early novels (see Ch. III, Sec. 3.1).

4 Violence as War: The Father

Mr. Quest, seen as a representative of society, is presented in different lights, in a way which recalls the characterization of Mrs. Quest. On the one hand his attitude to

his past experiences and to the social reality of Zambesia is characterized by an adherence to roles and conventions; on the other hand we are told that he had once been contemptuous of such matters (LL, p. 78). Like his wife, he appears to be a frustrated rebel, although in his case this more clearly takes the form of a split personality one part of which is associated with an authentic self and another seems to be the result of his subordination to collective pressures.

Mr. Quest's involvement in World War I is shown to be of crucial importance to him; his personality can be divided into a pre-war and a post-war self. Mr. Quest is not "'himself'" after the war (LL, p. 78); he has become a psychological invalid, a "dream-locked figure" (MQ, p. 39). His state of mental unfitness is further emphasized by his physical illness, his diabetes: "Mr. Quest was completely absorbed in the ritual of being ill, he talked of nothing else - his illness and the war, the war and illness . . ." (MQ, p. 40). The war turns him into one of the living dead. His personal identity is lost and instead he feels at one with history and society. This is exemplified in his conventional attitude to the accepted mores of Zambesia and in the stereotyped quality of his war memories which gives them the same "official" quality as that which Mrs. Quest exhibits to her past history. They are expressed through clichés such as "the Great Unmentionable" or in constant stereotyped reiteration of certain important war incidents such as the battle of Passchendaele (see MQ, pp. 40-41, 121, 309-310).[10]

However, there are residues in Mr. Quest of what is supposedly his pre-war self. For fleeting moments they manifest themselves in behaviour which is unconventional rather than conformist and personal and authentic rather than anonymous and stereotyped. In the early novels this behaviour is manifested in regard to sexuality. Mr. Quest opposes what is shown to be the accepted norms of Zambesian society by viewing Martha's marriage not in terms of social success or romantic love (cf. Ch. II, Sec. 2.2), but in terms of a deep sexual compatibility.[11] When Martha is about

to marry he warns her about the importance of sex in married
life (see MQ, p. 311), and when her marriage approaches its
final crisis he indirectly advises her to leave her husband,
since he is not a "man" but a "commercial traveller" (PM, pp.
342-343). On the latter occasion Mr. Quest's concern with
sexuality takes the form of reproaching Martha for having
married without being "in love":

> 'What did you do it for?' he said suddenly, in a low
> reproachful voice. 'It was so obvious it wouldn't be
> any good. You weren't even in love with him.' . . .
> 'You weren't in love with him, you've never been in love
> with anyone - anyone can tell it by looking at you,' he
> said. That last sentence, cool, direct, the judgment
> of no less than an experienced man, caused her to look
> at him in respectful surprise (PM, p. 342).

Martha's sexuality is connected with nature and both of
these forces are presented as potentially liberating and in
opposition to the norms of society.[12] In Mr. Quest's case
there is no direct link between nature and sex. Even so, his
feeling for nature is often emphasized and furthermore, his
love of nature and his appreciation of sexuality are the
aspects of his personality which are connected with his
pre-war self (see MQ, pp. 33-34; PM, pp. 166-168).[13] Like
Martha, he grew up in the country, and in both individuals
we find the combination of nature, sex and protest, whereas
Mrs. Quest, whose sexual puritanism is presented as an
important ingredient in her anxious adherence to the norms
of society, is never associated with nature. Mrs. Quest had
spent her childhood in London; she feels foreign to the
African landscape and wants to move her family back into a
city. Earlier I have pointed to her middle class family
situation, but her city background can be viewed as yet
another factor which accounts for her puritanism and social
conformism.

It is through Mr. Quest that war is introduced in
Children of Violence. War appears as a major shaping influence on him; the part of his personality which is not
related to the life-giving forces of nature and sexuality
is dominated by the death-bringing forces of war. This is
not so with Mrs. Quest. She served as a nurse during war

time but her character can largely be understood as a product of her family background.[14]

Because of his war experiences Mr. Quest adopts attitudes of escapism, passivity and an attraction to suffering and to the role of being a victim. These attitudes are also present in Martha and they may be viewed as influences from the war which she picks up through her contact with her father. While listening to her father's talk about his illness and the war, she becomes "absorbed in these twin litanies of suffering in spite of herself, for they had been murmuring down her childhood as far back as she could remember, and were twined with her deepest self" (MQ, p. 40). She feels that her personality contains a "morbid strain," a weakness for the "poetry of suffering," which is her father's "gift" (MQ, pp. 40, 59).

However, it is unclear to what extent Martha's attraction to the role of sufferer and submissive victim should be seen as an adoption of her father's attitude to his past or as a result of the dynamics of her family situation. Since Mrs. Quest is the major socializing agent for Martha the authoritarian conditions of the family which she represents would seem to better explain Martha's submissiveness than the destructive forces incarnated by her father. Martha's identification with Mr. Quest can be viewed as a result of the similarity of their position vis-à-vis Mrs. Quest in the family, where father and daughter are both subordinated to the influence of the mother. This family relationship in fact makes the characterization of Mr. Quest ambiguous in a way which is similar to that of Martha.

The quotation about the "nightmare" of "repetition" cited earlier in this chapter says that the woman's dominance within the family creates "shadowy" and "dependent" men (PM, p. 124). This seems mainly to refer to the relationship between the Quests, but other couples demonstrate a similar pattern, for instance Martha's friend Donovan's parents and Mr. and Mrs. Van der Bylt. As the war is not an issue in these latter relationships, they support my claim that the social and psychological pressures represented by the family

are more relevant if we want to explain the meaning of
violence in the early books of *Children of Violence*.

5 Martha

As a young woman Martha finds a counterbalance to the
reality communicated to her through her parents in her
private world which is made up of dreams and visions, her
reading, and contact with nature.

5.1 The Ideal City and the Mystical Experience

As a teenager Martha has a favourite dream of an ideal city,
a dream which will recur on numerous occasions in the novel
series. When she is still an adolescent it is associated with
her various dreams of ideal "brotherhoods" (MQ, pp. 106,
157-158); later it is connected with her socialist ideal
(RS, p. 36), and finally, in *The Four-Gated City*, the notion
of an ideal city becomes one of the symbols of the inner life
(FGC, pp. 160-163). The most detailed description of this
city presented in the first three novels is given when we are
first introduced to it at the beginning of *Martha Quest*:

> She |Martha| looked away over the ploughed land, across
> the veld to the Dumfries Hills; and refashioned that
> unused country to the scale of her imagination. There
> arose, glimmering whitely over the harsh scrub and the
> stunted trees, a noble city, set four-square and colon-
> naded along its falling, flower-bordered terraces. There
> were the sound of flutes, and splashing fountains; and
> its citizens moved, grave and beautiful, black and white
> and brown together; and these groups of elders paused,
> and smiled with pleasure at the sight of the children -
> the blue-eyed, fair-skinned children of the North
> playing hand in hand with the bronze-skinned, dark-eyed
> children of the South - yes, they smiled and approved
> these many-fathered children, running and playing among
> the flowers and the terraces, through the white pillars
> and tall trees of this fabulous and ancient city...
> (MQ, pp. 22-23).

Martha's adolescent dream of the city conveys an idea of how she envisions society. The dream contains an ideal of racial equality and of a harmonious relationship between the generations. Its ideological and political content is opposed to her social situation which is characterized by racism and oppressive family relationships. It also implies a longing for love and harmony and provides an emotional outlet for Martha in her conflict-ridden family situation.

When this dream is discussed by critics, they usually stress its ideal of racial equality.[15] To my mind the implied longing for a harmonious and loving family relationship is equally or more important. This aspect is strengthened by the fact that the dream is awakened by Martha's feeling of alienation from her mother which she projects toward a black child: "the pity she refused herself flooded out and surrounded the black child like a protective blanket. And again her mind swam and shook, . . . and now, instead of one black child, she saw a multitude, and so lapsed easily into her familiar daydream" (MQ, p. 22).

Martha's concern for the black child seems to create the fusion of racial and family matters which is expressed in her dream. However, her own sense of oppression appears to be based on her relationship to her parents, and racism seems to be a secondary or parallel phenomenon. Her dream suggests that to her the family is both an oppressive system and the basis for a desire for some sort of positive alternative. This I have touched upon in section 3.3 where I indicated that Martha's early visions of ideal social contexts contain the wish for a new home that is ideologically and emotionally satisfying. The emotional content is strong in these dreams, however. This may indicate the degree to which Martha misses a spontaneous interchange of emotions with her parents, especially her mother, where her typical stance is one of wariness and resistance. In the description of the city the elders' approval and delight at the sight of the children is stressed through repetition, which to underline Martha's psychological vulnerability and her need for emotional confirmation. Similarly, her intellectual communication with her friend Joss Cohen makes her long for

a "brotherhood" where she might enter as a "welcomed
daughter into that realm of generous and freely-exchanged
emotions for which she had been born" (MQ, p. 106). And
the result of her first meeting with the ideas of the *New
Statesman* is a feeling of "warmth" and "security," a sense
of being "at home," being "one of a brotherhood" with people
"altogether generous and warm," exchanging "generous emotions"
(MQ, p. 157).

Nature is another entity in *Martha Quest* which can be
said to serve as a home for Martha as well as to have the
function of creating ideals for her. The narrator suggests
that as a child Martha had a "religious phase" which contained experiences of a mystical unity with nature (MQ, p.
107). She is largely barred from this unity during her
adolescence when nature is said to be like a "loved country
which refused her citizenship" (MQ, p. 38).

A mystical experience is described only once in *Martha
Quest*. However, this event and others of the same kind which
are referred to in connection with her childhood are shown
to affect her consciousness in a significant way. Through
them she acquires a "lodestone" or a "conscience" which
helps her to orient herself towards reality:

> and the measure was that experience (she thought of
> it as one, though it was the fusion of many, of varying
> intensity) that was the gift of her solitary childhood
> on the veld: that knowledge of something painful and
> ecstatic, something central and fixed, but flowing; it
> was a sense of movement, of separate things interacting
> and finally becoming one, but greater - it was this that
> was her lodestone, even her conscience . . . (MQ, pp.
> 261-262).

The quotation indicates that the mystical experiences guide
her. But how? As the mystical experience is in fact described,
it contains certain elements which appear to clash with the
ideals represented by the imaginary city. It consists of a
painful integration with nature culminating in a "moment"
which cannot be recaptured afterwards:

> For during that space of time (which was timeless) she
> understood quite finally her smallness, the unimportance
> of humanity. In her ears was an inchoate grinding, the
> great wheels of movement, and it was inhuman, like the

blundering rocking movement of a bullock cart; and no part of that sound was Martha's voice. Yet she was part of it, reluctantly allowed to participate, though on terms - but what terms? For that moment, while space and time (but these are words, and if she understood anything it was that words, here, were like the sound of a baby crying in a whirlwind) kneaded her flesh, she knew futility; that is, what was futile, was her own idea of herself and her place in the chaos of matter. What was demanded of her, was that she should accept something quite different; it was as if something new was demanding conception, with her flesh as host; as if there were a necessity, which she must bring herself to accept, that she should allow herself to dissolve and be formed by that necessity (MQ, p. 74).

There are certain connections between the notion of the city and the implications of the mystical experience, the most important of which appears to be that both represent wholeness and unity. But the city stands for wholeness created in a meaningful human context, whereas the mystical experience points to the achievement of unity through human subordination, to certain elemental, natural powers. The integration model of mysticism seems to require an acknowledgment of human insignificance: Martha "understood quite finally her smallness, the unimportance of humanity." This lesson of futility would seem to be quite contrary to the aspiration for a better society which is contained in the ideal city.

In my discussion of Mr. Quest I maintained that in *Children of Violence* natural powers are socially liberating in that they foster a nonconformist attitude. This interpretation can be reconciled with the implications of Martha's mystical experience in the sense that as she is opened up to nature she partakes of a dimension of life which provides an ironic comment on human, social ambition. Having had this experience human beings may see through and defy social conventions and pretensions. Nature reminds them of their dependence on, and links with, forces greater than themselves and warns against individualism, self-assertion. Perhaps this is the "necessity" which it is demanded that Martha should accept during her mystical experience?

However, this type of humility does not seem to eliminate the complications which characterize Martha's mystical experience. The necessity that Martha must face appears not only to demand that she accepts her being part of nature but also that nature is all and humanity is nothing. Specifically human capacities such as language and reflection are presented as futile and pathetic, like "the sound of a baby crying in a whirlwind." Paradoxically, Martha can escape futility only by acknowledging it, that is by accepting that "her own idea of herself and her place in the chaos of matter" is without importance. Only by allowing herself to "dissolve" as a human being and be "formed" by "something new" that is "demanding conception with her flesh as host" would Martha be able to experience the powers of nature in a creative fashion.[16]

My intention in comparing the mystical experience with the idea of the city is to suggest certain tensions in the rendering of young Martha's relationship with the world. The city and the mystical experience not only provide different outlooks on human life but also concern different aspects of Martha's relationship to reality. Her dream of the city can be viewed as a response to the oppressive family situation; it is an attempt to find a solution to a social problem. The mystical experience, on the other hand, does not suggest a social conflict, but rather one which is based on a dichotomy between nature and culture. This dichotomy, as well as Martha's relationship to society, will be developed in the chapters which follow. In Martha's mystical experience nature appears as a basic force which is absolutely removed from human, cultural life but which still contains a creative aspect - an aspect which, however, is only suggested. On other occasions in the series nature is described as more easily accessible to the human being and more immediately creative. The various meanings of the role of nature should become clearer through my analysis of Martha's development in Chapters II and III.

The tensions between the city and the mystical experience of nature are not directly noticeable in the text. On the contrary, these entities are often combined in ways which suggest a harmonious rather than conflicting relationship between them. Martha's city exists in harmony with nature; it has "flower-bordered terraces" and "white pillars and tall trees" (MQ, p. 23). Her reading of poetry makes her think of the city as well as nature: "She read poetry . . . for the melodies which confirmed the rhythm of the moving grasses and the swaying of the leaves over her head, or that ideal landscape of white cities and noble people . . ." (MQ, p. 43). This close connection between the city and nature is also demonstrated further on in Martha's development. For example, her involvement with communism, which is one of the results of her social rebellion, is in her thinking combined with the memory of her mystical experience of nature; both are presented as entities which give a total picture of life and there is no indication of a potential conflict between them (see RS, pp. 65-66).

Although I regard the conflict discussed above as crucial for an understanding of Martha's development I would like to conclude this discussion by pointing to some ambiguous aspects as regards the city which to some extent modify the interpretation I have given of it. Earlier I have stressed the elements within the city which relate it to Martha's social situation, i.e., those parts of it which give it a concrete and specific content directly critical of her society. But the city can also be interpreted as an expression of a socially less defined longing for love and harmony.[17] The latter interpretation finds support in the narrator's stress on what is archetypal and eternally human in Martha's vision. Her city is said to be "fabulous" and "ancient" (MQ, p. 23), and her dream is declared to be "so much older than she knew" (MQ, pp. 157-158). The city can be viewed as symbolizing a wish to recreate an original state of harmony, which makes it take on a backward-looking as well as a forward-looking aspect. This duality is strengthened by a similar one which is contained in the notion of the city as an alternative home. This idea is also ambiguous in that it points both forwards to a change of the family and backwards towards an original experience of motherly love. Its regressive tendency is supported by the

strong emphasis on emotional confirmation which I noted in
Martha's ideal social situations.

The city viewed as a symbol of a lost state of harmony
appears to have certain connections with Martha's mystical
relationship to nature. Her mystical experiences happen in
her childhood, in a state of intuitive closeness to nature
which she is shown to lose when she develops her consciousness and becomes a cultural being. The mystical experience
which takes place during her adolescence can be looked upon
as her return to a primordial condition. Viewed in this light
it coheres with the backward-looking and regressive components comprised in the ideal of the city.[18]

5.2 Conscious Reflection and Intuitive Insight

A tension related to that which I have analysed in the preceding part of this section is the split between a reflective
and an intuitive approach to the world which characterizes
Martha as a young woman.[19] I intend to study this split as
it is manifested in her attitude to her reading, since books
provide her with an important means of orientation during
her adolescence.[20]

While she is still a teenager, Martha's rebellion
against her parents is supported by the growth of her reflective consciousness, which functions as a "dispassionate
eye" or a "detached observer, felt perhaps as a clear lit
space situated just behind the forehead" (MQ, p. 19). This
"detached observer" gives her a "weapon" with which she can
control her feelings, her "misery" (MQ, p. 19). Her consciousness is the "gift" of her friends the Cohen brothers,
who had lent her books on economics, sociology and psychology
from which Martha had "gained a clear picture of herself,
from the outside" (MQ, p. 20):

> She was adolescent, and therefore bound to be unhappy;
> British, and therefore uneasy and defensive; in the
> fourth decade of the twentieth century, and therefore
> inescapably beset with problems of race and class;
> female, and obliged to repudiate the shackled women
> of the past (MQ, p. 20).

The "outside" and "objective" image of herself (MQ, p. 20)
which Martha gains from the development of her reflective
consciousness is helpful to her as it gives her a tool
through which she can control her emotions, but it is also
painful as she experiences a gap between feeling and reason.
The ideas she receives from books give her "information"
about herself, but no idea of how to use it (MQ, p. 21).
She longs for books which can explain her "confusion of
violent feeling" (MQ, p. 78).

Martha's reading makes her "tormented with guilt and
responsibility and self-consciousness" (MQ, p. 20) - which
suggests that she wants to escape the implications of what
she learns from it. In the context of the quotation this
suggestion is qualified by the information that she did not
"regret the torment" (MQ, p. 20), but on another occasion
the narrator confirms the suggestion of escape by telling
us about Martha's relief at the rupture of her friendship
with the Cohen brothers, and indirectly, their books: "the
relief of escaping that barrage of criticism was . . .
great, there was no longer any necessity to read their
books, examine her own ideas" (MQ, p. 44). Martha is also
said to regard the picture of herself acquired from books
as a kind of magic wand which should deliver her from all
her troubles: "this sternly objective image of herself
merely made her think . . . If we *know* it, why do we have
to go through the painful business of living it? She felt
. . . the act of giving names to things should be enough"
(MQ, p. 20).

Martha's problematic relationship to factual literature can be compared with her attitude to fiction, especially poetry, to which she turns spontaneously, and from
which she seems to seek an easy, almost mindless, confirmation of her private world:

> She read the same books over and over again, in between
> intervals of distracted day-dreaming, in a trance of
> recognition. . . . She read poetry, not for the sense
> of the words, but for the melodies which confirmed the
> rhythm of the moving grasses and the swaying of the

> leaves over her head, or that ideal landscape of white
> cities and noble people which lay over the actual vistas
> of harsh grass and stunted trees like a golden mirage
> (MQ, p. 43).

Her early attempts at creating a sense of self is in this way
characterized by a tension between the forces with which she
can identify in an immediate, subjective and intuitive fashion
and those she can only embrace through self-consciousness and
reflection.

The narrator often points out Martha's lack of self-
awareness and stresses her emotional and romantic disposition
in ways which would seem to indicate a recommendation for
conscious reflection and self-scrutiny.[21] For example Martha
is made fun of in the description of her first reactions to
the *New Statesman*:

> Yet when she laid down the journal she could not have
> said in detail what she had read, what were the facts;
> but she gave, unconsciously, a great quivering sigh,
> and lay back on her bed, eating chocolate and dreaming
> of a large city - it did not matter which, for it shared
> features of London and New York and Paris, and even the
> Moscow of the great novelists - where people . . .
> altogether generous and warm exchanged generous emotions
> (MQ, p. 157).

Although the common attitude of the narrator appears to be
on the side of reason and self-awareness this is not unequivocal. Occasionally such heavy emphasis is put upon
Martha's intuitive and self-confirming approach to the world
that it tends to negate the value accorded to emotional
distance and conscious reflection.

I pointed out that Martha's mystical experiences have
given her a "lodestone" or a "conscience" through which she
understands her situation. The narrator exemplifies the
function of this conscience by relating it to Martha's
attitude to literature. In this context all her reading is
described as instinctive and self-confirming:

> And as she read, she asked herself: What has this got to
> do with me? Mostly, she rejected; what she accepted, she
> took instinctively, for it rang true with some tuning
> fork or guide within her; and the measure was that
> experience . . . that was the gift of her solitary
> childhood on the veld . . . (MQ, p. 261).

Although the narrator maintains a certain distance to the subjective quality of Martha's reading procedure, there is no indication of the conflict between her intuitive or instinctive approach to the world and that which is associated with "the detached observer." It is interesting to note that the narrator appears to give her instinctive reading habits a positive, creative quality when they are referred to her mystical experiences, whereas the same approach is given negative associations with a kind of numbing and deadening of the mind in the description of her as reading the same books "over and over again" in a "trance of recognition" in between intervals of "distracted daydreaming" (MQ, p. 43).

The ambiguities embedded in Martha's attitudes to her reading can be viewed as symptoms of a tension in the presentation of her orientation to the world. As a result of this one could either locate the centre of Martha's early identity in her reflective consciousness, "the detached observer," or in the intuitive "conscience" gained from her mystical experience of nature

Chapter II   The Outward Quest

1 Introduction

As indicated in the first chapter, Martha's search for identity starts from her feeling of being "exiled." On the one
hand she feels exiled from her parental family which she
rejects both in terms of social and political ideology and
as a model for personal relationships. On the other hand
she experiences herself as an exile from the kind of primary,
intuitive contact with nature which she had during her childhood. Martha's mystical experience as a teenager and her
dream of an ideal city can be viewed as solutions to this
twofold sense of alienation.

I look upon the mystical experience and the dream of
the city as the first manifestations of two different directions or tendencies within Martha's search for identity. The
quest suggested by the dream of the city is directed outwards; it indicates an ambition to find an alternative social
context, a new society. This outwards-directed tendency dominates Martha's search for identity in *Martha Quest* through
A Ripple from the Storm. *Landlocked* and *The Four-Gated City*,
on the other hand, are dominated by her search for an inner
identity through a mysticism which can be traced back to her
early mystical experience of nature. This identity is non-
social or extra-social; it implies a withdrawal from personal
relationships and social institutions. It is reached through
an identification with certain psycho-physical powers which
make up a kind of Jungian collective unconscious (see Ch. III,
Secs. 1, 2). The point which marks the break-through of the
inwards-directed tendency of Martha's quest is her love
affair with Thomas Stern in *Landlocked* (see Ch. III, Sec.
2.1), but this inclination is also present as an underlying
element in the first three volumes. After its manifestation

in the mystical incident it recurs in Martha's experiences
of sexuality, pregnancy and childbirth.

Martha's outwards-directed search is characterized by
a social or sociological outlook on her relationship to
reality. It is looked upon as a conflict between the individual and society: Martha forms her identity in answer to
social expectations on her which are related to her womanhood and her class. The world view which informs her search
for an inner identity, on the other hand, sees her conflict
as one which exists between nature and culture or between
conscious and unconscious forces. In other words, the latter
view dramatizes a conflict which exists between Martha as a
natural being and Martha as a cultural being, whereas the
former presents her as an essentially social being confronted with problems of society.

This chapter is mainly devoted to Martha's outwards-
directed search, although the early manifestations of her
inwards-directed quest will also be considered. Martha tries
to find alternatives to the society represented by her
parents, to build the ideal city. This attempt finds its
actual social manifestations in her first marriage and in
her involvement with a leftist group. There is a discrep-
ancy between these realizations and the vision contained in
her quest. My investigation will primarily be concerned with
the mechanisms which prevent Martha from finding a meaningful identity within society.

In *Martha Quest* through *A Ripple from the Storm*
Martha's identity as a woman is crucial. The woman's situation within the family is of vital importance: the family
serves as a microcosm of society not only in Martha's
relations with her parents and with married life but also
in her involvement with politics. Furthermore, the presentation of Martha's female self illustrates certain tensions
between the outwards-directed and the inwards-directed tendencies within her quest. Her womanhood is partly determined by her relationship to society and partly by her
relationship to nature, i.e., it is defined in social as
well as biological terms. Although the social definition

is dominant, there is an ambiguous treatment of her female self which elucidates the tension between the two approaches to reality that inform her quest. This ambiguity also involves conflicts between feeling or intuition and intellect, and between conscious and unconscious forces.

2 Martha and Married Life

2.1 Love and Marriage – Dream and Reality

Love constitutes Martha's first attempt to transcend what is socially given. She falls in love with Douglas because he seems to be different from other men who have courted her: he relates to her in a more open and less ritualized manner and he represents new ideas - he reads the *New Statesman*. To Martha her early relationship to Douglas represents the fusion of creative personal interaction and progressive ideas which characterizes her teenage dreams of the city and of the "brotherhood." Her love is awakened as she sees in their relationship a possibility of realizing the dream. Love incorporates the dream or becomes the dream. Love seems to have the potential of leading to change, of bringing about new ways of relating to people and new ideologies. It appears to offer her a new "home" and to end her state of alienation (see MQ, pp. 22-23, 157-158, 282-283).[1]

Love leads to marriage. Martha does not search for marriage, but she accepts it as the social form in which love can be realized. Through marriage she becomes the victim of the repetition of the family. She reproduces the social, political and psychological structures against which she had rebelled in her parental family. Marriage provides Martha with a social identity. Politically, socially and economically she becomes a member of the white colonial middle class. As a woman Martha like her mother becomes confined to the functions of wife, mother and lover, and is forced to adopt defined psychological attitudes which bind and divide her instead of bringing the freedom and wholeness she longs for.

Martha's marriage and motherhood demonstrate the triumph
of collective reality over the individual attempt to transcend
it. Martha's female self is formed in a way which can not
primarily be explained as a result of her individual psyche,
but rather as the outcome of social and biological demands
upon her as a woman. The social demands consist of external
expectations on Martha to perform a specific social function
and internal, or rather internalized, expectations on her
which manifest themselves as a female consciousness or sex
role. This sex role is shown to be adapted to the woman's
function in society. The biological demands consist of instincts to reproduce life and to strive for sexual fulfillment. The social as well as the biological demands upon Martha
can be called collective in the sense that they represent
forces which do not relate to her as an individual but as a
member of society on the one hand and as a member of the
human species on the other.[2]

2.2 Social Demands

Martha tries to form an identity in a society where the
division of labour between the sexes is strictly defined
according to the norms of the bourgeois family:[3] women are
confined to domestic life, they are wives, mothers and lovers,
whereas men have their main functions within the social and
political spheres of life. Marriage is a white middle class
woman's way of realizing her social potential, it is her
career, her way of doing "well" (MQ, pp. 24, 292). Society
is also shown to be patriarchal. The two sexes have a hierarchical relationship to each other. Men exercise authority
and power over women due to their control over the public
and political realm of life which determines the conditions
of the private lives of women. Although the hierarchy
between the sexes is sometimes overshadowed by the power
that the woman can reach within the family, Martha's
inferior position as a woman is clearly demonstrated,
particularly in the wartime part of *A Proper Marriage*.

Martha and her women friends are then relegated to a kind of
ghetto of domesticity while their husbands band together in
the world of "offices, bars and clubs" (PM, p. 108). Her
social reality is reduced to being the wife of "one of the
lads" (PM, p. 173).

Thus Martha's identity is formed in a society which has
quite definite demands upon her womanhood. These demands are
communicated to her through a number of institutions which
represent society, such as her parental home and her married
home, and the Sports Club, an institution which sets the
norms for the young unmarried people of Martha's generation.
The standards of society also reach Martha through certain
socially representative figures, which are her male
"mentors," notably Donovan, who attempts to provide her with
a model of womanhood during the period preceding her first
marriage, and Dr. Stern, the gynecologist, who ministers to
her needs as a married woman.

Donovan prepares Martha for her role as sexual object.
He teaches her to please, to make herself attractive, to
utilize both her mental and physical powers in order to make
herself desirable merchandise on the marriage market (see
MQ, pp. 131-133, 190-191). Martha adjusts to these demands
on her womanhood. Her need to please men is shown to be
stronger than her frustration at their manipulations of her
personality. This psychological tendency functions as a kind
of trap which manoeuvres Martha into the traditional female
life which marriage represents. She seems to be aware of
this in a vague fashion:

> She thought confusedly that there was always a point
> when men seemed to press a button, as it were, and one
> was expected to turn into something else for their
> amusement. This 'turning into something else' had
> landed her where she was now, married, signed and
> sealed away from what she was convinced she was (PM,
> p. 17).

Donovan brings Martha in touch with the Sports Club, an institution which is presented as normative for the sex role
behaviour of white young middle class men and women. Social
interaction in the Sports Club requires a strongly stereo-

typed behaviour. Men are active and boyish: they are constantly "giving it bang" or "tearing" the place to "pieces."
Women are passive and are furthermore expected to be
"responsible" for the men. Men treat women with a ritualized
adoration to which women respond in a maternally understanding manner; they receive the male homage with "maternal indulgence" or "all-experienced compassion" (MQ, pp. 179-181,
292).

The sexually pleasing and maternally understanding
attitudes which women are expected to display towards men
appear to be part of a specific female consciousness or sex
role which Martha has internalized. In erotic or potentially
erotic contacts she demonstrates a dependence on men which
manifests itself as a need to support and please them in
their roles as lovers and patriarchal authorities. In her
early sexual contacts, from Billy Van Rensberg to Douglas,
this dependence is described as a "claim" or a "compulsion"
which deprives her of her will power and her rational judge-
ment and makes her instinctively compliant and obedient
(see MQ, pp. 101, 131, 242, 285-288). During her marital
life Martha gradually develops an emotional distance to
Douglas but remains bound to this female dependence: "That
instinct to comply, to please, seemed to her more and more
unpleasant and false. Yet she had to reassure Douglas and
kiss him . . . if she was not to feel guilty and lacking as
a woman" (PM, p. 337).

The "instinct to please" as well as the maternally indulgent attitude present in Martha are attributed to a dream
for romantic love in the following quotation describing her
and Douglas making love during the first period of their
marriage:

> She was on the point of turning over away from him, when
> the instinct to please turned her towards him. Love had
> brought her here, to lie beside this young man; love was
> the key to every good; love lay like a mirage through
> the golden gates of sex. If this was not true, then
> nothing was true, and the beliefs of a whole generation
> were illusory. They made love. . . . Loyalty towards
> love was forcing her to pretend that she was not dis-
> appointed, and that she did not - at that moment she was
> sick with repulsion - find him repulsive. But already

> that image of a lover that a woman is offered by society,
> and carries with her so long, had divorced itself from
> Douglas, like the painted picture of a stencil floating
> off the paper in water. Because that image remained
> intact and unhurt, it was possible to be good-natured.
> It is that image which keeps so many marriages peace-
> able and friendly.
> She listened, smiling maternally. . . (PM, pp.
> 40-41).

A longing for love makes Martha adopt the role of pleasing
lover as well as repress her sexual frustrations and become
an indulgent, tolerant mother figure. For a time the claim
of love prevents Martha from rebelling against Douglas. Thus
he acquires power over her emotional reactions regardless of
whether he does or does not incarnate the image of the lover.
In this context love both creates and sanctions a female
consciousness which befits the woman's social function as
wife and sexual object. Romantic love is presented as a myth
which both binds woman to her roles and gives the roles an
illusory value. Love is shown to have the power of bringing
the woman into marriage and keeping her there. Within marriage
the idea of the lover functions as a safety mechanism which
maintains the stability of marriage.

In the early volumes of *Children of Violence* the myth
of love provides the most explicit explanation of compliant
female behaviour. Society offers women an "image of a lover"
- it keeps alive a tradition of romantic love which women in-
herit (cf. MQ, p. 239; RS, p. 226). This inheritance helps
women to develop a maternal attitude that is crucial in
marriage.[4] This is intimated in the quotation above as well
as in the description of the Sports Club where the exaggerated
adoration of women gives them a promise of romance, while the
behaviour actually expected from them is motherly. The Sports
Club seems to prepare women for marriage. The role as lover
dominates the premarital stage of Martha's life, while in
married life the roles as wife and mother become central and
require a psychological attitude which is first and foremost
maternal.

Practically all of the women in Mrs. Quest's generation
are dominated by their motherly function whether it is directed towards their husbands and children as in the case of

Mrs. Quest and Mrs. Knowell or towards social work as in the case of Mrs. Maynard. Even Mrs. Van der Bylt who is involved in politics as a social democratic member of parliament regards motherhood as her first priority. The function as mother is also central to the women of Martha's generation. Despite their conscious intentions not to have children Martha and her women friends soon find themselves pregnant. In the circle of civil servants' wives to which Martha is introduced through her marriage to Douglas all the women were "pregnant, or intended to be soon, or had just had a baby" (PM, p. 319). Female revolts against motherhood are controlled by the gynecologist, Dr. Stern, who has considerable power over women because of his "expert" knowledge of women and because of his identification with the male fabric of society. Dr. Stern tries to convince women that female unhappiness in marriage is a normal condition of "life," experienced and accepted by "everybody" (PM, pp. 348-349). It is also intimated that he wilfully lies about Martha's pregnancy in order to prevent her from carrying out an abortion (see PM, pp. 26, 107, 347).

But women also control themselves and each other through identification with motherhood and through adherence to the motherly tolerance that includes both men and children. Martha's women friends automatically treat their husbands with the maternal "indulgence" which women are trained to display in the Sports Club (PM, p. 21). This attitude is presented as the psychological factor which ultimately keeps marriage together. When Martha is about to leave Douglas he rallies his mother and Mrs. Talbot to the task of making her stay married to him. Mrs. Talbot tries to convince her that love and sex are unimportant in marriage (PM, pp. 409-410) and Mrs. Knowell demonstrates the maternal attitude that she is supposed to adjust to:

> His mother went to him and took him in her arms, and murmured: 'There, there my baby. She won't leave you, she won't.' . . . She |Martha| saw that what his mother wanted was for her to put her arms around Douglas, and promise in that maternal murmur that she would not leave him. This was what Douglas was waiting for (PM, p. 432).

2.3 Biological Demands

Martha's female identity is also formed by her biological
nature, by its sexual and reproductive needs. The existence
of a sexual instinct is a generally accepted idea, whereas
a reproductive instinct is a less established notion.[5] In
A Proper Marriage, however, reproductive as well as sexual
needs are treated in ways which make it reasonable to define
them as instincts. In fact, a reproductive impulse is more
clearly demonstrated than a sexual one in the early novels
of the series.

Despite Martha's intentions not to have children she is
already pregnant by the time she marries. An intricate process of reproductive needs and social pressures conspires to
make her unaware of her pregnancy. The social pressure in
the form of Dr. Stern's possible manipulation of her has
already been referred to; here it is more interesting to
note that her conscious wishes seem to be outwitted by strong
unconscious forces working against them. Five months pregnant she sat

> feeling the imprisoned thing moving in her flesh, and
> was made more miserable by the knowledge that it had
> been moving for at least a week, without her noticing
> it, than by anything. For what was the use of thinking,
> of planning, if emotions one did not recognise at all
> worked their own way against you? (PM, p. 134).

In this context it is worth pointing out that before the
birth of her daughter Martha thinks little of children as
social beings. She sees them as obstacles to her freedom as
a woman, and as the ultimate link in the cycle of repetition
which binds her to her family history (cf. MQ, p. 25; PM, p.
124).

While Martha has no interest in children as individuals
she exhibits a certain spontaneous feeling for them on a more
abstract level: they are fascinating to her as representatives of life, as wonders of creation as it were. Dr. Stern
appeals to this feeling when he compares her foetus to a
statue of a mermaidlike figure diving off a rock which he
keeps in his office. This comparison is effective. Despite

her bitterness "she was already weakening towards this baby.
She could not forget that diving creature, bent in moulded
bronze, about five inches long. In her bedroom, she found
herself standing as she had seen Alice stand, hands curiously
touching her stomach" (PM, p. 133). When Martha contemplates
having a second child she again displays this fascination
with the creation of life: "She thought that in nine months
from now, if she chose, she could hold in her arms something
new and extraordinary - a new creature created from her,
Martha" (PM, p. 392). This particular interest in children
might perhaps be termed a maternal feeling; however, its
origin would seem to be biological rather than psychological
as it is shown to be closely connected with the biological
process of reproduction:

> Caroline was three years old. Martha knew that her
> female self was sharply demanding that she should start
> the cycle of birth again. There were moods when a slow,
> warm, heavy longing came up, when the very sight of
> Caroline filled Martha with a deep physical satisfaction
> at her delightful little body and charming little face;
> and this was at the same time a desire to hold a small
> baby in her arms again. If she looked at one of her
> friend's babies in this mood, the craving was painful
> and insistent; and the adventure of being pregnant
> filled her entirely (PM, pp. 321-322).

In this quotation the narrator refers to a "female self,"
which makes itself known through a physical longing for a
child, which seems to return at certain time-bound intervals.
Considering the physical and cyclic quality of this longing,
it would seem to manifest a female instinct for reproduction.
In a closely allied context the narrator also stresses the
irrational element involved in the need to give birth which
supports the definition of it as an instinct. We are told
that the "sharp physical yearning for a baby" had confused
"young Letty Jones" out of her "efficiency" and made her
pregnant when she had not meant to be (PM, p. 323). Letty
Jones here represents every woman, hence the instinct for
reproduction is made into a generalized phenomenon common to
all women. This impulse seems to be a vital force in Martha's
pregnancy which to a large extent accounts for its irrational

and mysterious qualities.

In the early volumes of *Children of Violence* the sexual
instinct is described in a less distinct and defined manner
than is the reproductive impulse. The sexual instinct is one
component at work in the "claim," but this component is hard
to isolate: it is hard to determine to what extent a need for
sexual fulfillment or a dream of romantic love ultimately
determines Martha's contacts with men. Sexuality acquires a
power over her as it seems to lead to love: "Love was the
key to every good; love lay like a mirage through the golden
gates of sex" (PM, p. 40). However, sexuality is also presented as a force which in itself is strongly instrumental
in making her relationships to men so binding and irrational.

Especially in Martha's early contacts with men, for
example with Billy Van Rensberg and Donovan, an "outside
force" or "compulsion" is at work upon her which seems to
refer to the sexual instinct rather than to the concept of
romantic love (MQ, pp. 101, 131). During the dance at Van
Rensbergs Billy incarnates the "outside force," something
which puts Martha into a state of trance-like obedience to
him and makes it impossible for her to tear away from him,
despite her irritation with him as a person:

> it would have driven across the current of feeling
> which said that Billy, or rather, what he represented,
> had claimed her for the evening; for alcohol had
> strengthened the power of that outside force which
> had first claimed her four days before, at the moment
> she agreed to go to the dance. She was not herself,
> she was obedient to that force, which wore Billy's
> form and features . . . (MQ, p. 101).

It seems to me that the impersonal quality of the "force"
and of Martha's attachment to Billy (plus the rather trite
reference to alcohol) imply the workings of a sexual impulse.[6]

The binding force of sexuality can also be studied in
Martha's relationship to Adolph, her first lover. Although
they do not get along love-making with him turns her into
the compliant woman:

> they were increasingly uncomfortable together, except
> during those moments immediately after love-making,
> when she lay quietly beside him, in that devoted

> childlike way. She told him, then, that she loved him;
> she found herself saying all sorts of things that it
> embarrassed her afterwards to remember at all. For
> lying close up against that warm, sleek body, which
> apparently had such a powerful claim on her, waves of
> emotion came over her . . . (MQ, p. 242).

In contrast Donovan loses his power over Martha, when it
becomes obvious that he is unable to relate to her sexually.
It is vaguely indicated that his sexual identity is problematic, that perhaps he is a homosexual.

The sexual drive like the concept of romantic love thus
seems to turn Martha into an obedient and compliant woman.
This raises the issue of whether her compliance is, in fact,
presented as a social phenomenon as I have stated above or
whether it is looked upon as being biologically conditioned.
While it is clear that *Children of Violence*, 1-3, mainly
demonstrates a social understanding of Martha's female
identity, the importance accorded to reproductive and sexual
instincts poses the question of how her womanhood is ultimately defined. This question remains unanswered in the
first part of the novel series.[7]

2.4 Cooperation between Social and Biological Demands

Biological and social demands cooperate to form Martha's
identity as a woman according to the social norms of marriage.
Marriage provides the social structure in which instinctive
needs for reproduction and sexuality can be realized. These
instincts are sanctioned and controlled by social myths and
concepts of morality which are firmly lodged within Martha's
female consciousness.

The myth of love allows Martha to be sexual, but at the
same time it turns her into a sexual object who represses her
spontaneous erotic impulses (cf. PM, p. 40). She is also tied
to this role by a social code which recommends a technical
and performance-oriented approach to sexuality. This code is
represented by Van der Velde's sex manual which is often
referred to as simply "the book" (MQ, p. 296; PM, pp. 85, 357).

It encourages a "determined hedonism" or an "accomplished
athleticism." This attitude is presented as a reaction
against "the English puritan tradition," a rebellious stance
which is still bound by its origin because of its orientation towards technical sexual performances. In Martha's case
this means that her mother's puritanism turns her into a
sexual rebel who is still bound by the ideal of having to be
"good in bed" (MQ, pp. 306-307; PM, p. 357).

The female instinct for reproduction is socially manipulated in a similar fashion. Woman's biological longing for
a child is both sanctioned and confirmed by a myth of motherhood which gives an abstract image of the relationship
between mother and child and thus prevents the woman from
seeing its social implications. Martha articulates this myth
in the following way:

> That phrase, having a baby, which was every girl's way
> of thinking of a first child, was nothing but a mask
> to conceal the truth. One saw a flattering image of a
> madonnalike woman with a helpless infant in her arms;
> nothing could be more attractive. What one did not see,
> what everyone conspired to prevent one seeing, was the
> middle-aged woman, who had done nothing but produce two
> or three commonplace and tedious citizens in a world
> that was already too full of them (PM, pp. 349-350).

As the myth of love makes Martha feel guilty and "lacking"
if she admits her frustrations with men, the myth of motherhood makes her feel guilty and "unnatural" if she acknowledges
that the child binds her and limits her freedom (see PM, pp.
227, 258, 260, 322).

2.5 Sex Role Patterns in a Male-Dominated Society

The sexual division of labour and the male dominance within
society create unintegrated, fragmented male and female
identities and hierarchical relationships between the sexes.

Like women men have definite sex roles which correspond
to their social position. Like the female sex role the male
has two sides, one being the paternal, related to the male
function as upholder of the sphere of work and politics and

authority within the family, the other being the boyish, which
expresses a reaction against public and private demands,
routine, responsibility, and a desire for adventure and
excitement.[8]

When the male sex role is confronted with the female in
the interaction between the sexes a form of parent-child
relationship is established. Men are either decisive fathers
or irresponsible boys-sons, whereas women fluctuate between
the roles of understanding mothers and romantically obedient
girls-daughters. This interaction which may at first sight
seem complementary involves a hierarchy in that the male sex
role behaviour implies control of the woman, whereas her
function signifies adjustment to and support of the man.
Regardless of whether the man is fatherly-authoritative or
boyish-adventurous he dominates, while the woman is subservient both in her maternally understanding and her child-
ishly adoring roles.

This power structure is, however, modified in several
ways, mainly by the stress on male childishness and irre-
sponsibility. The male-female relationship most often alluded
to is that of mother and son.[9] And although the maternally
"indulgent" attitude is presented as binding to the woman,
the narrator often seems to share her tolerant attitude
towards male boyishness. Also occasionally the woman takes
on the dominant role, as in the case of Martha's and Donovan's parents. Still, Mr. Quest represents male authority
and is appealed to in this capacity by both his wife and his
daughter (see MQ, pp. 34, 94-95).

Whatever version of the male-female hierarchy we are
presented with the interaction between the sexes implies conflict and tension. Although male-female relationships are
pictured as less psychologically charged and threatening than
those between the generations, they ultimately form themselves
along the lines of oppression and submission, strength and
weakness and thus become reminiscent of the latently sado-
masochistic struggle between Martha and her mother. In the
male position there is an in-built need to control and master
which in its benevolent form is manifested as a proprietary

and complacent attitude towards women (cf. PM, pp. 81-82, 345). Its destructive, sadistic potential is most clearly demonstrated in Douglas's reactions to Martha when her decision to leave him challenges his mastery. During the long, drawn-out quarrel which precedes the break-up of their marriage, Douglas, the "sensible" man (PM, p. 337), turns into an aggressive, violent one, who attacks Martha physically, threatens to rape her and finally to kill her. His behaviour is not presented as an isolated phenomenon but seen as representative of male-female relationships. Martha's experience with Douglas is confirmed in her talks with other women: "She thought, Those women said there was a point when they started knocking you about. She remembered the satisfaction in their voices and thought: Oh no, not for me" (PM, p. 433). A masochistic streak in women would seem to be the logical outcome of the submissive and compliant female role, just as the sadistic impulse is latent in the mastering male role.[10] Martha's refusal to adapt to the female role in her fight with Douglas brings out masochistic as well as sadistic traits in him. Throughout his behaviour fluctuates between self-conscious displays of violence and suffering, enjoyment in strength on the one hand, in weakness on the other. In his masochistic mood he presents himself as a suffering victim, an anguished husband and father whose goodness is betrayed and outraged. By manipulating Martha's emotions he tries to make her submit to the subservient role. As in the fights between her and her mother an emotional blackmailing takes place which serves the purpose of securing power. In both instances she protects herself through her defence mechanism of cold and, by a large, rational uninvolvement (see PM, pp. 404-406, 423-424).

The character structure displayed by Douglas in his quarrel with Martha is demonstrated to exist not only in relationships between men and women but is seen as a prevalent, colonial social character. When Douglas and his fellow colonials are sent home from the front, declared unfit for active service, their mood ranges from violence to self-pity in a way which parallels the psychological attitude Douglas displays with Martha. The British doctor who is confronted with this behaviour sees it as typically colonial: "he could not understand these Colonials, so tough, masculine, violent - and then the sudden collapse into self-pity. It seemed a well of self-pity lay in all of them . . ." (PM, p. 281). An analogy is also made between Douglas's mentality and that of the official organ of Zambesian society, the *Zambesia News*:

> what did that state of self-displaying hysteria Douglas was in, have in common with that same shrill, maudlin self-pity of a leader in the *Zambesia News*, when it was complaining that the outside world did not understand the sacrifices the white population made in developing the blacks. . . . precisely that same note was struck in every issue of the local newspapers - goodness betrayed, self-righteousness on exhibition, heartless enemies discovered everywhere (PM, p. 424).

It might be assumed that the parallel between the male and the colonial character is due to the fact that both are re-flections of hierarchical social systems: the relationships between white and black and man and woman contain the same structure of mastery and subordination. Like the patriarchal the colonial mastery is hidden under a pretence of goodness and self-sacrifice, which when challenged, turns into the attitude of "goodness betrayed."11

The male sex role also has another socio-psychological implication, namely its connection with war. The extreme of the male desire for adventure seems to be the attraction to war. War combines the male need to escape the routine and responsibility of everyday life and the need to escape women, seen by the men as the enforcers of responsibility and order. Douglas thinks of his war experiences as "the real thing": "It seemed that his whole life had led . . . to the climax of being with those men, his fellows, his friends, parts of himself, in real fighting, real living, real experience at last" (PM, p. 285). Douglas's reaction to war is paralleled by that of Mr. Quest, who despite his bitterness about war is attracted by its excitement: "The comradeship," he would exclaim, "I've never experienced that since! . . . *It was the only time in my life I was really happy*" (PM, p. 92).

The female longing for romance becomes implicated with the male attraction towards war by upholding an image of masculinity which corresponds to the male dream for adventure. Martha comments on this mechanism in the following manner:

> The condition of being a woman in war-time, she thought . . . was that one should love not a man, but a man in relation to other men. Whether it was Douglas with the boys, or the boys of the air force, it was all the same: and it was precisely this thing, dangerous, and attractive, which fed the intoxication of war, heightened the pulse, and drugged them all into losing their heads (PM, pp. 303-304).

The description of constant festivities before and during the war in a city "given over to dancing, love and death" likewise stresses the connection between war and romance (PM, p. 234).

But women also stand for different kinds of needs which are presented as both more basic and more healthy and creative. Women are often presented as sceptical of the male attraction to wartime heroism (PM, pp. 110, 172), a scepticism which seems to issue from a closeness to certain lifegiving forces represented by sexuality and reproduction. These forces amount to a kind of female principle which finds its clearest expression in Martha's creative union with nature during her pregnancy (see Sec. 2.7). However, this principle functions underground, as it were, and is not given a social outlet.

2.6 Martha, her Mother, her Men and her Daughter

In the early volumes of *Children of Violence* Martha exhibits a strong fear of the family as well as a tendency to get caught in family-type relationships. Martha whose first "tenet" of belief was "the tyranny of the family" (PM, p. 109) marries twice without really intending to. Her marriage to Anton Hesse largely demonstrates the same negative dependence on a man as does her marriage to Douglas. I have tried to explain her first marriage by analysing the importance of the family as a unit which conditions her social and biological womanhood. However, this explanation can be given added force if Martha's relationship with her mother is also taken into account.

Martha's relationships to men are connected with her
interaction with her mother in various ways: for example, in
both cases she displays tendencies towards a negative
emotional dependence characterized by repressed aggression
which is manifested in guilt feelings and a kind of emotionally binding tenderness. The combination of pity and guilt
which Martha experiences in her conflicts with her mother is
comparable to the guilty maternal compassion which she shows
in relation to men. The similarities which mark her emotional
interaction with men and with her mother can be viewed as a
result of both being psychological expressions of similar
social structures. The authoritarian relationship between
mother and daughter might be assumed to give her a psychological readiness to adopt the submissive role which society
demands of her as a woman.

Martha's relationship to her mother makes her long for
freedom and personal integrity as well as safety and emotional
confirmation. To her Mrs. Quest represents both the tyranny
of the family and an ideal of a loving contact; the latter
aspect is manifested negatively in her sense of being unloved
and unwanted by her mother. Martha's feeling of being emotionally "exiled," of being "excluded from some good, some warmth,
that she had never known" (RS, p. 196), quite possibly
deepens her dependence on men and on romantic love.

In times of real crisis Martha turns to her mother which
seems to indicate that her need for love and safety is ultimately directed towards her. During the dramatic quarrel which
precedes the break-up of her marriage she turns to her mother
for support; during the pain of childbirth she calls out for
her mother and during her severe illness which happens in
A Ripple from the Storm she wants maternal care. Mrs. Quest
does visit her during this illness but is her usual critical
self, commenting on Martha's loose morals and pestering her
with stories about her daughter Caroline. Martha reacts with
the thought: "If my mother would come in again, and just be
kind, instead of hating me so much . . ." (RS. p. 108).

The kindness she wants she receives from Anton Hesse who
visits her sickbed shortly after her mother. This visit marks

the beginning of Martha's and Anton's relationship as a couple.
Despite her sense of panic over a love affair with him she
submits to it by convincing herself that she feels "safe" with
him because he is "kind" (RS, p. 108). Kindness was also an
important component with Douglas. With him she experienced a
"warm friendliness" which she had never known before and which
made her feel "altogether approved" (MQ, p. 284). Martha's
need for safety, kindness and approval points to the deep
insecurity which her conflict with her mother has created in
her and which might further explain her tendency to fall into
a negative dependence on a man.[12]

Like her relations to men, Martha's relationship to her
daughter Caroline is primarily determined by collective demands on her as a woman. As already indicated motherhood
appears as a central function in marriage, to which women
conform out of biological needs and social demands. The close
connection between motherhood and married life is demonstrated
when Martha automatically leaves her daughter as she breaks up
from her marriage in order to "live differently" (PM, p. 407).

However, Martha's separation from her daughter is also
the result of her own psychological reactions to the authoritarian relationship between her and her mother. In her fear
of repeating the past and turning into the oppressive mother,
she tries to protect her daughter from the effects of her
maternal function. During her pregnancy she promises the
future child that "freedom would be its gift. She, Martha,
the free spirit, would protect the creature from her, Martha,
the maternal force" (PM, pp. 145-146). She harbours the
notions that the only function of the parent is to be the
child's hate object and that the ideal condition of childhood
would be to do without parents altogether (see PM, pp. 146,
221, 261). When she eventually leaves her child her farewell
is expressed in the following manner: "You'll be perfectly
free, Caroline, I'm setting you free" (PM, p. 431). Martha
projects her relationship with her mother on her interaction
with Caroline. Her longing for freedom makes her see her
daughter as an image of her own freedom-loving self without
any further thought about the implication of freedom to
Caroline.

2.7 Martha's Split Identity

Martha experiences wifehood and motherhood as conditioning
structures which are threatening to her sense of identity,
her "real" self, which she often defines in terms of freedom
as "the free spirit" (PM, pp. 165, 146). Marriage shapes her
life according to a pre-established "pattern" (PM, p. 321),
the repetitious quality of which is symbolized by the fun
fair wheel whose movements accompany her married life.[13]
Motherhood makes her feel swallowed up by a natural cycle,
an "immense, impersonal tide, which paid no attention to
her, Martha" (PM, p. 132).

Martha defends her individuality and her potential freedom by relating to the roles that family life force upon her in
a critically reflective manner which enables her to keep an
emotional distance to her experiences. She uses her "intellectual's bastions of defence" in order to acquire a perspective
on her functions as wife and mother (PM, p. 123), she is scru-
tinizing and intellectualizing in relation to Douglas and Caroline. She draws a line between those parts of life which she
sees as pertaining to her real self and those which belong to
the institution of marriage which she looks upon as foreign to
herself. She refuses to identify emotionally with her role as
mother, for example: "she could not relax into Caroline; that
would be a disloyalty and even a danger to herself" (PM, p. 258)

Martha's attempt to keep up a distance to the dependence
which her womanhood creates in her is expressed most dramat-
ically during her pregnancy:

> She was essentially divided. One part of herself was
> sunk in the development of the creature, appallingly
> slow, frighteningly inevitable, a process which she
> could not alter or hasten, and which dragged her back
> into the impersonal blind urges of creation; with the
> other part she watched it; her mind was like a light-
> house, anxious and watchful that she, the free spirit,
> should not be implicated . . . (PM, p. 165).

This quotation suggests the tension between feeling and
intellect and between conscious and unconscious forces which
characterizes Martha during her marriage. She becomes the
watcher, the "detached observer," an attitude which also

characterizes her as a young woman in her parental family (cf. Ch. I, Secs. 3.3, 5.2). With the help of her mind she tries to control her emotional impulses and her unconscious needs. Through her emotional distance to her experiences she keeps alive a vision of an authentic identity but is unable to realize it within the context of marriage. Martha's detached attitude makes it possible for her to acquire a perspective on her emotions, but it does not help her to master them. Her attitude is split: she fluctuates between intellectualized distance and emotional dependence.

Martha tries to solve her conflicts by formulating an ideal of a woman as one who combines "a warm accepting femininity" with being a "person" (PM, p. 264). Martha's split attitude can be further elucidated through a comparison between her and two women characters who can be seen as representatives of the two poles of her ideal of womanhood. The person who stands for a "warm accepting femininity" is the black woman who exists in Martha's consciousness as an "invisible sister, simpler and wiser than herself . . ." (PM, p. 85). The woman who best corresponds to the idea of being a "person" is Mrs. Van der Bylt (usually referred to as just Mrs. Van) who manages to combine marriage and motherhood with a serious political involvement in the social democratic movement.[14]

From this description it might seem as though Mrs. Van fulfills both sides of Martha's ideal of a woman. However, the very point of the characterization of Mrs. Van is to illustrate that she has had to repress her womanhood in order to keep her integrity and become a "person." She is able to combine the traditional female functions with her political involvement as she rids herself of the emotional dependence on a man, which is shown to be the central, psychological content of her female sex role.

When Mrs. Van discovers that her husband disapproves of her political involvement she gets rid of her emotional dependence on him and indirectly on love. This she does since it constitutes a weakness which her husband can use to make her subservient and to force her to fail her personal in-

tegrity. This psychological process is described in a dramatic
episode which occurs during the early part of Mrs. Van's
marriage. It is referred to on two different occasions and
remains in her consciousness as a decisive event which she
thinks about as "that night" (RS, pp. 238, 226). What takes
place is a psychological battle between the sexes: Mrs. Van's
husband subjects his wife to emotional blackmailing by re-
fusing to make love to her as she has "better company" in
a book. During the struggle Mrs. Van refuses to feel guilty
and adopt the indulgent attitude described as instrumental
in keeping the woman under male control.

> Her |Mrs. Van's| cold bare arms lay at a skin's distance
> from her husband's muscular arm. But she did not move
> her arm; it lay still and trembled with the effort not
> to move it, while she thought: He wants me to let my
> arm touch his, but if I do, he will see it as a kind
> of an apology, a promise (RS, p. 238).

The following image of this battle between the sexes remains
in Mrs. Van's consciousness:

> Mrs. Van remembered the image that had filled the girl's
> mind through those long hours while she lay awake by a
> man who also lay awake, waiting for her to turn to him.
> The image was of something deep, soft, dark and vulner-
> able, and of a very sharp sword stabbing into it, again
> and again. She had not moved, had not let her arm relax
> into contact with her husband's, and so the sword had
> not stabbed into her, never again, the soft dark pain-
> ful place which she felt to be somewhere under her heart
> had remained untouched. She had remained herself (RS, p.
> 238).

The "soft, dark, painful place" could be seen as an image of
woman's emotional dependence upon a man. What Mrs. Van learns
from this experience is that "it was emotion . . . she must
ban from her life. Emotion was dangerous. It could destroy
her" (RS, p. 226).

The interaction between Mr. and Mrs. Van implies that
"emotion" refers both to the sexual and the maternal components
of the female dependence structure. The maternal element is
implied in the "apology" which Mr. Van expects from his wife
and the sexual element underlies the whole scene. It is a
sexual act which he withholds from his wife, and there are
sexual connotations to the image of the incident which Mrs.

Van recalls. She gets rid of her emotional dependence and
adopts a thoroughly rational attitude towards her husband
rather than keeping an image of a romantic lover as do so
many other women in *Children of Violence*: "she did not do
what nearly all women do . . . create an image and fight a
losing battle . . . in the no-man's-land between image and
the truth" (RS, p. 226).

The description of Mrs. Van gives an image of woman in
society who retains her personal integrity by adopting a
rational attitude to the demands which marriage puts upon
her.[15] The black woman on the other hand, who can be seen
as the incarnation of a "warm accepting femininity" lives
her life according to her instincts, in harmony with the
biological demands upon women which *Children of Violence*
postulates. The black woman is not an individualized character; rather, she is Martha's symbol of womanhood in harmony
with nature. Feeling torn in mind about sexuality and motherhood Martha conjures up the image of her as somebody who has
an attitude of acceptance and wholeness towards her biological womanhood (see PM, pp. 31, 42, 85).

Martha's sexual experiences are split partly by the
demands for technical sex which are related to her role as
sexual object and partly by her need to be critically aware
in order not to get emotionally tied to a man. This separates
her body from her mind:

> It was almost with the feeling of a rider who was
> wondering whether his horse would make the course that
> she regarded this body of hers, which was not only
> divided from her brain by the necessity of keeping
> open that cool and dispassionate eye, but separated
> into compartments of its own. . . . Martha had after
> all been provided with a map of her flesh by 'the
> book', in which each area was marked by the name of a
> different physical sensation. . . . She was beginning
> to feel that this view of herself was an offence
> against what was deepest and most real in her. And
> again she thought of the simple women of the country,
> who might be women in peace, according to their in-
> stincts, without being made to think and disintegrate
> themselves into fragments. During those first weeks of
> her marriage Martha was always accompanied by that
> other black woman, like an invisible sister, simpler
> and wiser than herself (PM, p. 85).

Martha is simultaneously attracted to and wary of the instinctive womanhood which the black woman represents. She is emotionally drawn to it while she intellectually guards herself against the traditional womanhood which it implies. She is also split in relation to the psychological dependence on love which Mrs. Van frees herself from. While Martha tries to get a rational perspective on this phenomenon her relationship to love is presented as more complicated than Mrs. Van's.

Martha cannot get rid of her emotional dependence on Douglas until her political involvement gives her a vision of a new social context which can replace the dream of the city. But this new involvement does not end her need for love. Martha's love affair with the leftist William and her second marriage to Anton Hesse demonstrate a continuing dependence on the emotional confirmation which love implies. Not until she has transferred her emotional involvement to William and leftist politics is she able to combine her critical distance to Douglas with the emotional coldness which, in the example of Mrs. Van, is presented as an important element in preservation of personal integrity.

If Martha is considered in comparison with Mrs. Van and the black woman her ambivalent attitude to feeling and intellect and consciousness and unconsciousness becomes manifest. A similar ambivalence also seems to characterize the textual treatment of these matters. On the one hand Martha's reflective awareness is described as a device which makes her retain her idea of an authentic identity, while her social and biological womanhood represents emotional and irrational forces which are threatening to her sense of self. On the other hand these very forces are seen as central to Martha's sense of identity and in this context her reflective awareness is viewed as an obstacle. In *Martha Quest* through *A Ripple from the Storm* consciousness is viewed as necessary for survival in society: women need it as a defence mechanism against social and biological pressures. At the same time its limitations are often demonstrated in a way which makes the realization of emotional and instinctive needs appear as a more creative attitude.

Martha's consciousness has a definite limit in that it does not lead to action. The narrator often displays an ironic, satirical attitude towards Martha's need to abstract and intellectualize her experiences which suggests that she uses her awareness to retain a status quo, that she rationalizes her emotions in order not to have to deal with them (cf. PM, pp. 83-84). The narrative voice hints that Martha's awareness is a fake; thus it could be argued that it recommends a more thoroughly conscious attitude rather than rejecting such a mentality. However, there are several other ways in which the weakness of consciousness are pinpointed. Taken together they point to a strong ambivalence about the use of a reflective and rational attitude. The ideology which permeates *A Proper Marriage* contains an implicit criticism of what could be called an "instrumental" attitude, i.e., a technical, rational, scientifically oriented way of relating to life. The instrumental view is mainly represented by the various handbooks which regulate Martha's marital life both as regards sexual matters, childbirth and childrearing. The criticism of their ideological influence is manifested by the fact that they force the characters to adapt to a kind of ritualized, superficial existence in which they are alienated from more deeply felt emotions.

On several occasions the instrumental attitude can be interpreted as one which women adapt to but feel basically foreign to. During her pregnancy Douglas and Martha agree that "the whole business of having a baby was . . . a minor incident, to be dealt with as practically as possible" (PM, p. 146). On her own, Martha reacts differently, however. Her sense of reality changes during the pregnancy: her body changes, teaches her that "strength of mind alone was not enough" - and her life becomes dominated by "that other time," the time of "the stranger in her flesh" (PM, p. 148). As Douglas adheres to the demand for rationality and practicality Martha cannot share her real experiences of her pregnancy with him. This is clearly demonstrated on the occasion when Martha is able to communicate with Douglas's mother because of their mutual interest in

children, a communication which is immediately destroyed by
Douglas's presence (PM, pp. 153-155).

The criticism of an instrumental, possibly male attitude
to life colours the descriptions of Martha's attempts to be
aware of her situation. This colouring makes her attitude seem
related to the rationalism which is objected to. Martha's
striving for a conscious attitude and the textual illustra-
tion of the limits of consciousness are most clearly demonstrated during Martha's childbirth.

When Martha gives birth she tries to control the physical
process by being conscious of what happens to her. Her method
consists of an attempt to be simultaneously conscious of both
the presence and absence of pain, but she fails:

> all her concentration, all her self-consciousness, could
> not succeed in creating either the state of pain or pain-
> lessness while its opposite was in her. It was a complete
> failure of her, that free and willed spirit. . . . There
> were two Marthas, and there was nothing to bridge them.
> Failure. Complete failure (PM, p. 187).

This deadlock is broken by a black woman who makes Martha give
in to the pain by singing an old nurse's song: "Martha let the
cold knot of determination loosen, she let herself go, she let
her mind go dark into the pain" (PM, p. 189).

In this context Martha's striving for consciousness is
presented as a kind of hubris, an absurd individualism which
fails when confronted with the laws of nature. Prominence is
given to the black woman's acceptance of the biological process as being more creative. Her singing seems to represent
a female knowledge which Martha lacks, something "simpler and
wiser." Her womanhood can be formulated as acceptance of and
unity with nature. Martha realizes such a womanhood on one
occasion during her pregnancy when she has an instinctive
experience of nature.

Martha and her friend Alice revolt against their husbands by going out into the countryside in a state of advanced
pregnancy in the middle of the rainy season. They undress and
throw themselves naked into a pot-hole on the veld. "Blindly"
and with shouts of "triumph" they give themselves over to it
(PM, p. 174), an experience which gives them both physical

and psychic release: "they were both free and comfortable in
their minds, their bodies felt relaxed and tired . . ."
(PM, p. 176).

The pot hole episode appears as a creative rite in which
fertile and sexual elements are combined. The sexual component
is underlined by the instinctive bodily release which Martha
achieves and by her encounter with a snake which appears to
function as a sexual symbol (PM, p. 175). This experience
signifies her first unequivocally positive realization of her
sexuality as an adult woman. In this fashion she appears to
find an outlet for the liberating sexual energy which she
manifests in the battle of the clothes and which is latent in
her occasional experiences of bodily strength and confidence
(see Ch. I, Sec. 3.3, and notes 11, 12).

The two pregnant women's instinctive union with nature
is a protest against the male war activities. It suggests a
claim for a female principle serving as a corrective against
a male-dominated culture which manifests itself in a scientifically rational attitude on the one hand and in an attraction
to violence and destruction on the other. The centre of the
female principle appears to be the biological womanhood represented by the black woman.[16] I have tried to demonstrate
the ambiguous presentation of this type of womanhood by
pointing out how it is related to Martha's reflective awareness. A similar ambiguity is also present in the treatment of
the specifically female consciousness that can be summarized
as directed towards love.

While it seems clear that the early novels of *Children
of Violence* mainly display an anti-romantic, rational attitude towards love this standpoint does not exhaust their
treatment of it. Love is not only presented as a myth which
is given to a woman by society but also as a deeply felt
inner need central to woman's sense of identity. Woman's
capacity for love is described as that "other veiled per-
sonage that waits, imprisoned, in every woman, to be released
by love, that person she feels to be (obstinately and against
the evidence of all experience) what is real and enduring in
her . . ." (MQ, p. 206). Martha is also said to belong to the

"type of woman who can never be, as they are likely to put it
'themselves' with anyone but the man to whom they have permanently or not given their hearts" (RS, p. 48). Furthermore
love is not only presented as a force which has the power to
maintain society through the institution of the family but
also as a power which transcends what is socially given. There
is a utopian element in Martha's way of relating to love which
is illustrated by the fact that love is intimately connected
with the dream of the city, the new, different society.
Martha's love for Douglas demonstrates this connection.
Likewise, when she leaves him love is one of the motivating
factors which inspires her to search for new forms of life.
It seems significant that Martha's dream for a new society
contains ideals of loving personal relationships as well as
new political concepts. The female concern for love attributed
to her seems to contain not only the potential of negative
dependence on others but also an intuitive openness and receptivity to human needs.

This means that Martha's tendency to comply takes on an
ambiguous aspect. *Martha Quest* refers to Martha's way of
"submitting herself to a person or a place, with a demure,
childish compliance," and *Landlocked* describes her "need
to say yes, to comply, to melt into situations." In *Martha
Quest* this attitude is mainly associated with passivity and
sensitivity to outside pressure: it is compared to being
"under a spell." In *Landlocked*, on the other hand, it is seen
as a creative receptivity. There Martha's need to comply is
termed "what was best in her" and exemplified as a "warm
response" to people, a need to lovingly comfort and support
them (MQ, p. 196, LL, pp. 24-25).

The tensions embodied in the treatment of Martha's female
identity may ultimately be viewed as symptoms of the conflict
between the outwards-directed and inwards-directed tendencies
contained in her quest. Martha's reflective awareness is a
central force in her outward search while her female biology
and consciousness threaten her abilities to realize a meaningful social identity; on the other hand this very womanhood allows her to reach the mystical experience of unity

with nature and with an unconscious dimension of life which
is central to the inward search.

When Martha goes into the pot-hole she joins with nature
in an instinctive fashion which recalls her adolescent contact with nature, although during the pot-hole episode nature
is not awsome and fearful and she is at one with it in a more
harmonious way than during the mystical experience. Nature's
challenge to Martha's humanity - its lesson of littleness and
insignificance - returns, however, during her pregnancy and
childbirth when she experiences biological and instinctive
forces which are shown to be stronger than her conscious ego
and threatening to her sense of self.

Martha's contact with natural and unconscious forces is
brought about partly by her biological womanhood and partly
by the intuitive and receptive components of her female consciousness. In *Martha Quest*, *A Proper Marriage* and *A Ripple
from the Storm*, where her main project is her attempt to
transcend given social reality, the negative aspect of her
female consciousness is stressed, i.e., its tendency to turn
her into the compliant female trapped by social conditions.
In *Landlocked* and *The Four-Gated City*, on the other hand,
where her quest aims at an inner, mystical transcendence,
her receptivity is looked upon as creative and is used both
in social life and in mystical experiences.[17]

3 Martha and the Group

3.1 Hopes and Frustrations

Martha's marriage breaks up because her dream of an ideal
city becomes attached to a communist group. To her the group
signifies a new way of life, it seems to be the answer to her
search for a "brotherhood" which will fulfill her needs for a
life style characterized by equality and intellectual and
emotional communication. Also, the group represents a new
philosophy, communism, which to Martha (as well as to other
group members) stands for a belief in the future which re-

places her sense of being bound by the past, a faith in change instead of the "nightmare of repetition," and a committed idealism instead of a dry cynicism (cf. RS, pp. 65-66).

However, actual social reality defeats the group's attempt to transcend it. Because of collective, social pressures the group becomes frustrated in its aims, both externally and internally. Colonialism prevents it from being effective in its fight against racism. Its inner harmony is torn apart by conflicts which to a large extent stem from the class consciousness and sex role patterns exhibited by its members.

The working-class RAF members of the group are in opposition to its middle class women: towards the women these men display a mixture of a working-class sense of inferiority and a patriarchal feeling of superiority (cf. RS, pp. 111-112, 155). Patriarchal traits are in fact present in most of the male members, which means that the conflict between men and women is a major one within the group. Another important tension springs from the opposition between intellect and feeling, or theorizing versus activism and emphasis on personal experiences. In this context the RAF members clash with Anton Hesse who, although he is working-class like them, is the intellectual and ideological leader of the group. In this capacity he also comes into conflict with the women who tend to share the RAF viewpoint of giving priority to feelings and to personal experiences rather than to intellectual analysis and to "correct" conclusions about the political situation (cf. RS, pp. 93-98).

The only character who approaches a synthesis of these conflicts is Athen, former peasant and guerilla fighter from Greece. He combines political activism and a non-sexist attitude towards women. Without adopting the overly emotional approach of some of the RAF members, he expresses a concern with human beings which is manifested as a personally involved, humanistic interpretation of communism.[18]

The internal conflicts and dreams of the group are most clearly brought out through the presentation of its couples, notably in the relationships between Anton and Martha and

between Andrew and Maisie. These couples dramatize a conflict
between the personal and the political, an issue that will be
the main focus of attention when I analyse Martha's political
identity.

3.2 The Personal and the Political: Martha, Politics, and the Family

According to group ideology "personal matters" are subordinated to strictly political ones. Martha welcomes such an outlook;
to her it is a relief to consider her personal problems as
minor and uninteresting in comparison with the overall political aims of the group. Thus, for example, she is supported
in her effort to leave Douglas by Jasmine's assurance that
the possibility of a "revolutionary situation" makes her
concern with "personal matters" ridiculous (PM, p. 428).
     Martha's attempt to disregard the personal implies that
she tries to disconnect herself from her past, i.e., from her
experiences of the family. Instead her energies are directed
towards the future, socialist society. She tries to politicize her individual life in so far as she attempts to become
a servant of humanity instead of keeping up close personal
relationships with a few people: Martha, like other group
members, is pervaded by a spirit of "all-comprehensive compassion for the whole of humanity" (RS, p. 47).
     There are, however, latent conflicts and inconsistencies
in Martha's position. Her political identity contains a deep
split: it is compared to a "bright shell" which protects her
from a "deep, impersonal pain," which still manifests itself
as a "shadow" deepening steadily. This "pain" is related to
her past, to those "personal matters" that she tries to repress, mainly her relationship to her daughter (RS, pp.
33-34). The contrast between the "bright shell" and the
shadow of pain points to the generally precarious nature
of Martha's political identity. Likewise, her longing for
her daughter demonstrates the somewhat theoretical nature
of her involvement with humanity instead of with individual
human beings. Martha not only misses Caroline, she also needs

a "close, complete intimacy" with a man so as not to feel
lacking in an important aspect of her sense of self (RS, p.
48).[19]

The tenuous quality of Martha's political identity is
further illustrated by her serious illness. As in the case
of her other momentous illnesses, this one should be viewed
as a symptom of a psychological crisis (cf. Ch. I, Sec. 3.3).
Her state of unhealth may be considered as a protest from
those parts of herself which she represses in her life with
the group. Her illness forces her into a state of loneliness and quietude which contrasts sharply with the constant
activism and collectivity of her political life. It also
brings out layers of her consciousness which are in opposition to group ideology. This is demonstrated in two dreams
one of which seems to stress the strength of the past in the
form of an ancient, mysterious lizard (RS, pp. 101-102),
whereas the other manifests a longing in Martha to escape
from the demanding political life to the "shallow shores of
nostalgia, where no responsibility existed" (RS, p. 104).

It is not only its deep split which makes Martha's
political identity so fragile, the identity is also shown
to be inconsistent in the sense that she simultaneously tries
to escape and to solve her personal problems by embracing
group life and group ideology. On the one hand her political
attitudes tend towards an anonymous and abstract interest in
humanity, on the other they indicate that her personal life
is the centre of her involvement. She is not primarily
engaged in a fight for clearly defined economic and social
goals, she has a more vaguely humanitarian aim, a dream of
a future when "pain would cease to exist" (RS, p. 35). This
aspiration can of course be seen as an indication of the
generally vague, utopian character of the politics of the
group, but as already suggested pain for Martha is intimately connected with the private sphere of life. This
dimension she tries to escape from in politics, but it still
seems to provide the basis for her political concern. She
demonstrates her interest in finding political solutions
to personal problems by her engagement in Maisie's unwanted

pregnancy and by her dreams of a different way of life for
women in the Soviet Union.

The relationship between Martha and Anton most explicitly illustrates the various tensions and conflicts inherent in
her political self. One reason for Martha's attraction to
Anton is the detached and theoretical quality of his political involvement - he may be said to incarnate the impersonal,
abstractly revolutionary spirit of the group. The ideological
aspect of her attraction is underlined by the quotation from
Olive Schreiner which precedes the section of the novel that
deals with the married life of Martha and Anton: "My friendship for him began by my being struck by the stand he took on
certain political questions" (RS, p. 177). But there is also
another motive for Martha's interest in Anton. For her he is
a parental figure from whom she expects safety and love. This
element in their relationship is stressed by the fact that it
is established during Martha's illness, i.e., at a time when
her personal problems are dominant (cf. Sec. 2.6).[20]

Anton's attitude to the relationship between personal
experiences and political ideology indirectly provides a
comment on the split in Martha's mind. The firmness of principle which he displays turns out to be a protection against
human relationships: his political ideology gives him an
excuse for not dealing with his own personal problems and
for being contemptuous of those of others. For example, his
revolutionary ideals about women serve as a cover-up for a
bourgeois and patriarchal practice in his private life with
Martha. Theoretically he claims to have an understanding of
the special problems of women in society, problems which he
considers not to have been given "sufficient thought" in the
socialist movement (RS, p. 60). But he is unable to look upon
Martha as a comrade and instead treats her in a paternally
complacent and vainly uxorious manner. Like Douglas he displays not only the strength but also the weakness inherent
in the patriarchal character structure: his behaviour ranges
from fatherly contempt and possessiveness to childish dependence and appeal (see RS, pp. 183-184, 202-203, 269).

Anton illustrates a conflict between theory and practice.

Basically, however, a connection rather than a division is
suggested between his political and personal lives: both in
his political and private capacities he is pictured as
authoritarian. His political leadership is presented as
oppressive in a way which coheres with rather than contra-
dicts his personal relationship with Martha. Martha's attraction to Anton indicates a tendency in her to be drawn to what
is authoritarian. Their relationship contains the role
pattern of the revolutionary leader and the devoted cadre
as well as that of the patriarch and the submissive woman.
By connecting these two patterns the text shows that a
revolutionary group like a family with bourgeois norms may
be hierarchical and characterized by oppression and submission.[21]

In the demand for the individual to adhere to the
collective ideology of the group there is a potential for
passive submission to an authoritarian structure. For example,
to be "ripe" to join the group is described as a state of
"utter self-abnegation" (RS, p. 48), a mental condition which
seems similar to the self-effacing dependence which Martha
develops with men. The absolutist and self-negating traits
in the group ideology may be assumed to strengthen rather
than counteract Martha's passivity and tendency to submit
herself to stereotyped role patterns. Probably this is what
is referred to when she summarizes her experience of the
group life in the following manner: "Why is it I listen for
the echoes of other people in my voice and what I do all the
time? The fact is, I'm not a person at all, I'm nothing yet
- perhaps I never will be" (RS, p. 302).

Still, this appraisal of Martha's political identity is
not clear-cut. It is also presented as a "rebirth into a
higher state of consciousness: "her eyes had been opened and
her ears made to hear. . . . For the first time in her life
she had been offered an ideal to live for" (PM, p. 364). This
pronouncement concerns Martha's introduction to communism, but
her reaction to the collapse of the group is described in a
similar fashion. Her two years of political life seem to
her "more important than all the time she had lived before"

(RS, p. 303); without the group she feels "cut off from everything that had fed her imagination" (RS, p. 301).

Like the marriage between Martha and Anton that between
Maisie and Andrew concerns the relationship between the personal and the political. Maisie must solve a personal problem:
she needs a father for her future child and Andrew declares
himself willing, initially for ideological reasons. However,
as love soon arises between them, their relationship ultimately points to the need for spontaneous feelings rather
than for principally correct actions.

This couple represents a type of communist or socialist
family in the sense that it challenges the bourgeois notion
of private ownership: it demonstrates that family relationships need not be based on the man's ownership of woman and
child. But this experiment fails. Like the relationship
between Martha and Anton it eventually illustrates the pervasiveness of bourgeois and patriarchal family patterns. With
the arrival of Binkie Maynard, the biological father, Andrew
is suddenly made aware that the child does not belong to him.
Once his sense of ownership is awakened it kills his love for
Maisie; her body starts to remind him of the other man and
becomes revolting to him. The relationship between Andrew
and Maisie changes into one which involves the two men:
Maisie turns into an object for their competition and
prestige. In Maisie's words: "They talked about each other
more than me. . . . suddenly it wasn't me any more that
either of them was fond of. But *I* feel just the same" (RS,
p. 297).[22]

Despite her attempt to escape the personal dimension by
becoming involved in leftist politics, Martha's political inclination tends towards a concern with human relationships.
Her involvement is primarily based on a need to find alternatives to the oppressive family patterns she has experienced.
The group relations between men and women and between parents
and children thus take on a political significance for her.
Her relationship to Anton and that between Andrew and Maisie
become to her deeply felt examples of the political failure
of the group.

Chapter III   The Inward Quest

1 Introduction

In *Landlocked* and *The Four-Gated City* Martha's search for an
identity turns inwards. Her search is helped by an inner self,
a "monitor" or "watcher" (LL, p. 24; FGC, pp. 270, 604), whose
function it is to guide her to mystical experience of wholeness by putting her in touch with certain elemental unconscious powers.[1] This endeavour is resisted by her social being
characterized by a special form of consciousness, which in
The Four-Gated City is called "ordinary" or "daytime" thinking
(FGC, pp. 48, 51, 76). To be ruled by the "ordinary" or "daytime" consciousness is to be fragmented: it is the nature of
this type of thought to divide reality into categories, to
generalize and abstract (see FGC, pp. 99, 495-496, 573).
Although this consciousness is sometimes described as some
sort of defect inherent in the human brain (see FGC, p. 573),
its mode of functioning seems to connect it with intellectual
and rational thought. Throughout *The Four-Gated City* this
"ordinary" consciousness is also contrasted with an intuitive
or visionary apprehension of reality.

A split identity can also be maintained by forces which
do not pertain to the intellect but to physical and biological
functions. It is suggested, for example, that too much food,
sleep and sex may hamper the experience of wholeness (see
Sec. 2). However, biology is not primarily viewed as a force
which inhibits Martha's quest. In *The Four-Gated City* the
basis of all existence is provided by a form of energy which
manifests itself in physical and social life as well as in
the unconscious. This energy can be manipulated by the individual in a way which leads to inner experience (see Sec. 2).

The conflict between intellect and feelings and
between rational and intuitive ways of perceiving reality

is given a more definite and precise content in *Landlocked*
and *The Four-Gated City*. Intellect and rationality are connected with an outer, cultural form of consciousness, whereas
intuition and irrationality are linked with the inner self,
the "watcher." In the earlier novels Martha's watching consciousness is mainly associated with the reflective and
rational "detached observer." In *The Four-Gated City* it
appears instead to be a development of her mystical "conscience" and her receptive and intuitive female consciousness (see Ch. I, Sec. 5.2; Ch. II, Sec. 2.7). This novel
thus resolves the ambiguity about what aspects of her consciousness are central to her identity. It may be argued
that instead of the tension between reason and intuition and
between conscious and unconscious powers which characterizes
the early novels, the later ones are informed by a dualism
where intuitive, irrational and unconscious powers are viewed
as leading to creativity and wholeness, whereas reflective,
rational and conscious ones are seen as destructive and
fragmenting.

In *Landlocked* and *The Four-Gated City* the theme of
violence concentrates on its significance in terms of war.
War is seen as the major destructive expression of a fundamental source of energy or force which informs all of life.
The late volumes of *Children of Violence* present a world
view based on a conflict between different types of forces
which emanate from a basic source of energy. These forces
manifest themselves as varying expressions of consciousness
within the individual and society. The conflict between them
can be interpreted in terms of nature versus culture: the
basic energy appears to be a potentially creative, natural
power which may, however, become deformed because of destructive cultural influences. In the early part of the
series biological womanhood represents a creative, natural
force in opposition to an oppressive cultural one. In that
context the nature-culture approach to reality clashed with
another view which saw life as determined by social categories. In the later books this tension is largely resolved
and nature versus culture remains the dominant mode of
understanding.

In this chapter I shall seek first of all to outline the realization of Martha's inner identity and then demonstrate the changed outlook on the family, politics and society which this concept of the inner life entails. In *The Four-Gated City* Martha is no longer concerned with a change of social institutions but aims instead at a transcendence of the "ordinary" consciousness which characterizes cultural existence. This pursuit still has social and political implications, however; the expanded or evolved consciousness which Martha tries to develop is presented as the solution both to her own and the whole human predicament.

2 The Way towards Inner Life

Martha's inner identity is developed with the assistance of certain other characters who seem to be in touch with elemental and unconscious sources of power. In this section I want to analyse her relationship with these characters.

2.1 Thomas Stern

In the beginning of *Landlocked* Martha's identity is described in the following manner: she has an inner, "real" identity, a "monitor" or "guardian," and an outer identity, a "shell." This "shell" consists partly of her "personality," i.e., her social being, and partly of her physical appearance (LL, pp. 23-24). Her real indentity manifests itself through a kind of area within her consciousness, "a tall lit space," which informs her of her state of mind: "Inside her opened up the lit space on to which . . . emotions would walk like actors and begin to speak without (apparently) any prompting from her" (LL, p. 39). This inner identity also communicates with her through dreams; early on in *Landlocked*, Martha has a recurring dream in which she sees herself as a house with many rooms which the monitor tells her to keep separate (LL, pp. 23-24). The dream demonstrates her split identity and the

relationship between its two parts: the many rooms illustrate
the various roles which make up her social being whereas the
monitor's advice seems to imply that to enter fully into one
of these roles would hamper the development of her inner self.

Martha harbours the view that a close relationship with
a man would make her whole: a man "would unify her elements,"
would be "like a roof, or like a fire burning in the centre
of the empty space" (LL, p. 41). This quotation indicates that
the search for a man would no longer contain the same social
significance as it had for Martha as a young woman. Love is
no longer a way of transcending the given society in order to
establish an alternative "brotherhood" or an ideal city.
Instead it is presented as leading to inner wholeness and
resurrection. Nor is it any longer romantic. Martha is looking
for a *man* - the sexual component of her longing is strongly
emphasized. In *Landlocked* she is driven towards various men
in an instinctive, almost impersonal way. First she is
attracted to Solly Cohen despite the fact that she opposes
his ideas and dislikes his personality; then she is drawn to
Joss in the same haphazard fashion. Her sexual instincts also
keep her from repairing her marriage with Anton Hesse (see
LL, p. 72).

Thomas Stern is the one man who corresponds to Martha's
partly unconscious demands. He is a Jewish communist refugee
from Poland who works with garden farming in Zambesia. Sexual
attraction rather than political beliefs brings Martha and
Thomas together. Their contact gives Martha a new mental
"room" which eliminates the division of her identity by
becoming the "centre" of her self (LL, p. 114). This symbolic
room is directly related to nature as it has its tangible
counterpart in the garden shed to which the love affair is
localized. The gardener and his shed are refuges of natural
life which are seen in contrast to the social, civilized
forms of existence represented by the family house of Thomas's
brother and other social "rooms" which Martha keeps in touch
with, for example her home life in the flat which she shares
with Anton, her parents' house and Johnny Lindsay's home.

Martha's contact with Thomas signifies her first

achievement of wholeness together with another human being.
Together with him she tears down the intellectualizing and
emotionally distancing defence mechanisms with which she
normally protects herself. Through him she also realizes the
sexual and sensuous components of herself which were latent,
expressed only in her contacts with nature. The reason why
she is able to communicate with Thomas appears to be the
non-social quality of their relationship. Their interaction
is not only non-social in the sense that it is connected with
unconscious, natural powers, but also in so far as it dis-
agrees with the social norms for relationships between men
and women in the early volumes of *Children of Violence* through
its lack of family orientation. As Martha and Thomas are already married, their love affair escapes the danger of
domesticity. With him Martha's emotional and sexual openness
will not result in her being tied to the traditional role of
the woman in the family, as in the case of Douglas and Anton.
Martha experiences her new openness as a painful dissolution
of the ego, which, however, leads to new insights which point
towards her final experience of an inner identity:

> what was this absolute giving up of herself, and his need
> for it; what was the prolonged almost unbearable look at
> each other, as if doors were being opened one after
> another inside their eyes as they looked - how was it
> that she was driven by him back and back into regions
> of herself she had not known existed . . . (LL, p. 117).

Martha's love life with Thomas is thematically linked with her
mystical experiences of nature as a child and as a teenager
and with the pot-hole episode during her pregnancy.[2] The
difference is that natural, instinctive life now becomes
central to her sense of identity instead of consisting of
incidental glimpses of a reality which conflicts with her
life as a social being.

Through her relationship with Thomas, Martha makes contact with a form of creative energy: "life" itself runs
through them, and their room contains a "softly-running
dynamo, to which, through him, she was connected" (LL, pp.
125, 168). By being in touch with this energy Martha changes
her understanding of herself and the surrounding world.

Whereas she earlier oriented herself mainly by means of the
intellect, systems of ideas, and books, she now develops her
capacity for irrational and emotional perception through
physical experiences, intuition, and dreams. She starts having
visions and overhearing the thoughts of others, a capacity
which she will fully develop in *The Four-Gated City*. Her inner
room, "the empty space," gets filled with pictures of people
in different situations and when Thomas is in Israel she
"hears" him and argues with him (LL, pp. 182-183, 220-222).
Also she has a dream which predicts his death (LL, pp.
229-231). Furthermore she starts using her irrational abilities politically - for example, her intuition serves as her
means for judging the truth of a book about Stalinism:

> Reading this book . . . it was her first experience,
> though a clumsy, unsure one, of using a capacity she
> had not known existed. She thought: I *feel* the book is
> true - although it is badly written, crude, sensational.
> Well, what does that mean, to *feel* something is true, as
> if I'm not even reading the words of the book, but
> responding to something else. She thought, vaguely: if
> this book were not on this subject, but about something
> else, well, the yardsticks I use would say: yes, this is
> true. One has an instinct one trusts, yes... (LL. p.
> 249).

Despite the fact that Martha develops her visionary powers
Landlocked suggests that the consciousness which she achieves
is incomplete. Martha is capable of profiting from only one
aspect of Thomas, the one which is in correspondence with
growth and creativity. But he also stands for the opposing
perspective, linked with death, violence and destruction.
As a Jew and a communist Thomas is intimately connected with
the violence and oppression of World War II; his life is
inextricably bound up with gas chambers and internment camps.
The hatred which this background has created in him gradually
emerges and is directed against a certain Sergeant Tressel,
a white Zambesian he had met during his military service in
Africa. Tressel's "good-natured" destructiveness incarnates
in Thomas's eyes all the meaningless and wanton violence he
encountered during the war (LL, p. 164). To exact his revenge
on Tressel, Thomas goes to Palestine to take part in the
Zionist struggle. Back in Zambesia he withdraws from his

earlier life; he is drawn into a kind of schizophrenic state of mind and lives with the blacks until he dies - a victim of the destructiveness within himself and others.

Before his withdrawal Thomas tries to communicate a world view to Martha which would seem to contain a constructive way of relating to violence. Thomas does this by means of two stories; he recounts one about an elm tree and one about his Polish teacher (LL, pp. 135, 219). The meaning of both is that the time when people lived, loved and died protected by an elm tree is definitely over. The time of safety, clear and calm perspectives, of having roots and enjoying peace, is over. Our time is ridden by atomic power, violence, chaos, and alienation. Thomas's message to Martha implies that his experiences and psyche should be seen as normal and sound whereas people who consider themselves untouched by such matters ought to be regarded as aberrant: "There are two kinds of people - those who know how easy it is to be dead, and those who think death can't happen to me... I told you, everything's changed. I'm the norm now. I told you, the elm tree and safety's finished. Who is the freak, the unusual person?" (LL, p. 193). Thomas further implies that a new type of person can develop who is capable of encompassing the changes of the times: "Perhaps there'll be a mutation though. Perhaps that's why we are all so sick. Something new is trying to get born through our thick skins. I tell you, Martha, if I see a sane person, then I know he's mad" (LL, pp. 134-135).

On one occasion Martha has an experience which contains something of what Thomas tries to tell her. During a dance when she is "high" on love and liquor she reaches a total state of mind which encompasses both love and death, creativity and destructiveness. Her consciousness grows until she becomes a "space of knowledge inside a shell of swaying drunkenness" (LL, p. 169). In this state of mind she sees her relationship with Thomas as related to the war in Europe and acknowledges Tressel's presence as a sign of the continuous existence of violence:

> She and Thomas would soon part, and soon this love . . .
> which had taught her what loving a man was, would have
> gone, been blown apart. Like a town in Europe, dark
> under a sky bursting with bits of flying flame and
> steel. And the Tressels, . . . their appearance this
> evening could have been foreseen. Martha felt as if she
> had known all her life that on this evening . . . she
> would sit by a man she loved with her whole heart, and
> look past flaring braziers at a red-faced fattish man
> in a badly-cut dinner suit, and know that he was an
> enemy too strong for her (LL, pp. 168-169).

On this particular occasion Martha experiences violence as
something which exists within herself not just within others.

> Martha had again discovered her hand. . . . It was
> monstrously, unbelievably ugly, like a weapon. . . .
> The shape made by her forefinger and thumb, touching
> each other - it was like a revelation of brutality.
> Her hand was like a pair of pincers, the claw of a
> lobster, something cold and predatory. She looked at
> her left hand, astounded by its cruelty. . . .
>   Her left hand, her hand - never had there been
> such an extraordinary thing . . . (LL, pp. 173-174).

Violence is, however, rejected by Martha in her everyday life.
In her arguments with Thomas, away in Palestine, she advises
him not to give in to it. The narrator hints that Martha is
naive:

> The soul of the human race, that part of the mind which
> has no name, is not called Thomas and Martha, which
> holds the human race as frogspawn is held in jelly -
> that part of Martha and of Thomas was twisted and
> warped, was part of a twist and a damage - she could
> no more disassociate herself from the violence done
> her, done by her, than a tadpole can live out of
> water (LL, pp. 222-223).

Landlocked appears to argue that both Martha and Thomas
display failures of consciousness as regards violence. Thomas
lets himself be engulfed by it, Martha pushes it aside.
Neither of them is able to grasp its meaning and transcend
it. It is further implied that Martha is partly guilty of
Thomas's destructive development through her unwillingness
to allow herself to be connected with the forces of violence.
Martha's lack of insight into the dark part of Thomas is
described as a "failure" of "imagination" and "sympathy"
(LL, p. 213), a phrase which recurs as an interpretation of
the violence committed during the war: "forty-odd million

human beings had been murdered, deliberately or from care-
lessness, from lack of imagination . . ." (LL, p. 223).[3]

Martha's relationship with Thomas prefigures the development of her inner identity in *The Four-Gated City*.
His character encompasses aspects which will be more fully
developed in Jack and Lynda with whom Martha continues on
the way towards the inner life. Thomas shares with Jack the
sensuousness and experience of violence; he and Lynda are
both familiar with madness, and in a rudimentary form he
also represents the expansion of the human consciousness
which in *The Four-Gated City* is presented as the solution
to social and cultural problems.

2.2 Jack and Lynda

In *The Four-Gated City* the inner life is more developed than
in *Landlocked*. The conflict between inner identity and social
being remains, although in a somewhat different form. Now the
agent of inner life is called "the watcher" or "the permanent
person" (FGC, p. 395), and the social identity is associated
with "ordinary" or "daytime" thinking. Furthermore a new category of inner life is introduced, "the human mind" (FGC, p.
546), which can be seen as a kind of "collective unconscious."[4] The conflict between inner and outer identities is
also placed in a more defined philosophical context. "Ordinary" consciousness is connected with Western rationalism,
whereas inner life is related to various forms of mysticism
(see FGC, pp. 560-564).

Martha's experiences during the first part of her life
in London are centred around her sexual contacts with Jack.
They are a prologue to her later experiments with inner life
together with Lynda. As a newcomer to London Martha stands
apart from all social contexts; she experiments with different
identities and experiences the tenuous quality of her social
identity. This brings her closer to her inner identity: she
is no longer Martha, a particular personality, but a watching consciousness, "a soft dark receptive intelligence" (FGC,

p. 51). But before reaching this stage she must free herself
from the fear of loneliness which is brought out by her lack
of social and personal identity. She must give up her desire
to belong and quiet her heart:

> And her heart, ... well, that was the point, it was
> always her heart that first fought off the pain of not
> belonging anywhere, and then, resisted, told to be quiet,
> it quietened and stilled. Her heart as it were came to
> heel; and after that, the current of her ordinary
> thought switched off (FGC, p. 51).

In this detached state of mind Martha can communicate with
Jack; they then inhabit the same region of "the human mind"
(FGC, p. 54). Jack is described as an outsider whose painful
childhood and war experiences have made him withdraw from
all social responsibility and live a life concentrated
around sexual experiences. To him sexual intercourse consists of a building up of energy whose aim is to break through
the "ordinary" frame of mind. Through sexuality he learns to
master his "enemy," i.e., the hatred which his childhood has
created in him (FGC, p. 74). He discovers that hatred and
love both stem from forces that human beings can learn to
control.

> Martha, do you know what I've discovered - making love?
> I understood what hating is. You say all your life
> 'I hate' 'I love'. But then you discover hatred is a
> sort of wavelength you can tune into. . . . If you can
> get beyond 'I hate' - then you find - *there is hatred,
> always there*. You can say, *I am going into hatred now,
> it's just a force*. That's all, it's not anything, not
> good or bad. . . . it's like a thousand volts of elec-
> tricity (FGC, 75-76).

Here *The Four-Gated City* introduces the idea that love and
hatred, good and evil are different forms of energy. This
was hinted at in the relationship between Martha and Thomas
but not explicitly formulated. Later in *The Four-Gated City*
when Martha experiences a transfer of energy from Lynda, the
same notion recurs in an even more defined way.

> We don't understand the first thing about what goes on,
> not the first thing. 'Make love.' 'Make sex.' . . .
> It was all nonsense, words, sounds, invented by half-
> animals who understood nothing at all. Great forces
> as impersonal as thunder or lightning or sunlight or

> the movements of the oceans being contracted and heaped
> and rolled in their beds by the moon, swept through
> bodies, . . . being in the grip of this force - or *a*
> force, one of them. Not sex. Not necessarily. . . .
>   Jack had once said: 'the thousand volts.' He had
> been talking of hate. . . . A thousand volts of love?
> A thousand volts of - compassion? of charity? (FGC,
> p. 543).

Martha's sexual experiences with Jack are connected with her
interaction with Thomas and her early sense of unity with
nature, or some similar force. But with Jack her search for
mystical experience is made explicit. Sex with Jack is
described as a "ritual" with clearly defined phases (FGC,
p. 75). The accumulation of energy is followed by a stage in
which Martha and Jack investigate each other's bodies. This
is portrayed as a therapeutic act, a way in which they can
relive their personal past and liberate themselves from it.
Martha touches the scars from the wounds which Jack received
as a child and in war, and Jack examines the marks of her
pregnancy. They are then ready for the contact with the unconscious: "a power, a force, which when held and controlled,
took both up and over and away from any ordinary consciousness into an area where no words could be of use" (FGC, p.
76). In this context sexual union is described as a means
for experiencing inner wholeness, which is set in contrast
to the compartmentalized condition of ordinary life.

> Breath flows on, blood beats on, separately from each
> other; my sex lives on there, responding, or not; my
> heart feels this and that, and my mind up here goes
> working on, quite different from the heart; yet when
> the real high place of sex is reached, everything moves
> together, it is just that moment when everything does
> move together that makes the gears shift up. Yet people
> regarded sex as the drainer, the emptier, instead of the
> maker of energy. . . . There was a knowledge that was no
> part of our culture, hinted at merely; you could come
> across references (FGC, pp. 79-80).

Martha's relationship with Jack takes place within a context
of social freedom, which is presented as being premature.
Martha is still bound to ordinary, social life; she has "debts
to pay" to her mother, her husbands and her daughter (FGC, p.
54). Jack's position is likewise untenable. He finally
surrenders to the power which he tries to control. His fate

may be a warning against individualistic experiments with
inner life. This seems reasonable if he is compared with
Martha who eventually aims at reaching a consciousness which
can be of use to the human collective.

Lynda is part of the Coldridge family who provide the
basis for Martha's social life in *The Four-Gated City*. The
various members of this family correspond to different needs
in Martha's life. Lynda, who is classified as a schizophrenic,
helps Martha to reach a form of consciousness outside of the
ordinary, whereas Mark represents an attempt to comprehend
reality through the use of reason. The children serve as
mirrors to Martha in which she can see aspects of her earlier
life; by witnessing their development towards adulthood she
receives a new image of her own childhood and adolescence.

Martha's life with the Coldridges is relevant to the
treatment of the family in *Children of Violence*. In *The
Four-Gated City* family and sex role patterns are described
in a way which differs from that which predominated in the
early novels. This will be dealt with in a separate section;
what is relevant in the context of Martha's inner development is that she must liberate herself from her family experiences before she is ready for the definite movement inwards.
Martha's existence with the Coldridges is presented as an
acceptance of the family in terms of social responsibility
and as a type of therapy; she "pays her debts" to her past
by devoting herself to this family, at the same time as she
uses family life as a means of dealing with her past, defined
in *The Four-Gated City*, as "what we've been given" or are
"landed with": "'You start growing on your own account when
you've worked through what you're landed with. Until then,
you're paying off debts,' said Martha" (FGC, pp. 497-498).

With Jack Martha experienced in a concentrated form the
therapeutic exploration of the past which her life with the
Coldridges signifies. Martha's family problems have primarily
concerned her relationship with her mother and thus the
settlement with the past starts with her. When Mrs. Quest
announces her arrival in London Martha gets into a state of
depression which forces her to engage in a "salvage operation"

(FGC, p. 321) of her memory which she has repressed in order
to avoid the pain of her relationship with her mother: "her
mother - ah, yes, here it was, and she knew it. She had been
blocking off the pain, and had blocked off half of her life
with it. Her memory had gone" (FGC, p. 243).

In this context the division in Martha between an outer
and an inner identity is strongly emphasized. The latter
becomes instrumental in regaining and mastering her past.
It is described as a kind of essence of life, neither human
nor animal, neither male nor female but all these things
simultaneously: "Who are you then? Why, me, of course, who
else, horse, woman, man, or tree, a glittering faceted
individuality of breathing green, here is the sense of me,
nameless, recognizable only to me. Who, what?" (FGC, p.
260). The pain which Martha struggles against is connected
with her identity as a particular and individual personality:
"This being |the inner self| moved in and out of the house
on the kopje. . . . But, let this person become Martha - she
was swallowed in a wash of hot pain" (FGC, p. 260). With the
help of her inner self Martha is able to relive her relationship with her mother and thereby re-experience the feeling
of being unloved and unwanted: "She wept, while a small girl
wept with her, mamma, mamma, why are you so cold, so unkind,
why did you never love me?" (FGC, p. 261).

The aim of Martha's therapy is to break loose both from
her personal past and her individuality in order to be at one
with her inner identity. To achieve this she must liberate
herself from her need to be loved and to belong; in the same
way as when she was first in London, she must seek to "quiet"
her "heart." She practises this in her relationship not only
with her mother but also with men. During her depression she
has turned to Mark for comfort and a love affair develops,
which Martha then rejects so as not to become transformed
into a woman "in love" who is tied to social and personal
life through her demands for emotional confirmation:

> to herself she was able to say precisely what she feared.
> It was the rebirth of the woman in love. If one is with
> a man, 'in love', or in the condition of loving, then

> there comes to life that hungry, never-to-be-fed, never
> at peace, woman who needs and wants and must have. . . .
> God forbid (FGC, pp. 334-335).

Martha's affair with Mark is her last important relationship
with a man. Her movement away from love is already noticeable
in the comparison between her relationships with Thomas and
Jack. Martha loves Thomas, whereas Jack is only a means to
an end, an "instrument" in her search for wholeness (FGC,
p. 77).

The process of making Martha anonymous and depersonalized
is continued in her interaction with the young generation in
the Coldridge home. By recognizing aspects of herself in the
young girls Martha acquires a distance to herself:

> It was as if a shell or a skin had been peeled off, as
> if an aspect of one's self had floated away and become
> part of that timeless and fluid creature, A Young Girl,
> whose features were as little Gwen's or Jill's as they
> were hers. . . . The rejuvenation a young girl gives her
> mother or an older woman is a setting free into imper-
> sonality, a setting free, also, from her personal past
> (FGC, p. 428-429).

Her contact with the young people also enables her to cultivate
a detached attitude towards the function of being a mother,
both as regards her own mother and herself. She sees herself
as acting predictably in a play: "There were lines written
to be spoken; there was a play set like a duty" (FGC, p. 429).
Through her contact with Mark and his communist friends,
mainly Patty Samuels, Martha also detaches herself from her
earlier political self (see FGC, p. 229). Family and political
roles provide a picture of the combination of inevitability
and coincidence which characterizes social and biological
life. Freedom lies elsewhere; it is warranted by the existence
of the "watcher" or "permanent person" that can be realized
within all human beings:

> When a small baby looked straight at you, . . . you
> looked into eyes that would stay the same for as long
> as it lived. . . . Oneself, or Paul, had to be, for as
> long as it was necessary, screaming baby, sulking
> adolescent, then middle-aged woman. . . . And it was
> not so silly, not so absurd after all, to insist on
> the right to feel, while one played these ridiculous
> games . . . that all the time one communicated with

> somebody else, that person who looked steadily, always
> the same, from eyes only temporarily glazed over with
> anger, sorrow, sulk ... Because, once the necessary
> allowance of sulk, or sorrow, or pain had been dealt
> out, then the reward was that in fact one did speak to
> the permanent person in Paul, or Francis, or anybody
> else (FGC, pp. 394-395).

Martha's fight with her past is called a struggle for "survival" (FGC, p. 333). In the context of her development towards inner freedom this probably means that she avoids
getting stuck with what is given, with what she is "landed
with," and succeeds in transcending social roles and biological necessity. Her means of achieving liberation from social
life is experience followed by a sense of detachment, and her
method for overcoming her biology consists in various prac-
tices such as eating and sleeping less in order to avoid
lethargy and density. In this way she makes progress: "She
had found doors she had not known existed. She had wrestled
herself out of the dark because she had had to, and had
entered places in herself she had not known were there" (FGC,
p. 334). Her consciousness being raised, she has visions and
overhears the thoughts of others; what was earlier the result
of extra-ordinary states of mind, such as those together
with Thomas and Jack, now occurs in her daily life. So, for
example, she has a vision predicting the suicide of Lynda's
friend Dorothy and she "hears" Paul's thoughts.

Freed from her personal crisis Martha continues
"working" on her mind together with Lynda (FGC, p. 415).
Through her depression she has moved closer to Lynda's world
of mental illness and psychiatry which she used to regard as
alien to herself. By being "mad" Lynda possesses a certain
awareness which makes her function as Martha's guide: together
they expand their irrational capacities through mental exercises and through the reading of mystical literature. With
Lynda's help Martha prepares herself for her final "inner
journeys."[5]

Martha's first journey is a result of her being with
Lynda when the latter is "silly," i.e., acutely psychotic.
Martha's official capacity is to be Lynda's surveillant and
to use her "sense" in order to keep Lynda in touch with outer

reality (FGC, p. 531). But instead she identifies with Lynda
and understands her intuitively. Once she grasps that Lynda
is involved in finding means for transcending the barriers
of ordinary consciousness she stops worrying about Lynda's
behaviour, which consists in not eating or sleeping and instead
constantly circling the room. From her own visionary experiences Martha remembers that this is a way of containing energy.

   In all the descriptions of the approach to inner, unconscious life, the building-up of energy is presented as its
first phase. The body is said to be an "engine" which can
bring the human being out of the "small dim prison of every
day" (FGC, p. 545). This occurs when the body is submitted
to an extraordinary state in which physical energy is concentrated and transformed into psychic energy: *A body is a
machine for the conversion of one kind of energy into another*"
(FGC, p. 601).

   Having passed through this first phase Martha enters a
state of mind where her consciousness is characterized by
a highly increased receptivity. She then "hears" Lynda; she
thinks Lynda's thoughts as if they were her own: "it was not
far off being inside Lynda's head. . . ." At this point she
is close to "the human mind," which makes itself known as a
"great chaos of sound." She wonders if these sounds belong to
her mind or to Lynda's but then realizes that all such distinc-
tions are spurious: "it is not a question of 'Lynda's mind' or
'Martha's mind'; it is the human mind, or part of it, and Lynda,
Martha, can choose to plug in or not" (FGC, p. 546). The sound
region of the human mind contains violence and destruction. It
is dominated by a creature that incarnates evil and that is
sometimes called the "self-hater," sometimes the "Devil" (FGC,
pp. 585, 595). Martha's last and lonely inner journey is a
confrontation with this figure who must be overcome in order
for her consciousness to achieve its full potential.

   The "self-hater" makes Martha face the "underneath" of
herself (FGC, p. 604), i.e., all the hatred and violence
that she is shown to share with the human race. She confronts
sado-masochistic aspects of her own self and is in turn made
into an antisemite, a nazi, a racist etc. All of these forms

of hatred are referred to a principle or force of evil which
Martha must experience in order to attain a total view of
herself and humanity:

> *I am switched in to Hating, which is the underside of*
> *all this lovely liberalism. But just because we are all*
> *such lovely liberals it doesn't mean ... well why does*
> *he (who?) tell me that? Don't I know it already? Why,*
> *I don't ... it's because I keep forgetting I can't say,*
> *reasonable, civilized, etc. etc. Thinking that I am.*
> *I am what the human race is. I am 'The Germans are the*
> *mirror and catalyst of Europe' and also: 'Dirty Hun,*
> *Filthy Nazi'* (FGC, p. 590).

Hatred is presented as part of a basic power within which
opposite forces unite and are resolved. The part that is hate
cannot be separated from the totality without deforming it:
"Is this what all those books call 'the pairs of opposites'?
Love, hate, black, white, good, bad, man, woman" (FGC, p.
590). By experiencing hatred and admitting its existence
Martha transcends the principle of evil and completes her
inner educational process. She is free from her personal ego
as well as her unconscious, collective self. What remains is
"the watcher": "I've seen the underneath of myself. Which
isn't me - any more than my surface is me. I am the watcher,
the listener ..." (FGC, p. 604).

3 Inner Life and Social Life

The notion of an inner life leads to an altered outlook on
society in *Landlocked* and *The Four-Gated City*. This will be
dealt with below; as earlier the focus will be on the family
since the family or family-like group emerges as the primary
symbol of social life in *The Four-Gated City*.

3.1 The Family

In *The Four-Gated City* Martha accepts the family. This is
communicated to the reader through two dreams which she has
during her contact with Jack:

> she saw in front of her eyelids a picture of a man and
> a woman, walking in a high place under a blue sky holding
> children by the hand, and with them all kinds of wild
> animals, but they were not wild at all: a lion, a leopard,
> a tiger, deer, lambs, all as tame as house-pets, walking
> with the man and the woman and the lovely children, and
> she wanted to cry out with loss. . . . And then, out of
> the pain of loss, came another picture . . . she saw a
> large layered house . . . it had a London feel to it, and
> it was full of children, not children, half-grown people,
> and their faces as they turned them towards her were
> tortured and hurt, and she saw herself, a middle-aged
> woman, thickened and slowed, with the face of a middle-
> aged woman. An anxious face, a face set to endure, to
> hold on - there was such pain in this vision, such hurt,
> and she heard herself crying . . . (FGC, pp. 77-78).

These dreams depict the family in relation to the antithesis
of nature and culture. The first dream demonstrates a state
of natural harmony, an Eden, whereas the second dream which
predicts Martha's actual life with the Coldridges suggests a
"fallen" humanity. Together they suggest the idea that humanity was originally good and unspoilt but became corrupted by
an evil society, represented by the family. This is further
brought out by Martha's reflections upon her dreams: here she
describes the socializing of the child within the family in
terms of a fall from grace, a nightmarish descent into a
lower form of existence which she contrasts with her vision
of a "golden age":

> Last night again - the nightmare. But at the same time,
> the marvellous family walking with their friendly
> animals. The golden age. . . . What's the use of
> imagining impossibly marvellous ways of living, they
> aren't anywhere near us, are they? . . . Babies are
> born into this, what there is. A baby is born with
> infinite possibilities for being good. But there's
> no escaping it, it's like having to go down into a
> pit, a terrible dark blind pit . . . (FGC, p. 88).

The individual's relationship to the family consists of first
going "down into a pit" and then fighting one's way up and
out: "and your parents are part of it, of what you fight
out of. The mistake is, to think there is a way of not having
to fight your way out" (FGC, p. 88). In this context it is
suggested that it is the duty of the individual to come to
terms with the family, but the idea of collective liberation
through social change is rejected. In a bitter statement,

which signifies her departure from the idea that a new,
socialist society would create alternative, unexploiting
family relationships, Martha is ironical about her former
communist involvement:

> Oh, sometimes I think communism . . . was a kind of
> litmus paper, a holdall - you took from it what you
> wanted. But for us it went without saying that the
> family was a dreadful tyranny, a doomed institution,
> a kind of mechanism for destroying everyone. . . .
> And so we abolished the family. In our minds, and when
> the war was over and there was communism everywhere,
> the family would be abolished. You know - by decree.
> Clause 25 of a new Magna Carta. 'We decree the family
> at an end.' And then there would be the golden age,
> no family, no neurosis. Because the family was the
> source of the neurosis (FGC, p. 86).

Martha is shown to be mistaken in her earlier assumption that
there was a social means of escape from the family. Because
of this she has got "debts to pay": she must relive her life
and make up for her crimes against her mother, her husbands
and her daughter in order to liberate herself from her past
and regain the original state of freedom which she lost when
she became a social being.

Accepting the family as a cultural and psychological
necessity, Martha assumes responsibility for the Coldridges.
By doing this she submits to the "nightmare" of "repetition."
She accepts the norms of womanhood against which she was
earlier struggling both socially and psychologically. Although the Coldridge family is non-conventional in the sense
of being a form of extended family, the social roles of men
and women and parents and children correspond largely to the
ones described in the early novels of the series. In *The Four-
Gated City* the woman's main function in the family is to be a
mother; Martha plays this role both in relation to the
children and to Mark, although her relationship to the
Coldridges is nominally based on her job as Mark's secretary.
As during Martha's married life, confinement to the role as
mother represents a threat to her sense of self; likewise
the relationships between parents and children are again
centred around the conflict between rebellion and authority
(see FGC, pp. 390-395, 428-430). The main difference in the

portrayal of family roles in *The Four-Gated City* as compared
to the early novels is that in *The Four-Gated City* they are
presented as an inevitable necessity: children must revolt,
parents have to be authoritarian, Martha must "pay" her
"debts" by being a mother. Earlier family functions were
mainly rendered from a social or sociological perspective
which contained the possibility of change given other social
conditions; in *The Four-Gated City* they appear to be
characterized by a biological outlook which results in
social and cultural determinism.[6]

In *The Four-Gated City* the "nightmare" of "repetition"
is connected with a biological view of the human predicament.
Martha's life with the Coldridges repeats her past; while
before her life had been directed at change, now its cyclic
quality is stressed. The young Coldridges develop according
to certain given phases, which makes their growth appear
closely related to the biological cycle of life. To a great
extent biological necessity also seems to rule the relationships between the sexes. In my discussion of Martha's identity
as a woman I indicated a vacillation between a social and a
biological definition of her womanhood. In *Landlocked* and
The Four-Gated City the latter view appears to be dominant.
In *Landlocked*, for example, Martha is physically ill from
simultaneously having two sexual relationships: "Her stomach,
her intestines, her bladder complained that she was the wife
of one man and they did not like her making love with
another" (LL, p. 132). Female dependence on one man is
viewed as conditioned by biological nature rather than, as
earlier, by the cultural myth of love. Such an outlook also
seems to have inspired the description of the "woman in
love" in *The Four-Gated City* as a "hungry" creature, "never-
to-be-fed, never-at-peace."[7] A biological interpretation
fits this novel's conception of life as ultimately reducible
to a form of energy. But the physical phenomena that are
part of "ordinary," social existence are viewed as compulsory
and thus lack the creative dimension sometimes inherent in
this energy.

Whereas in the early novels the basis for the relation-

ship between the individual and society fluctuates between
a socio-psychological and a biological-psychological definition, in the late books biological and psychological modes of
explanation dominate. The psychological understanding of the
characters which is given in *Martha Quest* through *A Ripple
from the Storm* is deepened in various ways in *Landlocked* and
The Four-Gated City. For example, in the latter novel the
importance of Martha's relationship with her mother is made
explicit and the connections between her family experiences
and her political involvement are articulated.[8] But while
the psychological insight into Martha's relationship with
the family is expanded, its social dimension disappears.

The Four-Gated City presents the family in terms of a
private "neurosis," Martha's relationship to which is summarized by the notion of "debts" that she is said to owe to
her mother, her daughter, and her husbands. According to
this view her life with the Coldridges is a sign of her
maturity and sense of realism; she has finally given up her
idealistic dreams of a better future and accepts instead the
responsibility for her past experiences. This view contains
an element of psychological truth in that Martha's previous
reactions to her family experiences display certain romantic
and escapist tendencies, demonstrated, for example, in her
hopes of setting her daughter "free" and in her longing to
escape from "personal matters" in the political group. However, this approach is based on an exclusively psychological
understanding of her relationship to the family. In the early
novels Martha's longing for freedom and her emotional detachment in family relationships were primarily looked upon
as a social protest against the bourgeois view of woman
which threatened her genuine humanity. Now this definition
of her position has disappeared and her former attitude is
only regarded as an expression of misdirected idealism and
escapism.[9]

The tendency to see reality only in terms of psychology
comes out quite clearly in the redefinition of the relationship between mother and daughter which occurs in *Landlocked*
and *The Four-Gated City*. In the first two novels of the

series the presentation of the conflict between Martha and
Mrs. Quest, between Mrs. Quest and her mother, and between
Martha and Caroline concentrates on the deforming effects
of social structures. In the last two books, on the other
hand, this conflict is seen as based on a lack of love that
is perpetuated from one generation to the next. That Martha
was not loved by her mother is alleged to be at the centre
of their mutual opposition, whereas that part of it which is
related to Mrs. Quest's class consciousness and sex role
behaviour is eliminated. When Martha expresses her need for
motherly love she is at one with her daughter in a way which
points to the perpetuation of this longing throughout the
generations:

> She |Martha's daughter Caroline| turned her face towards
> Martha, a small rather sharp face, watchful. Her smile
> was strained. Martha reached towards the smile, saw it
> dissolve in tears: Martha heard herself crying. She wept,
> while a small girl wept with her, mamma, mamma, why are
> you so cold, so unkind, why did you never love me?
> (FGC, p. 261).

As mentioned in the first chapter, in *Landlocked* this lack
of motherly love is presented as the reason why Mrs. Quest
becomes fit for "nursing" only. The change from a social to
a psychological interpretation of Mrs. Quest's character
leads to shifting, even contradictory representations of her
background. Mrs. Quest's revolt against her family is directed mainly at her father, but in *A Proper Marriage* her
mother is said to have been a domineering woman against whom
her daughter had to rebel even as an adult (PM, p. 332).
In *Landlocked*, on the other hand, this same mother is pictured as a mysterious incarnation of "beauty" who died when
giving birth to Mrs. Quest (see LL, pp. 76-77).

The accentuated psychological outlook on the relationship between the individual and society is closely connected
with tendencies towards reductionism and abstraction. As has
already been suggested, the complex and concretely portrayed
relationship between Martha and Mrs. Quest is ultimately
reduced to a question of love. All of these tendencies are
also present in the sado-masochistic structure which in the

early novels was mainly connected with the institution of the
family but which was also seen as a manifestation of racist
society. This pattern is also relevant to Martha's inner life
in that it provides the content of her last inner journey.
The "self-hater," who is said to be an aspect of her "hating,
self-hating self" (FGC, p. 602), turns her confrontation with
evil into a lesson in sado-masochism, during which she is
forced to experience both sides of the pattern.

Martha's meeting with the "self-hater" can be viewed as
a sign of the deeper insight into her psyche which is contained in *The Four-Gated City*. The sado-masochistic pattern
is seen as an inner, psychological structure; simultaneously,
however, as its connection with the family is lost or repressed, [10] it is related to a general and abstract cultural
tendency towards violence. Furthermore, the biological thinking which appears to be the fundamental mode of consciousness
in *The Four-Gated City* ultimately reduces the concept of
sado-masochism to the basic source of energy or force, neither
good nor evil, but which can be materialized in destructive
forms.

Given the biological determinism of *The Four-Gated City*,
there is no social solution to the pattern of dependence,
with its sado-masochistic components, which characterizes
Martha's contacts, both with her mother and with men. It
becomes simply an inevitable necessity. In this novel the
actual interaction between mother and daughter is marked by
their usual conflicts, and even their final separation takes
on an unresolved character:

> Then, as she vanished from her daughter's life for
> ever Mrs. Quest gave a small tight smile, and said:
> 'Well, I wonder what all that was about really?'
> 'Yes,' said Martha, 'so do I' (FGC, p. 321).

Martha's relationships with men are treated in a similar
fashion. Both with regard to her mother and to men Martha
tears herself free from her dependence on love in order not
to prevent the development of her inner identity, but the
actual pattern of dependence is not questioned. [11]

The problems resulting from Martha's search for a social
identity remain socially unresolved and are dissolved rather

than solved in relation to her inner life. In the sense that
the inner identity implies the dissolution of her individuality, it appears to do away with her conflicts rather than
solve them. As an end to Martha's quest the inner identity
is also ambiguous as it can be interpreted as a logical
development of her tendency towards dependence. Her fusion
with forces greater than herself, i.e., a submissive and
assimilative union, is comparable to that which was latent
in her relationships with her mother, with men and with
political life.

As a socializing institution the family incarnates the
restrictions of culture. But it also has another significance
which relates it to the sphere of the inner life. Martha's
acceptance of the family allows her to realize the creative
aspect of her female consciousness which consists of a
receptive and intuitive openness to human beings. Earlier
she had repressed this dimension of herself as it could
make her passive and compliant and thus undermine her determination to transcend the family as a social structure. Now
she has abandoned this objective and feels free to develop
her receptivity and intuition in the close personal contacts
which she experiences with the members of the Coldridge
family. By providing a context where this female consciousness can be cultivated, family life implies not only compulsion and necessity but also a possibility to develop an
approach to the world which helps her to achieve the inner
experience of wholeness.

The family-like group based on intuitive and emotional
understanding rather than intellectual, idea-orientated
communication is also presented as an alternative to the
predominant organization of society in *The Four-Gated City*.
Examples of such groups are Francis's commune and Martha's
survival community, which are both initiated through non-
verbal, intuitive means of communication (see FGC, pp.
650-651, 691).

However, there is a clear ambiguity in the presentation
of the female consciousness and the personal sphere of life.
On the one hand close personal relationships based on intui-

tion and empathy are looked upon as models of human communication, on the other hand the inner identity involves detachment from the personal dimension both as regards individual development and human interaction. From the point of
view of the inner identity personal, everyday life is often
presented in a clinically cold and ironically distant manner.
The analysis of the kiss as a phenomenon is a good example
of this attitude (FGC, p. 540; cf. FGC, pp. 554-556, LL, p.
267). The use of technological terms such as to "plug in,"
and "volts of love" (FGC, pp. 545, 543), to describe states
of experience also gives them an instrumental quality which
clashes with the emotional and intuitive elements contained
in Martha's expansion of consciousness. An ambiguous treatment of woman's specific consciousness and personal life is
present throughout *Children of Violence* and will be further
commented on in the next chapter.[12]

3.2 The Politics of Inner Life

In *Landlocked* and *The Four-Gated City* the political focus of
attention is no longer directed towards family structures
and racial patterns but towards the two World Wars. The theme
of violence which was earlier expressed mainly through
racial tensions and conflicts between the generations and
the sexes now becomes attached to the issue of war, introduced through Martha's father and then existing as a background to her first marriage and her political life.
Violence takes on a wider and at the same time more abstract
character in the last two novels of the series. The two
World Wars appear as symbols of an interminable violence
which finds its most dramatic manifestation in wars, but
which also expresses itself in extreme technological expansion and in global environmental destruction (see FGC, pp.
527, 606). Violence is seen as the common denominator in
20th century history and the central conditioning factor
in Martha's development:

> Every fibre of Martha's body, everything she thought,
> every movement she made, everything she was, was be-
> cause she had been born at the end of one world war,
> and had spent all her adolescence in the atmosphere
> of preparation for another. . . .
>   Martha was the essence of violence, she had been
> conceived, bred, fed and reared on violence (LL, p. 222).

In this view of history and of Martha's part in it there is
the same generalizing and reductionist tendency which I have
discussed in relation to the family. It is further strengthened by the fact that violence is not given a social explanation as in the early novels but is seen as part of a basic
source of energy or force.

   This power acquires a destructive social form through
the predominance of constraining cultural phenomena, notably
through the prevalence of "ordinary" thinking. This form of
consciousness is seen as leading to violence in that it
splits and categorizes: it divides humanity into groups and
separates man from nature. It further implies a strict division between rational and irrational forms of consciousness.
The unconscious powers are repressed and therefore manifest
themselves in a negative and destructive form. As a result
the individual becomes torn between a civilized, "liberal"
surface consciousness and a primitive and hateful unconscious, which can accidentally be "plugged" into "Hater" or
be manipulated by anyone who incarnates the destructive
forces (FGC, pp. 592, 604). Class divisions, racial and
sexual conflicts are seen as collective expressions of this
splitting and repressing form of consciousness (see FGC, pp.
99, 590). Social violence is a sign of a collective failure
to see humanity as a whole. Socially, the individual tendency towards repression and compartmentalization acquires
institutionalized forms. Society is presented as based on a
hierarchical power structure with fascist components which
upholds the dominance of the prevalent form of consciousness
through the use of technology, mass media and psychiatry
(see FGC, pp. 644, 495-496, 574).

   The expansion or evolution of human consciousness in
inner life is presented as the solution to this state of
affairs. The aim of Martha's project is not only personal

liberation but the liberation of mankind. Her expanded consciousness attempts to conquer the divisive mentality of the
"ordinary" state of mind and to reach a total view of life
where none of its aspects are repressed. Furthermore it aims
at outwitting the social control mechanisms represented by
technology. When Martha and Lynda become "watchers" and
"listeners," i.e., when they develop extra-sensory perception,
their minds are compared to machines, to "radios" and "tele-
vision sets," but of a superior kind:

> If we didn't have the machines and someone told us,
> You don't need machines, it's in your minds, you don't
> need computers, there are human computers, perhaps we'd
> never have to make the machines. What do we need
> machines for? . . . our brains could be rockets and
> space probes, if they can be radios and television
> sets. . . . But you must be careful, Martha, careful,
> you mustn't say what you know, they'll lock you up,
> they want machines, they don't want people ... (FGC,
> pp. 550-551).

The social and political implications of Martha's inner
search are further brought out through a comparison between
her and Mark and through the vision of the "new" children of
the future. Mark first adopts a leftist position which is
practically identical with the one which Martha formerly
embraced. The description of his political stance demonstrates
the view on communism given in *The Four-Gated City*. To be a
communist means that one adopts a given personality with a
given state of mind and a given set of ideas. It is a
mechanical process which repeats itself at certain time-
bound intervals (see FGC, pp. 206-207, 210). This interpretation of the communist position gives it the same fatalistic
quality as that which characterizes family relationships.
A similar outlook is also demonstrated in *Landlocked* when
Martha attends a meeting of a new socialist group which
turns out to be an exact copy of her own: she finds the same
atmosphere, the same personalities, the same conflicts.
Martha also predicts that their political developments will
be identical: "So if history was repeating itself - and why
not? If the dramatis personae were the same, presumably the
plot was also . . ." (LL, p. 310).

Communism is further said to be part of the fragmenting
and repressing mentality in that it identifies everything
that is good with its own cause and everything that is bad
with the enemy. No difference exists between leftist and
rightist positions: both are self-righteous and potentially
linked with forces of violence (see FGC, pp. 206, 228-229).
The history of the 20th century is presented as "sudden
eruptions of violent mass feeling, like red hot lava, that
destroy everything in its path - First World War, fascism,
communism, Second World War" (FGC, p. 527).

When Mark becomes disillusioned with communism he
embraces another political creed which is supposed to be
free from ideology and which also attempts to reach a total
view of life. It is represented by the maps in his study on
which he registers facts about society. These maps pay no
attention to "nationalisms" or "politics" but aim at showing
what is "*really* happening." He gathers information about the
war industry, about mental illness, about the breakdown of
technology and about "Famine, Riots, Poverty, Prisons" (FGC,
pp. 329-330, 478-480). This study project leads him to the
same conclusion as that which Martha reaches during her inner
journey, namely that violence is a constant phenomenon (see
FGC, pp. 605-606). But unlike her, he tries to remove it by
developing a new society. He fails and his failure implicitly points to the correctness of Martha's method. Although
Mark has freed himself from what is considered to be the
limitations of an ideological attitude, he still attempts
to deal with society through "ordinary" means, through
organized collective actions and through the use of rationality. "I can't stand that nasty mixture of irony and St.
John of the Cross and the Arabian nights they all. . .
went in for" (FGC, p. 708), is Mark's detached comment on
Martha's, Lynda's and finally Francis's experiments with
their inner life. Mark's shortcomings also underline the
need for liberation from one's personal past since his vision
is severely limited by his stubborn love for "Lynda and
England" (FGC, p. 709).[13]

The most explicit recommendation of inner consciousness

as a solution to social problems is contained in the vision
of the future presented at the end of *The Four-Gated City*.
There we meet a number of children who are born with the
"higher" consciousness which Martha finally reaches. These
"new" children – biological mutations whose minds are the
results of exposure to radioactive power – are looked upon
as the new humanity embodying the concept of inner life
(FGC, p. 702). Their evolved consciousness gives promise
of an alternative future which has transcended the collective history of mankind: "they are beings who include that
history in themselves and who have transcended it. They
include us in a comprehension we can't begin to imagine.
These seven children are our – but we have no word for it.
The nearest to it is that they are our guardians" (FGC, p.
703).

What a society based on the concept of inner life
would look like is intimated by the rudimentary ideal communities in *The Four-Gated City*, for example, Martha's survival community and the mythic city in the desert which is
imagined by Martha and Mark. These societies are part of the
city symbolism in *Children of Violence*; in different ways
they are related to Martha's first dream of a city which has
now become transformed by the ideals of inner life.[14]

In these communities human beings live in harmony with
each other and with nature. This harmony is based on a force
which in the mythic city is represented by certain people
whose function it is to form a "centre," a "variety of power-
house" (FGC, p. 161). On Martha's island it is compared to a
mysterious symphony made up of human beings as well as nature:
"And the texture of our lives, eating, sleeping, being together, has a note in it that can't be quite caught, as if
we were all of us a halftone or a bridging chord in some
symphony being played out of earshot with icebergs and
forests and mountains for instruments" (FGC, p. 701).

Both of these societies are inspired by an organic view
of life; they are both based on unity between man and nature
which leads to social harmony. The people who make up the
core of the imagined city are said to be recruited from its

gardeners; thus their function as guardians seems to be
founded on their closeness to nature. The "new" children
perform the same role because of their evolved consciousness, which, although it is not clearly defined, implies
contact with a creative force connected with nature.

The idea of society as an organism can be looked upon
as one of the results of the biological thinking which informs *The Four-Gated City*. Organic thought also colours the
description of Martha's development in this novel;[15] it is
quite clearly expressed in the following quotation where the
idea of man seems to find a social projection in the communities discussed above:

> In every life there is a curve of growth, or a falling
> away from it; there is a central pressure, like sap
> forcing up a trunk, along a branch, into last year's
> wood, and there, from a dead-looking eye, or knot, it
> bursts again in a new branch, in a shape that is
> inevitable but known only to itself until it becomes
> visible (FGC, pp. 226-227).

Chapter IV   Expressions of Consciousness in *Children of Violence* and Other Works by Doris Lessing

1 Introduction

In this chapter I will try to interpret and to some extent evaluate the expressions of consciousness which determine the *Children of Violence* novels. In order to do this I feel obliged to alter my analytical point of view and treatment of *Children of Violence* as a self-contained unit by relating it instead to various external phenomena.

The chapter can be divided into two parts. The first concerns primarily *Children of Violence* and is predominantly confined to an examination of the literary text itself. The concept of "female consciousness" is introduced in the course of section 3, and in section 4 the analysis combines with an interpretation of *Children of Violence* from the standpoint of its intellectual background. I will also briefly incorporate *The Golden Notebook* into the discussion in order to try and deepen the understanding of the *Children of Violence* series. The introduction of external material is meant to indicate a fundamental acknowledgment of the writer Doris Lessing as the person whose individual consciousness informs and pervades *Children of Violence*, whereas my previous preoccupations have been with what consciousness the text of the novel series itself gives expression to.

In the second part of the chapter I will try to broaden and expand my perspective in relation to *Children of Violence* by linking it with other novels by Lessing, primarily with those which followed the series, and with non-literary statements which Lessing has made in articles and interviews. The closing section differs somewhat from the others in that I attempt to develop a contemporary reading of Lessing's work which complements and to some extent qualifies the interpretations made earlier.

2 Martha and the Collective. A Short Resumé. The Two Forms of Consciousness in *Children of Violence*

Martha's attempts to go beyond the family and create a social alternative are redirected into efforts to change the expressions of human consciousness. Throughout the series she seeks to achieve a sense of wholeness and harmony, but her outward search is towards social unity, while inwardly she concentrates on reaching a unified consciousness. Her methods of realizing her aims change as well. In her extroverted endeavours her reflective consciousness becomes a means for both social knowledge and self-knowledge. Her introverted project, however, is realized through a special, inner self through which she makes contact with certain basic psycho-physical powers. This self is related to her intuitive, receptive consciousness and conflicts with her analytical and rational mind.

Martha's two identity quests are represented by two different forms of consciousness. That which dominates from *Martha Quest* through *A Ripple from the Storm* I have called the social or sociological consciousness. It could also be called materialist, since it sees Martha as a primarily social being, formed by categories such as sex roles, class membership, family background. It also contains elements of social criticism, which imply that humanity can change its social situation and, consequently, its consciousness.

The other type of consciousness I have called nature-versus-culture since it underscores the "nature" in Martha and sets it in opposition to "culture." What the concepts nature and culture consist of shifts throughout the series. In the first three books the concept of nature is in part identified with concrete nature, in part with the unconscious, with sexuality and female reproduction, and with intuitive mystical and female consciousness. Nature represents force and creativity. The concept of culture on the other hand is linked with stereotypes and mechanical role patterns, with masculinity, with the intellectual and rational, with violence and death. In *Landlocked* and *The*

Four-Gated City, "nature" is expanded and abstracted into a generalized, comprehensive source of power or energy, neutral in value, which becomes destructive through a fragmented cultural consciousness. The idea of a basic neutral force is first suggested in Martha's early mystical experience of nature but it is not developed until *Landlocked*, where Thomas's personality represents both life-bringing and death-bringing forces. Thomas stands for the creative forces of sexuality and nature as well as the destructive force of war, but it seems clear that both aspects of his character stem from the same fundamental power.

According to the pattern of nature versus culture, humanity is influenced by impulses or unconscious forces. This concept contains elements of biological materialism, in which at the extreme, mankind is seen as bound by its biology and the unconscious. In this sense this mode of consciousness strikes one as deterministic in contrast to the social mode of consciousness. Like the social form, the nature-culture mode of consciousness contains a socially - or rather culturally - critical dimension. It issues from a possible unity between mankind and nature which can correct the fragmented existence that cultural life implies.

Nature and culture are represented in turn by two different types of consciousness within the individual: the inner and unified, and the outer, or "ordinary." The emphasis placed on these types of consciousness in *The Four-Gated City* indicates a change within the concept nature-culture from materialism to idealism in the sense that social reality is seen as a product of consciousness. This idealism is however unclear because consciousness is ultimately seen as a product of basic, elementary forces.

In the above I have isolated social consciousness and thought according to the pattern of nature versus culture. However, they should not be taken as parallel lines in the novel series but as different aspects of one consciousness. The isolation of forms of consciousness underlines a tension, which leads to a transition from one way of seeing to another. In *Martha Quest* through *A Ripple from the Storm* the social thinking in terms of roles, class, and institutions conflicts with the nature versus culture outlook which emphasizes instincts and basic forces. The different forms of consciousness also have different evaluations of feeling, intellect, and the intuitive and analytical approaches to experience. These tensions are largely dissolved in the last two books in favour of a general biological view of mankind, with priorities given to the instinctive, intuitive and irrational.

The tensions of consciousness in *Children of Violence* can be further elucidated through a study of *The Golden Notebook*, published between *A Ripple from the Storm* and *Landlocked*. For reasons which are given in the Introduction no detailed analysis will be made of *The Golden Notebook*. However, a few comments which confirm the changes in *Children of Violence* are worth making.

The basic structure of *The Golden Notebook* indicates an opposition between an intuitive experience of violence, destructiveness and chaos, and an attempt to rationally order and control reality according to certain categories. The four notebooks in which Anna Wulf writes about politics, love, psychoanalysis and art signify this principle of order. As the novel progresses the sense of violence grows stronger (it manifests itself increasingly in love as well as politics and art) until it destroys the function of the ordering consciousness. In the fifth "golden" notebook the boundaries between different areas of life break down and Anna Wulf experiences the unity of certain elemental forces within which destructiveness plays an integral part.

As in *Children of Violence* the consciousness displayed in *The Golden Notebook* demonstrates a movement from a rational understanding of existence to an intuitive apprehension of it. *The Golden Notebook* further illustrates a change from an analysis of life in terms of separate social categories to an experience of it as an inner metaphysical totality which can be compared with the movement from the social approach to the world to thinking in terms of nature versus culture in *Children of Violence*. Perhaps most impor-

tantly, however, *The Golden Notebook* demonstrates the same
concern with violence as a force which can be found in the
late volumes of *Children of Violence*. The strong emphasis on
evil in connection with the metaphysical content of *The
Golden Notebook* and *A Four-Gated City* makes it possible to
see the mysticism of these works as both released by an
awareness of violence as a power and as a means to acknowledge, explain and master it.[1]

The Golden Notebook does not add anything to the understanding of the development of consciousness in *Children of
Violence*. However, as it demonstrates the break-through of
a metaphysical consciousness it serves as a link between the
early and late volumes of the series.

3 Female Consciousness in *Children of Violence*

In this section I intend to argue that the social or sociological consciousness and that which is based on the conflict
between nature and culture are both informed by a female perspective. By this I mean partly that the novels tend to select
features which are specifically female or particularly relevant to women, and partly that the chosen material is
structured from a female point of view. These are two independent factors; a text may focus on a female subject matter
but not portray it from a woman's point of view, i.e., through
concepts that issue from the life that women, but not men,
lead and that are employed in a way typical of women.

The female perspective on social consciousness is
exemplified in the central role that family and private life
play for Martha. Her relationship to society, history and
politics is portrayed largely through her contact with family
and private life. In this context Doris Lessing's work may
be said to mirror the general situation of women in Western
society where despite all the formal possibilities of equal
participation in work and politics woman's primary areas of
work and responsibility remain the family and private life.
The socialization of women is mainly oriented towards their

function in the private sphere of society which means that
these functions are pivotal for how women experience their
identities, even if their lives are influenced by other
social contexts.

However, I do not wish to claim that the occurrence of the
family and the private sphere of life in *Children of Violence*
is enough to give it a female perspective. The novel as a
genre has always concerned itself with private existence and
the treatment of the family is an important part of the
Bildungsroman tradition.[2] But in *Children of Violence* Lessing
may be said to give the Bildungsroman a female structure:
female experiences such as the relationship between mother
and daughter, for example, are made central to the formation
of the identity of the heroine and are projected from within
a woman's consciousness.

Most importantly, the central opposition within *Children
of Violence* between the social consciousness and its nature-
culture counterpart may be interpreted as a tension within female consciousness. This conflict between a social and a non-
social approach to reality may be assumed to be more pertinent
to women than men. Women more than men may tend to experience
themselves as "natural," non-social beings, confronted with a
foreign culture, partly because women are still more conditioned by their biology, and partly because women may to a large
extent be regarded as "outsiders" in male-dominated society.

"Social female consciousness" will be my term for social
consciousness filtered through a female perspective. When the
nature-culture conflict is filtered through a female perspective the resulting point of view will be called "biological female consciousness."

According to biological female consciousness woman is
close to nature or embodies nature due to the fact that she
is determined by her sexuality and her reproductive function.
This outlook is clearest in *A Proper Marriage* where Martha's
instinctive life represents a life-giving female principle,
which stands in opposition to destructive male-dominated
culture. Moreover, Martha's intuitive and receptive consciousness is related to the "nature" or "natural" dimension

of her self, although it is unclear whether it is in fact viewed as socially or biologically conditioned.

The social female consciousness appears in Martha's battle against the family as a microcosm of society. This battle implies her overcoming her social and biological womanhood, since it binds her to the family and thus threatens what she sees as her "true" self. This is not feminine in essence, but consists of a potential humanity which is supported by her analytical and reflective consciousness. This aspect of Martha defends her personal integrity through providing a distance, an overview and a mechanism for control over her emotional life, instincts, and unconscious. As suggested in Chapter II, the social female consciousness conflicts with the biological which considers femininity central to Martha's identity, and the analytical consciousness an alien, devisive, male, cultural phenomenon. It is the biological consciousness which gives rise to the following description of Martha: "And again she thought of the simple women of the country, who might be women in peace, according to their instincts, without being made to think and disintegrate themselves into fragments" (PM, p. 85).

Although the social female consciousness dominates the character of Martha's female identity in the earlier books, it is clear that the biological element represents even at that stage something important, which however is repressed because it conflicts with the social counterpart. The biological consciousness seems for example often to have more affinity with what could be called Martha's female subjectivity, that is with what is shown to be her own experience of herself as a woman.

Martha's relationship to the black woman, who represents the instinctive character of women, is characterized by a spontaneous attraction which she represses to avoid social confinement, and because she professes a rational view of life. She is, however, throughout basically ambivalent about that view and the analytical mode of consciousness. She certainly sees reflective consciousness as necessary, but more of a necessary evil than a benefit. From the

beginning her analytical awareness provides her with an
objective and unfamiliar picture of herself. Other aspects
of her consciousness, such as her feelings, her ability to
love, and her intuition and receptivity appear in contrast
as deeply anchored in her conception of her own identity.
The social female consciousness has an anti-romantic,
rational relation to love, which is seen as a social, perhaps bourgeois myth. It disputes that consciousness which
shapes Martha's subjectivity and which also clearly argues
that love is central to Martha's and all women's sense of
identity. If this consciousness is to be identified as
biological or as one which contains an additional interpretation of the connection between women and love seems
unclear. As far as the female consiousness in the later
books in the series is concerned, when the biological connections are clear, this consciousness can be attributed
to biology.

When the biological consciousness becomes dominant,
those aspects of Martha's female identity which she had
earlier repressed in order to escape domesticity are manifested. Aspects of sexuality, and the intuitive and receptive areas of her identity become paths for her personal
and political development: both in *Landlocked* and *The Four-
Gated City* Martha's relation to her environment is informed
by her receptivity, intuition, and her instinctive physical
reactions. The special level of consciousness which Martha
achieves when she becomes a "watcher" and a "listener" can
be seen as a further development of her receptive and
intuitive consciousness, her "soft dark receptive intelligence" (FGC, p. 51). Likewise, in *The Four-Gated City* there
is a polarization between the male and female psyche, which
resembles that of *A Proper Marriage* and *A Ripple from the
Storm*.

Generally in *The Four-Gated City* women's consciousness
is presented as more creative and natural than that of men.
A sign of this are the numerous breakdowns which women suffer:
apart from Martha and Lynda, these are experienced by, for
example, Patty Samuels and Phoebe Coldridge. The last-

mentioned, however, is unable to utilize the creative dimension which according to *The Four-Gated City* is contained in
mental illness. Men, on the other hand, are generally described as stuck with a rational, technical, and instrumental
attitude to the world which makes them represent "ordinary"
thinking. The most extreme example of this is Jimmy Wood who
is shown to be more like a machine than a human being.
Although he is familiar with the esoteric knowledge that
Martha and Lynda utilize, his attitude to it is purely instrumental. It inspires him to technical innovations, but it
neither influences him psychologically, socially nor politically. Mark Coldridge displays similar shortcomings. He
does try to reach an all-inclusive knowledge - his study is
devoted to empirically observable as well as metaphysical
entities - but he is finally constricted by his rationalism.

The biological female consciousness provides fertile
ground for the inner life's mental growth in several different
ways. It creates a foundation for a generally biological or
instinctive way of thinking, which anticipates speculations
about energy and violence as a destructive power. There is
also the notion of women's unity with nature, which heralds
the organic view of society in *The Four-Gated City*. Finally,
the biological consciousness sees the analytical and reflective consciousness as splitting or fragmenting, while
intuition, instincts and the forces of the unconscious are
all seen as unifying.

However, female consciousness in *The Four-Gated City*
has a more abstract, philosophical character. What in *A
Proper Marriage* is a life-giving female principle has in
The Four-Gated City become an elemental source of power or
energy. Likewise, what was male rationalism and intellectual-
ism becomes "ordinary thinking," a general analytical and
rational attitude which in *The Four-Gated City* characterizes
Western thinking. In the later books female consciousness
becomes a form of mysticism, touching at various points the
ideas of Jung, Laing, and the islamic Sufis. I shall return
to the intellectual background of *Children of Violence* in a
separate section.

The abstraction of the biological female consciousness results in Martha's concrete and personal experiences as a woman becoming less and less important for the development towards mysticism in *Children of Violence*. Martha's development from Thomas to Jack indicates that realization of herself as a woman becomes less stressed, while the mystical dimension, contained in female experience, becomes increasingly central. Love is disconnected from sexuality; sexuality becomes an instrument until it has completed its role as bearer of mystical experience in the relationship with Mark, when Martha finally renounces it. Of the creative femaleness only the intuitive and receptive consciousness remains, and even this is mainly manifested in impersonal ways through inner experience.

The abstraction of the female consciousness issues not only from the exhaustion of the mystic dimension of concrete female life, but also because female identity in *Children of Violence* is always portrayed as destructive in social and family contexts. Throughout the novel series Martha is only able to realize herself as a woman in non-social contexts – in contact with nature and in her relationships with Thomas and Jack. Love and sexuality, which in her relations with Thomas lead to new insights, create in the family-like relationship with Mark, a dependent, potentially masochistic woman. Martha's role as mother in the Coldridge family to a certain extent activates the creative aspects of understanding and empathy in her receptive consciousness. But this is still described as mainly negative, partly as power – when she becomes the oppressor through her insights into others' psyche; and partly as a threat to her inner self – she risks losing contact with it through constant empathy with the needs of others (see FGC, pp. 390-395, 399). Her specific female consciousness functions unequivocally creatively only when it has become a part of the mysticism of the inner life. Only when translated into ESP are female receptivity and intuition presented positively as an expansion of human consciousness.

Despite the abstraction of the female consciousness in

The Four-Gated City, the mysticism of *Children of Violence* has clear points of contact with Martha's female identity. On the one hand Martha's development of a visionary apprehension is aided by her biological womanhood and her intuitive and receptive consciousness, on the other hand mysticism appears to provide an outlet for her identity as a woman: in mystical inner life Martha's sexuality and female mode of perception are creative, whereas in social life her femininity is constantly distorted. The picture of a deformed womanhood in *The Four-Gated City* occurs as a remainder of the struggle of the social female consciousness against the family. This mentality continues although the family in that novel is presented as woman's biological and cultural destiny.[3]

Until now I have related the shift of consciousness in *Children of Violence* to a female problematic. Another way of interpreting changes in the series is to concentrate on social and political implications which are not specific to women. The social and the biological consciousness encompass different views of society. The opposition of the social consciousness to the family involves a struggle against present existing society and for socialism. When the biological perspective is dominant, the political element becomes both wider and narrower - wider because it includes a general cultural criticism; narrower because all negative phenomena are reduced to one common entity: Violence. The perspective also shifts, so that the analytical consciousness, which from *Martha Quest* to *A Ripple from the Storm* aids Martha in the struggle against social oppression, becomes in *Landlocked* and *The Four-Gated City* a foundation of evil. This shift is, as I have mentioned before, prepared for by the mentality represented by biological female consciousness. However, the change in *Children of Violence* is not total until socialism is rejected.

Defence of the analytical and rational consciousness is closely connected with socially critical attitudes in the novel series. Martha's role as the reflective "detached observer" is from the outset associated with her reading of socially critical literature. Through this she receives

a picture of herself in terms of class, sex, nationality,
and race. The way of orienting oneself within reality contained in this literature finds its logical extension when
Martha involves herself with the communist group. Her role
of detached observer is complemented by the narrator's perspective as omniscient and corrective. Martha's attachment
to analytical and radical literature is parallelled by the
narrator's belief in rationalism and social explanations.
When disillusion with socialism begins in *Children of
Violence* it leads to a crisis in the reflective consciousness, its language and social explanations which then allows
the biological dimension, with its special wholeness and
thinking in terms of instincts, to take over.

4 Marxism, Depth Psychology, Sufism. An Intellectual Background of *Children of Violence*

The tensions of consciousness in *Children of Violence* referred to in the previous section can also be attributed to
Doris Lessing's intellectual background. The social view of
reality can be connected to her contact with Marxism, while
the opposition of nature and culture can be related to the
influence of depth psychology.[4]

The depiction of family patterns in the first part of
Children of Violence shows similarities with Marxist theories
of the family in its stress on authoritarian and repressive
family relationships which are related to the social division
of labour between the sexes and the patriarchal organization
of society. According to the Marxist view the bourgeois
family is organized along the lines of private ownership,
an arrangement which makes women and children subservient
to men as they have economic power.[5] In the middle class
family described in *Children of Violence* the emphasis on
the authoritarian pattern is often moved from the man to
the woman. Still, the oppression exercised by Mrs. Quest,
for example, is presented as a result of bourgeois and
patriarchal norms which confine the woman to the domestic
sphere of life.

Like Marxist family critics, Doris Lessing also de-
mystifies love as a basis for marriage and instead points
to its socio-economic foundations. By and large she displays
an anti-romantic view of love and the woman's social function, a view critical of bourgeois ideology of the family,
which sees the woman's special capacity as that of being
loving, caring and altruistic.[6] Particularly in the portrait of Mrs. Quest Lessing demonstrates how these characteristics are perverted into a striving for power and control due to her narrow and subordinated position as a
woman.

The treatment in *Children of Violence* of Martha as a
social being whose identity is conditioned by her functions
in the family can thus be related to Marxist theory. The
conflict between nature and culture and the notion of a
biologically defined womanhood, on the other hand, point
to inspiration from depth psychology.

Both Freud and Jung can be traced in *Children of
Violence*. In the theories of both there is the opposition
between nature and culture, but Doris Lessing's adaptation
of that particular conflict is closer to Jung than to Freud.
Like Jung, she accepts the powers of nature and the unconscious as positive and creative, while Freud stresses the
idea that human life as a cultural entity demands sublimation of these powers.[7] The biological view of women and the
concentration on the importance of sexuality for the development of the personality seem however more Freudian than
Jungian - Jung has a more "spiritual" view of mankind and
lacks Freud's biological emphasis.[8]

Marxist and Freudian influences often overlap in *Martha
Quest* through *A Ripple from the Storm*; for example, when the
Marxist-inspired picture of the authoritarian family structure
is combined with psychoanalytic ideas about the importance of
sexuality for the growth of the individual. The depiction of
Mrs. Quest suggests that a patriarchal family situation and
a repressed sexuality together create an authoritarian type of
personality. The analysis of Anton Hesse also indicates that
authoritarian political behaviour can be linked with sexual

repression. In these instances Marxist and psychoanalytic concepts are united, but in general conflicts exist between the sociological ideas of Marxism and the biological and instinctive view of psychoanalysis.

In its view of mankind as ultimately conditioned by instinctive and unconscious forces, depth psychology can be a point of departure for the philosophy which dominates *Landlocked* and *The Four-Gated City*. Jungian theory is close to religion and mysticism in seeing the unconscious as an independent creative force through which the human being can get in touch with a transcendental reality.[9] It may be assumed to serve as a bridge to the mysticism which the idea of the inner life implies. Jung's ideas are present in *The Golden Notebook*,[10] which is, as we have seen, the first work by Doris Lessing to display the authority of a mystical way of thinking. The fully developed mysticism of *The Four-Gated City* and other later works by Doris Lessing, notably *Briefing for a Descent into Hell* and *The Memoirs of a Survivor*, can be related to a variety of thought which contains idealist and metaphysical tendencies - for instance romanticism and certain psychiatric and religious conceptions. However, the most directly noticeable influences on Doris Lessing's work seem to stem from Jung, whose presence is still felt in the later works, from the psychiatrist R.D. Laing and from Idries Shah, a contemporary exponent of Islamic Sufi mysticism.[11]

Martha's development of an inner life may be viewed as a Jungian "individuation process." In this type of process people become at one with their inner identity - what Jung calls the "self" - by a liberation from their social individuality, the "persona" in Jungian terms, and by coming to terms with the personal and collective unconscious.[12] According to Jung the unconscious makes itself known through dreams; they are important to the individuation process as they guide the conscious ego and compensate it for its shortcomings.[13] Such dreams are common in both *Landlocked* and *The Four-Gated City* and have been attributed to influences from Jung.[14] Their function is perhaps most clearly demonstrated in *The Summer Before the Dark*, where

Kate's inner liberation involves working through a series
of dreams representing the inner self.

There are many more affinities between Jung and Lessing.
Most importantly perhaps, like him, she conceives of unconscious powers as a neutral energy which turns destructive
through the prevalence of a repressive, devisive, rational
consciousness. Like Jung, Lessing sees social violence as a
kind of revenge on the part of the maltreated unconscious,
and both of them may be said to view history as individual
psychology projected into the collective.[15]

In *Landlocked* and *The Four-Gated City* Jung's influence
is implicit; it is not explicitly demonstrated as is that of
Idries Shah, who is directly cited (see FGC, p. 492). In
The Golden Notebook Doris Lessing criticizes Jung for being
too myth-oriented and not observant enough of historical
change (see GN, pp. 401-405). As regards what she sees as
specific problems of our times, Lessing seems less inspired
by Jung and more by Idries Shah and Laing.

It is primarily the Laing of *The Politics of Experience*
who is of direct interest to Doris Lessing. In this work he
demonstrates his adherence to a metaphysical tradition of
thought, for example by apostrophizing Jung as a great pre-
cursor with respect to the ways of the inner life. In Laing's
opinion Western man is alienated and split and can only be
saved from this condition through contact with a transcendental reality: mental illness, primarily schizophrenia,
could serve as a psychological break-through since it could
lead to a healing journey through "inner space and time."[16]
Laing's view of mental illness as well as his judgment of
Western culture are analogous with Doris Lessing's.[17]

Laing's theory of the family may also have inspired
her. According to him the family is a closed organism
defending itself against the outside world through an
intricate control system which often takes the form of
"reciprocal terrorism" among the members of the family.
This destructive control mechanism is seen by Laing as
instrumental in the creation of schizophrenia. It creates
what he calls "double-bind" situations, i.e., situations

in which children are exposed to contradictory and paradoxical demands from their parents to which they can find
no solution except through mental illness. Lynda Coldridge's
case history includes her exposure to this kind of "schizophrenic" family. Here Laing may have appealed to independent insights in Lessing. Long before Laing made the concept
of the "double-bind" situation central to his study of the
family, Lessing illustrates such a situation through the
relationship between Martha and Mrs. Quest, for example
in the "pink-eye" episode.[18]

Doris Lessing, however, pushes her interpretation of
mental illness further than Laing. She does not see mental
illness as a potentially healing psychic reaction only, but
also as a sign of an evolutionary development of human consciousness. The notion of an evolution of the human mind
appears to be the most important idea Lessing has received
from Idries Shah's version of Sufism. In a motto which introduces the fourth section of *The Four-Gated City*, she
quotes Shah's evolutionary thesis of the human being as an
organism able to develop a new consciousness with the
ability to transcend time and space:

> Sufis believe that . . . humanity is evolving to-
> wards a certain destiny. . . . Organs come into being
> as a result of a need for specific organs. The human
> being's organism is producing a new complex of organs
> in response to such a need. In this age of the tran-
> scending of time and space, the complex of organs is
> concerned with the transcending of time and space.
> What ordinary people regard as sporadic and occa-
> sional bursts of telepathic and prophetic power are
> seen by the Sufi as nothing less than the first stir-
> rings of these same organs. The difference between all
> evolution up to date and the present need for evolu-
> tion is that for the past ten thousand years or so
> we have been given the possibility of a conscious
> evolution. So essential is this more rarefied evolu-
> tion that our future depends on it (FGC, p. 492).[19]

Shah's ideas may have inspired the mixture of organic, biological thinking and the technical, natural-science orientation in *The Four-Gated City*. The quotation above also points
to an ambiguous view of the expansion of the human consciousness likewise contained in *The Four-Gated City*. Shah on the

one hand describes this process as strictly evolutionary; on the other, he states that it is conscious, which I take to mean that it can be influenced by human effort. This ambiguity is also found in *The Four-Gated City*, where the new children appear as products of an evolutionary process, whereas Martha's expanded consciousness is presented as largely the result of her own efforts.

Shah's evolutionism is combined with a struggle against what he calls "pattern-thinking." This stands for conformist, predictable, and categorizing thinking, based on the logical and rational capacities of the mind. Intuitive insights and emotional experiences are viewed as potentials for "real" knowledge. The "patterned" mentality is quite possibly a source of inspiration for the idea of "ordinary" thinking in *The Four-Gated City*, although the preference for intuition rather than reason, and feeling rather than intellect, which is contained in both of these concepts emerges as a general characteristic of mysticism.[20] The physical and psychic rituals which are part of inner life in *The Four-Gated City* may also be attributed to a Sufic influence, although such exercises are general properties of mysticism as well.[21]

There are many more parallels between the mysticism of the Sufis and that of Doris Lessing. Among them could be mentioned the similarity between their legend of a lost paradise and the mythic city in *The Four-Gated City*,[22] and the connection between the Sufis' conception of a teacher of inner life and Doris Lessing's rendering of Martha's relationships with Thomas and Lynda. The initiatory character of Martha's affair with Thomas fits the Sufic notion of love as a means of approaching the inner life. As physical love appears to represent a "low," preparatory stage of inner education to the Sufis, Martha's progression from Thomas to Lynda is logical seen from their perspective.[23]

Doris Lessing's connections with Jung, Laing and Idries Shah demonstrate her dependence on idealistic, metaphysical currents of thought. Under the influence of these thinkers her mysticism becomes progressively more developed and acquires more spectacular characteristics.

5 Doris Lessing and Women

In this section I shall deal with various aspects of the
subject of women which are pertinent to *Children of Violence*,
The Summer Before the Dark and *The Memoirs of a Survivor* -
aspects such as what sort of consciousness of women prevails
in these texts, whether that consciousness could be called
feminist and to some extent how it corresponds with the
view of women that Doris Lessing herself has revealed.
Woman's relationship to the family is, as elsewhere in this
study, a main theme in the analysis: since the family does
not figure centrally in *The Golden Notebook*, that particular
text will largely be omitted from my discussion. In this
section I do not have the ambition to give comprehensive
interpretations of Lessing's works based on their female
perspectives. Therefore, I will not use the same terminology
as in section 3. Nevertheless, the tension between what I
have earlier called social and biological female consciousness serves as a starting-point for my analysis in this
section as well.

Despite the fact that Doris Lessing has a reputation
of being a writer who concerns herself primarily with the
problems of women, in her own statements about her work she
gives no prominence to this subject. For example, in her
comments about *Children of Violence* she does not say a word
about how the novel series is influenced by having a female
main character, despite the fact that this obviously determines the relationship between individual and society in
the novel. Judging from the Preface to the second edition
of *The Golden Notebook*, where Lessing confronts the issue
of whether she is a feminist writer, she chooses not to
underline the female dimension of her work partly out of
a fear of being categorized as a writer for women only, and
partly because she regards the female aspect of her work as
so self-evident that it needs no comment.

She argues that *The Golden Notebook* has been "belittled"
by reviewers as well as female readers as all of them saw
this book only as a tract about the "sex war." At the same

time as she makes clear that her novel was not intended to
be a "trumpet for Women's Liberation," she also expresses,
however, her sympathy for the feminist struggle and declares that her work was created from within a female point
of view: "Of course this attempt on my part assumed that
that filter which is a woman's way of looking at life has
the same validity as the filter which is a man's way ...
Setting that problem aside, or rather, not even considering
it. . . ."24

In spite of Lessing's wish to disassociate herself from
the feminist impact of her work, several critics have chosen
to discuss whether her female "filter" can be defined as
feminist. This is a complicated question, the answer to
which depends partly on what one means by feminism and
partly on how one considers feminist consciousness to function in a literary form. For example, one may argue that
the very fact that Doris Lessing maintains a female point
of view could give her work an emancipatory character
regardless of whatever ideological, political standpoint
is contained within her perspective. Lessing may serve the
feminist cause simply by giving her female readers access
to experiences and attitudes which are still scarce in
literature and which may help women to better understand
their predicament.25 In the discussion which follows I will,
however, be concerned with the ideology contained within
Lessing's female perspective. I will try to demonstrate that
her work displays two types of attitudes which have points
of contact with tendencies within historical feminism.

The first attitude agrees with what is generally meant
by feminism. It is a militant attitude directed against
female opression in the sense of economic, political and
psychological mechanisms which prevent women from realizing
their full potential as human beings. Lessing demonstrates
her critical awareness of the oppression of women primarily
through her portrait of the family as an institution which
binds women to a distorted social function and a deformed
consciousness. Her focus on the family allies her mainly
with the "new" women's movement. This movement which has

been growing in Western society since the beginning of the
1970's considers the family absolutely central to the understanding of the oppression of women.[26]

The earlier books in *Children of Violence* are characterized by the idea that the family can be struggled against
and surmounted. That type of militancy disappears in the
later books and the family is presented as woman's cultural
destiny, as something to which she has to adapt. The
disappearance of militancy is prepared for by the fatalistic
atmosphere which occurs early in *Children of Violence* in
the depiction of the repetition of family patterns. Already
then Martha is to a considerable extent bound by her biology, her unconscious, and her particular female orientation
towards love. The presentation of a special female nature,
determined by biology, which ties woman to the family, becomes more pronounced from *The Golden Notebook* onwards.

In *The Summer Before the Dark* Kate's attachment to the
family had begun "when her nature had demanded she must get
herself a man" (Summer, p. 126). "Nature" here refers to
sexuality, and in *The Golden Notebook* as well it is described
as woman's fate, awakened through the man she loves. Woman
can only reach sexual satisfaction through a monogamous
relationship to one man and thus becomes bound to a couple-
family relationship: "for women like me, integrity isn't
chastity, it isn't fidelity, it isn't any of the old words.
Integrity is the orgasm," says Ella, Anna Wulf's alter ego
(GN, p. 279).

The biological exposition of women is also present in
The Memoirs of a Survivor, where the girl Emily's development through puberty is described similarly to the depiction
of adolescence in *The Four-Gated City*, although in an even
more unequivocally biological way:

> the biological demands of her age took a precise and
> predictable and clocklike stake on her life, making
> her exactly like this and that. And so it would go on,
> it had to go on, . . . and in due time . . . she would
> become mature, that ideal condition envisaged as the
> justification of all previous experience, an apex
> of achievement, inevitable and peculiar to her. This
> apex is how we see things, it is a biological summit

> we see: growth, the achievement on the top of the
> curve of her existence as an animal, then a falling
> away towards death (Memoirs, p. 81).

As in the case of other women in Lessing's fiction, Emily's
biological nature ties her to one man, her lover Gerald, for
whom she becomes a supportive mother figure (see Memoirs,
p. 94).

The biological views that Doris Lessing manifests in
her novels she has also expressed in an interview where she
says:

> We're very biological animals. . . . Anna and Molly
> |in *The Golden Notebook*| are women who are conditioned
> to be one way who are trying to be another. I know a
> lot of girls who don't want to get married or have
> children. . . . Well, they're trying to cheat on
> their biology. . . . It will be interesting to see
> how they're thinking at thirty.[27]

This attitude is however not immediately noticeable in
Doris Lessing's work because even in the later books it is
combined with a social or sociological interest and with
an awareness of the oppression of women, which, however,
lacks the militancy which she expressed earlier. This combination of views is most obvious in *The Summer Before the
Dark*, which on the surface can be read as a critical
account of the family as a social structure and of the
destructive female consciousness which it creates. But
in its underlying structure, the novel portrays a biologically determined female life cycle, within which Kate
has reached middle age and is therefore compelled to take
a stand vis-à-vis her earlier life as a maternal and
sexual being.[28]

The combination of a biological interpretation, social
observations and awareness of oppression in Doris Lessing
can, I think, be confusing and lead the reader to believe
that she is more radical and militant than she really is.
Her biological ideas manifest themselves primarily in the
type of social determinism which dominates her later work,
and which turns the family into an unavoidable fate for
the woman. The result of this biological interpretation
is non-feminist consciousness.[29] However, at the same

time, from Doris Lessing's presentation of female nature
emanates a feminism of another sort than that which I have
already considered, and which I shall examine later. But
first a few examples of the consequences of the determinist
view of the family.

The Four-Gated City, *The Summer Before the Dark* and
The Memoirs of a Survivor are all characterized by a common
structure which presents inner liberation as the only
alternative to constraint through the family. In *The Summer
Before the Dark* as in *Children of Violence* there is a
frustrated revolt against the family. Kate like Martha
achieves inner freedom only. Her inner identity is symbolically portrayed as a seal which she manages to restore
to a free life in the sea during a dream sequence; but she
returns to the family situation she initially rebelled
against. The futility of rebelling against the family is
also illustrated by the figure of Maureen, the young woman
with whom Kate lives during a period of her crisis. Maureen,
who represents the future generation, is doubtful about
marriage, but seems unable to resist it. *The Summer Before
the Dark* ends with a strong suggestion that Maureen is on
the verge of beginning the sort of life from which Kate
has just reached inner, but not outer, release.[30]

Like Martha in *The Four-Gated City*, the anonymous female main character in *The Memoirs of a Survivor* is forced
to re-experience her childhood and youth through her contact with a young woman, Emily. The "survivor's" confrontation with her past is carried out through her mental
experience of a mythical, symbolic family. This family
seems to represent not only her own and Emily's past, but
that of all women; it appears to be archetypal and part of
a collective unconscious. The family represents a dimension
of life called the "personal" which is contrasted against
an inner sphere of existence. The family, or "personal"
dimension is compared to a "prison" where "nothing could
happen but what one saw happening," whereas the inner dimension is characterized by "freedom, a feeling of possibility" (Memoirs, p. 39).

That the family stands for the "personal dimension" I interpret to mean that it does not only represent a special social pattern of life but also personal private experience of life in general. Also in *The Four-Gated City* there is a tendency towards this view of the family. It is not only the family itself that is revealed to be oppressive but personal relations in general. Family life in *The Four-Gated City* is expanded to encompass a picture of "ordinary" life. Martha's liberation from that life involves a kind of "death" for her as an individual personality. The same "death," although more clearly marked, occurs in *The Memoirs of a Survivor*. It ends with the narrator, Emily, the mythical parents and other important people leaving the ordinary world, which is annihilated, to enter the inner sphere.

This inner sphere is made incarnate by a "Presence" which the narrator feels but does not see until the last scene (Memoirs, p. 87). The "Presence" is revealed to be a female spirit or goddess:

> But the one person I had been looking for all this time was there: there she was.
>   No, I am not able to say clearly what she was like. She was beautiful: it is a word that will do. I only saw her for a moment, in a time like the fading of a spark on dark air - a glimpse: she turned her face just once to me, and all I can say is ... nothing at all (Memoirs, p. 182).

The female divinity confirms my idea that the inner life involves an assertion of a female principle (see Sec. 3). This principle also represents a type of feminist consciousness in Doris Lessing's work which is, however, entirely different from that represented by the struggle against the family in the earlier books.

The earlier feminism sees woman as a social being, formed by role patterns defined by society. The later feminism is based on the proposition that woman's biology gives her a specific female nature. The former is oriented towards overriding sex roles, while the latter asserts the creativity of a female nature.

The earlier feminism can be related to Marxist thought

(see Sec. 4), and also to ideas expressed by Simon de
Beauvoir in *The Second Sex*. Martha's struggle to go beyond
femininity and realize herself as a person illustrates the
problem Simone de Beauvoir discusses in the Sartrean terms
of a conflict between subject and object, transcendence
and immanence. According to de Beauvoir all human beings
strive to be subjects through conquering or transcending
their given conditions. Woman's particular problem is
that she is seen by men and by society as at one with
her sex and is therefore forced into a static, passive,
repetitive "immanent" life, through which she becomes an
"object." The resultant conflict leads to a struggle
against immanence, and de Beauvoir stresses those aspects
of women which can make them into "subjects" - for example,
their reflective consciousness - and gives less attention
to their biological and sexual functions since they con-
tribute to turning women into objects. Doris Lessing's
rendering of how Martha defends her role of reflective
"detached observer," and "free spirit" resembles Simone de
Beauvoir's view of the struggle against immanence.[31]

Lessing's notion of a specific female nature gives
rise to a feminist criticism of culture in the sense that
women represent a creative, life-giving principle which
opposes a mechanistic, destructive, male, cultural influence.
Through their intuitive, receptive and irrational capacities
women can develop a unified consciousness, whereas men stand
for the rationalistic, fragmenting mentality, which in
Lessing's view is linked with technological expansion and
environmental destruction (cf. Sec. 3). Lessing's later
feminism includes an ecological awareness: in her later
works she appears as a sibyl, prophesying the fall of male-
dominated Western culture, searching for an alternative to
its technocratic, instrumental world view.[32]

The idea of a unique female nature which gives women
a life-preserving attitude is not unusual in the "old"
feminist movement. Virginia Woolf, for example, claimed
that if woman's nature was allowed to pervade society
it would become more peaceful.[33] Similarly the Swedish

feminist Elin Wägner believed that women, peace and earth belong together. Through safeguarding life women also protect peace and fight against the destruction of the environment.[34]

Usually, the idea of woman as a preserver of life is related to her ability to give birth and to her nurturing role in the family. Wägner's ideas can be compared with that of a "social mother" launched by other well-known Swedish thinkers about women such as Fredrika Bremer and Ellen Key. The concept of the "social mother" is founded upon the view that women have a motherly, caring nature which, diffused in society, can ennoble it.[35] The thoughts of Wägner, Bremer and Key have been re-activated by the new women's movement in Sweden through the idea of a special "female culture." The contemporary idea differs from the earlier notions by being based on women's work and not upon their nature. Still, it resembles them through its claim that the traditional work of women in the home has created in them a socially creative attitude which makes it natural for them to react against violence wreaked against both mankind and nature.[36]

The idea of the "social mother" is related to the bourgeois notion of women as altruistic mothers who have a special spiritual mission to fulfill within the family and in society.[37] It is possible that the concept of a "female culture" contains points of contact with this intellectual tradition; however, this is too complicated an issue to be dealt with here, nor is it my purpose to try to establish such connections within the history of ideas. The reason why I have brought up the question of motherhood and its bourgeois interpretation is that I wish to investigate in what ways Lessing's later feminism is related to her acceptance of the family. Is Martha's role as a mother in the Coldridge family instrumental in shaping the creative female mentality which Lessing postulates, and if so, does this mean that Lessing has adopted the idealizing, bourgeois view of woman in the family, which she earlier rejected?

As I have suggested earlier Martha's role as mother has a spiritual dimension as it gives her an ability to cultivate those intuitive and receptive faculties which help to bring about inner experience (see Ch. III, Sec. 3.1). But the actual social function of being a mother is not idealized; Lessing neither romanticizes the relationship between women and children nor the mentality which this contact demands from women.

In spite of the social awareness which is contained in Lessing's consistently critical description of the female identity developed in the family, this critical attitude makes her later feminism seem abstract and ambiguous. As I have indicated in section 3, this feminism is never realized socially but only through the inner dimension of mysticism. And that realization is combined with a detachment from concrete female experience, and from the traditionally female sphere of personal and emotional life, which means that the feminism gives an ambiguous impression. In both Martha's life with the Coldridges and in the text as a whole *The Four-Gated City* expresses an abstraction of the female perspective in *Children of Violence*. Martha achieves an identity which is an essence of life - impersonal, asexual, shared by people, animals, and nature (cf. FGC, p. 260). The novel as a whole abstracts all things into "forces." *The Summer Before the Dark* and *The Memoirs of a Survivor* likewise support the interpretation of mysticism as a final point of liberation from the social and personal dimensions of female life.[38]

Doris Lessing's image of the mother appears pivotal in explaining why she portrays the family, and finally the entire area of personal existence, as oppressive and constricting. Instead of being affectionate and understanding her main mother figures are despotic and exploitive. Mrs. Quest is the clearest example of this, but such mother types also appear in *The Summer Before the Dark* and *The Memoirs of a Survivor*. Kate's liberation is depicted as an intensive struggle with motherhood, which is revealed to be stifling both for her and for those around her. This

applies both to her function in the family, where motherhood is portrayed as a part in a destructive "family *folie*"
(Summer, p. 89), and in her work where Kate is expected to
function as a "social mother."

The relationship between Anna and her daughter Janet
in *The Golden Notebook* is a positive one and thus provides
the exception to the rule of significant mothers in
Lessing's novels. But then on the other hand Anna's need
to take care of men is presented as a potentially exploitive
motherliness, which threatens the man's integrity as well
as her own (see GN, pp. 547-548).

The most interesting portrait of a mother in relation
to *Children of Violence* is, however, the characterization
of the mother of the mythical family in *The Memoirs of a
Survivor*. This mother and this whole family resemble the
Quest family, even though the former is more symbolically
drawn. The mother and father resemble Mr. and Mrs. Quest
in appearance and manner. The father is a soldier, "con-
ventionally handsome," harrassed and henpecked by his
wife (Memoirs, p. 60; cf. MQ, p. 33). The mother has Mrs.
Quest's athletic build and healthy, competent looks, and
she indulges in constant fretting and nagging (Memoirs,
pp. 59-60; cf. MQ, p. 14). Like the Quests, the couple
have two children, a baby boy and a girl, Emily, who is
5 or 6 years old.

It is the same girl Emily who as a teenager is left
with the narrator to look after. The narrator and Emily
share many traits and characteristics and can very well
be the same person. The teenage Emily in turn is reminiscent of Martha as a young woman: like Martha, Emily
is a "bright, attractive girl," who plays up to other
people, but whose outer personality is compared to "a
shell" from within which "she watched and listened"
(Memoirs, p. 63).

The similarities between Emily and Martha and Mr.
and Mrs. Quest and the couple in *The Memoirs of a Survivor*
can lead to an interpretation of Emily's childhood as representing an image of Martha's, not included in *Children*

of Violence. One could even go a step further and see the
portrait of the family in *The Memoirs of a Survivor* and
consequently in *Children of Violence* as a portrayal of Doris
Lessing's family. Doris Lessing actually calls *The Memoirs
of a Survivor* "an attempt at autobiography" (book cover).
However, the mythical, archetypal rendering of the family
in this novel makes it unclear in what way it is autobiographical. The characterization of the family is hardly
individualized; but perhaps it stands for a sort of essence
of Doris Lessing's view of the family. This is conditioned
by the fact that *The Memoirs of a Survivor* belongs to her
later work - even so, it is significant for further understanding of *Children of Violence.*

The most important contribution of *The Memoirs of a
Survivor* to the issue of the relationship between mother
and daughter is that through her lack of love and her constant harping, the mother creates "GUILT" in the daughter
(Memoirs, p. 60):

> The hard accusing voice went on and on, would always
> go on, had always gone on, nothing could stop it, could
> stop these emotions, this pain, this guilt at ever having
> been born at all, born to cause such pain and annoyance
> and difficulty. The voice would nag on there for ever,
> could never be turned off, and even when the sound was
> turned low in memory, there must be a permanent pressure
> of dislike, resentment (Memoirs, p. 62).

The mother's "accusing voice" becomes an internalized "self-
hater" which the daughter bears forever within her. She
inherits a guilty conscience and self-destructive attitudes;
she becomes a potential masochist, who awaits punishment.
The Memoirs of a Survivor restores the correspondence between
the family and sado-masochism, which was present in the
early books of *Children of Violence*, but which was suspended
in *The Four-Gated City*. In a recent interview Doris Lessing
herself associates the "self-hater" with the relationship
between mother and daughter through describing the "self-
hater" as a form of "super-ego" created in the daughter
through the mother.[39]

The picture of the destructive mother links Doris
Lessing's early and later presentation of the family. The

problems concerning the relationship between men and women are presented in *Children of Violence* as a parallel to the conflicts between mother and daughter. The relationship between men and women seems less basic; it is shown to be secondary, while the disharmonious relationship between mother and daughter is primary. Both relationships reveal, however, the same psychological pattern – the need for a submissive form of love combined with fears of dependence and disintegration of the identity.

The presentation of the mother as destructive and oppressive means that Doris Lessing tends to diminish the father's role as an authority in the family. In her work there is a more indulgent attitude towards men than women, which I think can be explained by the fact that she sees the mother more than the father as the true threat to the child's – and particularly the daughter's – integrity. This can also be a reason for the lack of militancy in Lessing's portrayal of the oppression of women. Earlier I have referred to her biological view of women to account for this attitude. But her picture of the mother also seems important in this context: the negative attitude towards the mother can lead to a critical view of women in general and thus hamper a militant stance in favour of them.[40]

Children of Violence, *The Summer Before the Dark* and *The Memoirs of a Survivor* give a very dark picture of Doris Lessing's outlook on women. Her texts illustrate neither the possibility of overcoming the female role in social life nor of creating a positive social existence based on that role. The only positively portrayed womanhood is the mystical female principle, which in various ways provides a problematic solution to the question of women. The development of the mystical inner identity is associated with de-personalization and rendering the individual anonymous, which constitutes a sort of "death" for the concrete individual woman. Furthermore, it involves abandoning "ordinary" life for transcendence into the inner dimension.

In Chapter III, section 3, I suggested that Martha's

dissolution of the self and communion with elemental powers
could be seen as a logical conclusion of her longing for subjection and assimilation which existed in her relationship
with her mother. These elements are underlined in *The
Memoirs of a Survivor* where the entrance of the narrator
into the inner dimension, represented by a female deity,
is conceived of as a re-uniting with the immemorial mother
or "earth mother" and annihilation of her former life. Her
unification with mother earth or the mother as a life-giving
principle contains a regressive aspect of the return to a
state of nature, which is a realization of similar tendencies in Martha's earlier experience of mysticism and in her
dreams of a city resembling a mother's embrace.

Interpreted in this way mysticism becomes flight - an
escape from both social and human life, from conflicts,
emotional dependence, and the demands on consciousness, to
the harmony of the inner dimension, all-encompassing but
impersonal love, and the extinction of individual consciousness.

But one can also interpret the mystical female principle more positively. The female deity in *The Memoirs of
a Survivor* may be seen as a representative of the "good"
mother, whom the narrator reaches when she has lived through
her confrontation with the evil mother. Psychologically the
mystical female can be construed as a life-giving, creative
potential, and socially and culturally as a vision of harmonious unity between mankind and nature. However, even if
one isolates that interpretation, which I shall do later,
the split between the inner dimension and that of reality
remains disturbing.

6 Doris Lessing and Society

In the following pages I shall deal with Doris Lessing's
view of society at large and her general political consciousness. In part I shall touch upon some of the same
questions as in the section on women, but they will be

treated in a somewhat different way. Lessing has made more
interesting and directly relevant non-literary statements
concerning her general social views than concerning women.
There is also straight-forward factual information - e.g.,
that she was an organized communist. In my discussion I shall
use some of this material, which I shall try to relate to her
literary works.

Doris Lessing was a communist from the beginning of the
1940's until 1957, first as a member of a left group in
Rhodesia (where there was no official Communist Party),
and secondly as a member of the British Communist Party
during the 50's.[41] Judging from her own statements - both
from the time when she was a communist and later - it would
seem that her political involvement was a product of her
life in Africa. In her travel book, *Going Home* (1957), she
mentions that racial oppression turned her into a communist,
which she perhaps might not have been in England. She underlines that the word communist in certain ways is a mis-
nomer since the political climate in Rhodesia is such that
"the sort of work a Communist does . . . is exactly the
same sort of work a liberal or a progressive churchman
does. It is a fight for basic human rights" (GH, p. 103).
Another consideration which made her political experience
untypical is that according to her own testimony it was
made in a group that was "pure" and that consisted of
"enormously idealistic and mostly extremely intellectual
people." This group "created a Communist party . . . which
no real Communist party anywhere in the world would have
recognized as such."[42]

Doris Lessing's descriptions of her political life in
Africa indicate that the fact that she was a communist does
not give an exact picture of her view of society and her
political consciousness. Her comments about the content of
the concepts communism, socialism and Marxism also give a
rather vague impression. For the most part she uses them
as synonymous terms, a expressions for one and the same
political attitude. This attitude involves working for
human rights and freedom, and it encompasses a kind of

morality or ethics based on the idea of solidarity and
equality amongst all people. I consider the following
statement typical of Lessing's leftist approach:

> Communism . . . was a great, marvelous vision which
> was much bigger than merely eliminating poverty and
> redistributing wealth and that sort of thing. It was
> a vision of a society where every individual was
> immensely important, where there was no emphasis on
> color, class or creed, there was no hurting each
> other. Every person had a chance and the right to
> develop himself. This was the dream, and it's why
> people are socialists, why I was.[43]

While Doris Lessing often comments on the rights and possibilities of individuals, she seldom talks in Marxist terms
of class and class struggle. By that observation I do not
mean to indicate that she was neither communist nor socialist but a liberal. I can name several reasons that account
for her political vagueness. If one examines the social
questions which engage her - racial problems which she herself professes an interest in, the problems of women which
her literary works bear witness to her involvement in - they
are questions which are difficult to analyse purely in terms
of class. The socio-political categories of sex and race
exceed class boundaries and demand additional terms of
explanation. That she is an intellectual and a middle class
woman can also explain her emphasis on the human rights
aspects of communism and socialism. Finally, most of her
remarks about communism are informed by disappointment in
the kind of socialism practised in the Soviet Union. This
may also lead her to underline the egalitarian vision of
communism.[44]

I shall return shortly to some of the hypotheses I
have offered and try to investigate them more closely.
Above I have chosen to stress that for various reasons it
is difficult to draw precise conclusions about Doris
Lessing's politics from her political affiliation and her
own statements about it. It seems clear that she was a
leftist or socialist of some sort, but exactly of what kind
is difficult to determine. Better than trying to define her
development in terms of communism versus non-communism

would be to see it as a change from social radicalism to interest in mysticism and inner, psychic expansion. In the following pages I shall illustrate my view of Lessing's ideological development in more detail through first discussing her essay, "The Small Personal Voice," from 1957, in relation to *Children of Violence*, I-III, and then analysing later statements by her in relation to her later literary works.

Several critics use "The Small Personal Voice" as the point of departure for analysing Doris Lessing's entire production.[45] I believe this to be questionable because the essay is markedly "dated," with ideas clearly applicable to the early volumes of *Children of Violence* but which are more problematical when it comes to the later books in the series or other later works.

"The Small Personal Voice" is primarily a literary credo, but it is also quite illuminating about Doris Lessing's social and political opinions. In the essay Lessing declares that she is a humanist and not a communist. However, it is obvious that her humanism is founded upon a socialist consciousness, and consequently, I propose that humanistic socialism is a more adequate description of her position than simply humanism. In my view "The Small Personal Voice" documents in an unusually precise manner Doris Lessing's socialist awareness.

For a start, she maintains staunchly that she is a Marxist, that she identifies herself with a class analysis of society and of art. However, she dissociates herself from simplistic collectivism and from socialist bureaucracy, both of which she sees as characteristic of Soviet society. In art these characteristics give rise to the false optimism and "simple economic view of man" of social realism. But she also condemns the Western economic and social system, and its individualism and pessimism which as expressed in literature tend toward "the pleasurable luxury of despair, the acceptance of disgust." Both ideologies dominating the East and West are, according to Lessing, "aspects of cowardice, both fallings-away from a central vision, the two

easy escapes of our time into false innocence." And she
continues:

> One sees man as the isolated individual unable to com-
> municate, helpless and solitary; the other as collec-
> tive man with a collective conscience. Somewhere between
> these two, I believe, is a resting point, a place of
> decision, hard to reach and precariously balanced. . . .
> The point of rest should be the writer's recognition of
> man, the responsible individual, voluntarily submitting
> his will to the collective, but never finally; and in-
> sisting on making his personal and private judgements
> before every act of submission.[46]

Doris Lessing's humanism, her belief in critical, conscious
individuals should be seen in relation to the fact that her
essay was published the year after the Soviet Communist
Party's 20th Party Congress, which revealed Stalin's terror,
and the year after the Soviet intervention in Hungary.[47]
Lessing's criticism of Stalinism does not, however, mean
that she takes exception to socialism or Marxism, or to the
nations which attempt to practise them. On the contrary, she
speaks of the development of the Soviet Union and China as
"the greatest event of our time, . . . one in which we are
all involved."[48] She sharply condemns the literary generation of the 50's in England for being so indifferent to this
important social development - which is also occurring in the
Third World:

> There is Mr. Colin Wilson, who sees no reason why he
> should not state that: 'Like all my generation I am anti-
> humanist and anti-materialist.' . . . The fact is that
> outside the very small sub-class of humanity Mr. Wilson
> belongs to, vast numbers of young people are both human-
> ist and materialist. Millions of young people in China,
> the Soviet Union, and India, for instance. . . . Mr.
> Wilson may find the desire of backward people not to
> starve, not to remain illiterate, rather uninteresting,
> but he and people like him should at least try and
> understand it exists, and what a great and creative
> force it is, one which will affect us all.[49]

Doris Lessing claims that she has tried to portray in *Children
of Violence* the relationship between the individual and the
collective which was sought after in "The Small Personal
Voice."[50] Undoubtedly it is this statement which makes critics
use her essay as a starting-point for an analysis of the whole

series. I would personally maintain that Lessing's ideas in the essay are mainly relevant to the early part of the series, which was completed in 1958. The first three books are dominated by the sort of dialectic between the individual and society which Lessing strives after, even though, as I have already indicated, they also contain an undialectical element which is connected to a biological determinism, present already at that stage. The materialist and socially critical awareness governing these novels agrees with the basic socialist attitudes expressed in "The Small Personal Voice."

Certain critics dilute and reduce Doris Lessing's ideological development by concentrating exclusively on her humanism in "The Small Personal Voice." A similar attitude is displayed by those critics who, from an analysis of communism in Doris Lessing's early fictional characters, conclude that they, and by extension Lessing herself, do not embrace communism but humanism. The critics refer to, for example, the lack of economic content in Martha's communism in *A Ripple from the Storm*, and the attacks on Anton Hesse for his dogmatism and lack of humanitarian interest.[51] It is true that *A Ripple from the Storm* does not stress economics and even in the strictest sense the political content of communism but concentrates on how a group of people in their personal lives practise their communist convictions. Consequently, the work tends to emphasize the individual and his/her personal relationships, which can be labelled humanistic, but this can hardly hold as a pretext for assuming an anti- or non-communist stance on the part of the author.

As a totality *A Ripple from the Storm* is pervaded by the socialistically oriented criticism of society that is typical of the early volumes of the series. This attitude is combined with a humanist consciousness about the need to politicize psychological and ideological issues. This is consistent with the political questions Doris Lessing deals with in her fiction. As I have suggested above, racism and the oppression of women are both issues which are not immediately explicable by a strictly Marxist, economic analysis of society; they also need a study of elements within the so-called ideological superstructure, i.e., socially conditioned myths and attitudes about women and black people. Also, the conditions of women cannot be understood simply on the basis of their position in public life but must include their private relationships, and their relationship to the family as an institution. In *A Ripple from the Storm* Doris Lessing is primarily concerned with the relevance of communism to Martha, i.e., to a middle-class woman who is not submitted to direct economic exploitation in the Marxist sense. She shows that Martha's main problem lies in an oppression rooted in a bourgeois family structure. Considering Martha's relationship to society, Doris Lessing's concern with whether communism can change bourgeois and patriarchal sex role patterns seems consistent.

Through her criticism of Anton, Lessing seems to want to say that a political struggle must include the personality of the individual communist, i.e., lead to personal practice consistent with theory. Anton is mainly attacked for his treatment of women, but indirectly also for his position in racial matters: his lack of personal interest in the coloured people in the Location can be compared with his detached attitude to Maisie's problems and to "personal matters" in general.

Doris Lessing's portrayal of relationships in the family and in the communist group shows that the "private is political," to borrow a phrase from the contemporary women's movement. That is, the putative private existence has a social and political content. What I have called humanistic socialism in Doris Lessing could, in many ways, also be called feminist socialism. By this I mean not only that Doris Lessing's socialism appears most strongly in her portrayal of the oppression of women, but also that her own experience as a woman has influenced her picture of political experiences. In my own experience it is more typical of leftist women to engage themselves in questions pertaining to the private sphere of life than it is of men. For example, it is the new women's movement which has compelled leftist political parties to take notice of the political content of issues like the family and sexuality. In this connection, it is also appropriate to mention that interest in psychological mechanisms of oppression was also present in the socialist movement of the 20's and 30's, primarily among Marxist Freudians like Reich and Fromm.52

I have pointed out on several occasions that *Landlocked* and *The Four-Gated City* are marked by a consciousness that sees violence as a ubiquitous destructive power. As I have also mentioned earlier this mentality is first conveyed in *The Golden Notebook*. When she describes the time when she wrote this novel, Doris Lessing indicates it was a time of ideological re-orientation for her:

> An epoch of our society, and of socialism, was breaking up at that time. It had been falling apart since the Bomb was dropped on Hiroshima. We didn't know that this was a watershed. . . . Slowly, it began to sink into our consciousness, and to this day the shock penetrates deeper into our minds. . . . I feel as if the Bomb has gone off inside myself, and in people around me. . . . Some terrible new thing is happening. Maybe it'll be marvellous. . . . Maybe out of destruction there will be born some new creature. I don't mean physically. What interests me more than anything is how our minds are changing, how our ways of perceiving reality are changing. The substance of life receives shocks all the time, every place, from bombs, from the all-pervasive violence. Inevitably the mind changes.53

In this quotation Doris Lessing not only intimates her disillusionment about socialism and describes her experience of violence, but also indicates her interest in the Sufi theory of the evolution of human consciousness. It seems to have been the political mentality of the 50's, characterized by awareness of atomic power, the cold war, the controversy over Stalinism, which compelled Lessing to take the definite step from socialism to mysticism. As I have tried to show, the tendency towards mysticism is present very early in *Children of Violence*. It does not become dominant, however, before the later books and then appears for the most part as a means of understanding and mastering violence as a

destructive power. In the above I have given differing interpretations of the movement towards mysticism in Lessing's
works. To those can be added a more directly political explanation, which emphasizes the vagueness which characterizes
Lessing's socialism. Without, for that reason, interpreting
her socialism in religious terms,[54] it is relevant to point
out that it contains an idealistic element which can explain
why it could not resist the political upheavals and the doomsday mentality of the post-war period. However, in addition,
as I hope to show subsequently, in her later works Lessing
reveals a powerful awareness of environmental destruction, an
issue which to some extent demands new political ideas.

That Doris Lessing's present view of society is influenced by the political climate of the 50's is also
evidenced by the fact that recent political radicalization,
beginning in the West at the end of the 1960's, is alien to
her. Even though in 1969 she commented positively on the revolutionary developments in Vietnam, Cuba and various African
states, she also strongly stressed that she was convinced
that the "Bomb," not liberation movements, ruled the development of the world. She sees the student revolts in the
West as temporary occurrences, which will disappear as the
political climate hardens. In this context she also confirms
her belief in the view of history evident in *The Four-Gated
City*; to her history is a "series of explosions," moving
towards apocalypse. Her only hope in the face of annihilation is contained in the prospect of a new consciousness,
which can possibly be created out of the catastrophe.[55]

Through her mysticism, Doris Lessing embraces a new form
of collective thinking which would seem to replace socialism.
But in contrast to socialism, the collectivity of mysticism
for Doris Lessing is not combined with an interest in the
single individual. In mysticism it is the inner, impersonal,
non-individual self or identity which is significant, not
the individual personality.

This view does not yet prevail in *The Golden Notebook*,
where the individual personality is still central. *The Golden
Notebook* contains a humanistic consciousness, which has

certain points of agreement with that expressed in "The
Small Personal Voice" - but with the important difference
that belief in socialism has already been passed through.
"The Small Personal Voice" is also full of optimism about
the future, while *The Golden Notebook* is a pessimistic book.
Despite the diffident title - "The Small Personal Voice" -
Doris Lessing appears as a heroic individual, "an architect
of the soul;"[56] whereas the fighting individual that Anna
Wulf represents in *The Golden Notebook* is chastened - some-
one who has perceived the strength of the destructive forces,
but who continues to fight as though positive development
were possible.

Anna Wulf is described as a "boulder-pusher," as one
who struggles tirelessly as Sisyphus, without heroism (GN,
p. 537). She practises "a small painful sort of courage which
is at the root of every life, because injustice and cruelty
is at the root of life" (GN, p. 543). This struggle is
pursued by individuals, all equally devoid of illusion, who
together form a "team." Saul Green, Anna's lover, explains
what that means: "There are a few of us around in the world,
we rely on each other even though we don't know each other's
names. . . . We're a team, we're the ones who haven't given
in, who'll go on fighting" (GN, p. 549). This belief in individuals, their humble but unremitting struggle manifested
in *The Golden Notebook*, returns in statements made by Doris
Lessing after the appearance of this novel. Her political
contentions are then limited to liberty and freedom of
rights because these are fundamental for the continuing
function of the "team":

> The individual - democracy, liberty - I am concerned
> now with these more than with anything. . . . No govern-
> ment, no political party anywhere cares a damn about
> the individual. . . . So I believe in the ginger-groups,
> the temporarily associated minorities, the Don
> Quixotes, the takers-of-stands-on-principle, the do-
> gooders and the defenders of lost causes. . . . So -
> to the barricades, citizens! if we don't fight every
> inch of the way, we'll find ourselves with our numbers
> tattooed on our wrists yet.[57]

Humanism and liberalism can also be found in *The Four-Gated City*, but become ambiguous because they conflict with the collectivism and lack of interest in the single individual which mysticism entails. The interest in extra-sensory perception, ESP, which occurs in *The Four Gated City*, contains a humanistic and liberal element. Through ESP, "the old right of the individual human conscience which must know better than any authority, secular or religious, had been restored, but on a higher level, and in a new form which was untouchable by any legal formulas" (FGC, p. 677). This view of the social and political potential of the individual consciousness must however be placed in relation to the erosion of the concept of the individual in this novel, and in later books like *Briefing for a Descent into Hell*, *The Summer Before the Dark* and *The Memoirs of a Survivor*. "Since writing *The Golden Notebook* I've become less personal," Doris Lessing states. "I've floated away from the personal. I've stopped saying 'This is *mine*, this is *my* experience.' . . . I don't believe any more that I have a thought. There is a thought around."[58]

This statement can be taken to mean that she has considered herself representative through recognizing her own thoughts and experiences in others. There is support for this interpretation in other statements by her.[59] Equally, she has described the experience of being representative in her novels, in for example Martha's contact with the younger generation in the Coldridge family, and in Kate Brown's insights about what is typical in her life as a woman. But the presentation of the representative in the individual leads to a total reduction of that individual in Doris Lessing's later work, to eradication of the individual self, which I have already referred to as a "death" of the personality. I think that Doris Lessing's experience of no thought being personal can be connected with ideas of energy in *The Four-Gated City*, according to which in the final analysis all individual experiences, thoughts and feelings, are seen as a product of a collective energy, which the individual can receive and participate in through "the human mind." The presentation of the "death" of the individual as a basis for realizing the inner, impersonal, and collective identity is the paramount feature of Doris Lessing's work from *The Four-Gated City* onwards and, I think, reveals the demise of a humanistic point of view and not a new form of humanism. Most critics dealing with Doris Lessing's humanism argue that the humanistic pathos contained in her attitudes towards ESP is consistent with the humanism expressed in the earlier volumes of *Children of Violence*. I would argue that the question of her humanism becomes meaningless if it is not related to the total consciousness expressed in her work. From my point of view there is then a critical difference in the perception of the individual and his/her relationship to reality between the first and second half of *Children of Violence*.[60]

The nullification of the concept of the individual shows a lack of trust in the individual's value and potential which is alien to a humanistic attitude. The individual is not an asset nor a resource in Doris Lessing's work after *The Golden Notebook*. The "personal dimension" is pictured as a prison, from which the human being can escape only by realizing the inner identity. One reason why the "personal" or "ordinary" is a prison for Lessing is that it is imbued with the reflective and categorizing mentality, which thwarts the experience of inner unity. Disagreement with this consciousness is another anti-humanistic element in Doris Lessing that disputes the presentation of the critical, thinking individual as a social power, which is an important aspect of the early books in *Children of Violence* and which also is found in the later ones, although in ambiguous ways.

Doris Lessing's work, from *The Four-Gated City* onwards is extremely anti-individualistic. Neither the presentation of the outer nor the inner life gives any real latitude for individuality, but is based upon two different forms of collectivism, where the outer sphere involves biological, and the inner psychic communality. Perhaps the most extreme result of this collectivism occurs in *Briefing*

for a Descent into Hell, where humanity is described in
animalistic terms - as a mass of "microbes" whose only worth
lies in its function as a "note in the harmony":

> this *is* its point and function, and where the scummy
> film |humanity|transcends itself, here and here only,
> and never where these mad microbes say I,I,I,I,I, for
> saying I,I,I,I is their madness, this is where they
> have been struck lunatic, made moonmad, round the bend,
> crazy, for these microbes are a whole, they form a
> unity, they have a single mind, a single being . . .
> (Briefing, pp. 102-103).

The relationship between outer and inner life is also
problematic in regard to political and social consciousness
expressed in Doris Lessing's later work. On the one hand
there is an absolute difference between inner and outer life.
The outer stands for being bound to biology, for violence,
oppression, and fragmentation. The inner represents freedom,
harmony, and unity in a psychic communion. On the other hand
both dimensions seem to be ruled by biological laws, both
are products of primary energy. The transition from one to
the other occurs fundamentally through evolutionary laws:
the outer dimension moves inexorably towards the apocalypse,
the final annihilation, from which the inner dimension is
created. Or in other words, "violence" in culture - partly
physical, for example radioactivity, and partly psychic
for example mental illness - gives grounds for an evolution
of humanity, a new human being with a new consciousness.

However, this evolutionary idea is not unequivocal.
I have mentioned earlier that Doris Lessing, like Idries
Shah, labours under both an evolutionary view of the development of this new consciousness, and a volitional view,
where the individual creates his/her own new consciousness.
The evolutionary tendency is however sufficiently prominent
to make the cultural transformation which, according to
Lessing, is engendered through volitional expansion of
consciousness, seem highly ambiguous. In *The Four-Gated City*
the main hope resides in the new children, described as
biological mutations, not as products of a culture stamped
with a new consciousness. The presentation of a new human
being, who like a phoenix rises out of the ashes of

civilization, indicates to me a utopia more ridden with doubt
about the potential of mankind than belief in it. But it is a
logical utopia considering Doris Lessing's evolutionary
determinism, which gives rise to a non-dialectic, static
attitude towards mankind's relationship to cultural and
social development.[61]

Politically, the most interesting aspect of Doris
Lessing's utopia is its ecological aspect, its vision of
potential harmony between mankind and nature, which I shall
return to in the next section. Here I wish to continue my
discussion of the erosion of humanism through examining a
hierarchical, potentially totalitarian tendency in those
social utopias which are a result of her general utopia.

Doris Lessing's vision of a harmonious unity between
mankind and nature is based on ideas which treat human beings
as organisms like plants and animals: "I think we are an
organism like a plant is an organism. Humanity is part of
organic life and we are all one."[62] This view is extended
into an organic view of society which can be studied in the
utopian social formations that occur in *The Four-Gated City*.
As I have mentioned in Chapter III, these societies are
marked by a social harmony based upon mankind's closeness
to nature. Class conflict, sexual and ethnic differences as
well as individual upheavals are exempt from these societies
due to natural, collective communality between all peoples.
In the mystical city, which has the most detailed description
of its social structure, everyone has a given place and
function. Despite the fact that this society is said to
allow social mobility, it is founded upon a basic hierarchy
because those people who are so to speak closest to nature
by incarnating its creative powers, form a "natural" leadership. The mystical city is consequently a hierarchical
utopia and also quiescent since all social and human conflict has ceased.

This picture of society is an example of the general
static and dualistic thinking which Doris Lessing expresses
in her later books. The mystical city is the opposite of
the vision of the "ordinary" world's violence and oppression,

but one containing the same non-dialectic ways of thinking.
The absolute oppression and disintegration is parallelled
by the absolute transcendence in an infinite harmony.
Mystical consciousness leads to social nullity, to a utopia
where all social categories are denounced in favour of
association based on what is "natural" in humanity.

7 Doris Lessing Today

This section consists of an attempt at a "contemporary
reading" of Doris Lessing, which in parts shifts the perspective used earlier. During the time I have worked with
Lessing's texts, my understanding of the consciousness they
express has to a certain extent changed. This has led to a
desire to review some of my original ideas about Lessing and
also to attempt to explain their evolution. This is in no
way intended to satisfy an egocentric whim but hopefully
to disclose what has been historically determined or even
personally "dated" in my treatment.

What originally fascinated me in Doris Lessing was that
she seemed to be both socialist and feminist, that she was
a representative of both the Left and women's struggles.
This attracted me and continues to do so, although my
attitude to these two concerns is now more complex than
it was when I first read *Children of Violence* in 1973. I was
myself at that time filled with the revolutionary enthusiasm
of the the student revolt of the late 60's and of the new
women's movement. Consequently I became exceedingly
frustrated with the ideological development in *Children of
Violence*. In her later books Doris Lessing seemed to become
disloyal to both women and ideas of socialism. That I understand Lessing in a somewhat different way today is mainly
due to shifts in the leftist political climate during the
70's, which I briefly want to touch upon here and try to
relate to Lessing's later books, particularly *The Four-Gated
City*. It is her later work in particular that have become
a new challenge for me because of recent changes in the
political climate.

It is difficult to write about ongoing transformations in society and politics. My attempt to do so will be rather "intuitive" - it will be based on material difficult to define, which encompasses debates in the media, conversations with friends, my own experiences of political activity. All of this relates to a Swedish environment, but I think that in essence what I examine corresponds to a general development in Western society.

Risking simplification I would claim that the political tendencies of the last decade resemble those which can be traced in *Children of Violence*. I would underline the word "resemble," as history does not repeat itself. When, as some people do, one says today that we find ourselves once again reliving the 30's or 50's, one is not far from Doris Lessing's deterministic, cyclical view of history, according to which it is impossible to influence or affect our social environment.

Thus, although the political developments of the last 10 years are far from identical with those of the 40's and 50's reflected in *Children of Violence*, there are similarities. *A Ripple from the Storm* describes how enthusiasm over the Battle of Stalingrad (1942) leads to Martha's whole-hearted support of the Russian revolution. This can be compared with the significance the liberation struggles in Vietnam had for turning the leftist generation of 1968 into communists. Equally, the disillusion over Stalinism in *Landlocked* and *The Four-Gated City*, and even more clearly in *The Golden Notebook*, can be compared with the political sobriety which has marked the '68 generation during the 70's, when the revolutionary glow is dampened by the awareness of conflicts between different socialist states, by the continuing Stalinism in eastern Europe, by the inertia of revolutionary advance in the West. But what above all makes it easier to understand Lessing's post-war mentality, her fixation on Violence, is that the doomsday atmosphere of the 50's has begun to seep in again. The 50's fear of the atom bomb has been reactivated in the fear of atomic energy and in the consciousness of global environmental destruction

which threatens to annihilate life itself. This consciousness in combination with a more complicated relationship to
socialism among the Left today, has also resulted in the
arms race between the United States and The Soviet Union,
which has existed since the 50's, becoming noticeable again.
The Cold War atmosphere and fear of a third World War have
been resuscitated.

Doris Lessing has progressed from a socialist orientation with a concern for the relations between the individual
and the collective to being a cultural critic, concentrating
on the connections between nature and culture. Today her
development is primarily relevant to a discussion of the
relationship between ecological and socialist or Marxist
thought.

I would contend that Doris Lessing's utopia of the new
human being is first and foremost an ecological utopia, aiming
to demonstrate that life in harmonious unity with nature is
possible. Indeed, it seems that her attitude towards Violence
arose from her experience of the World Wars, but the origins
of violence issue from the alienation of man from nature -
partly concrete physical nature, partly the nature in man's
psyche, which she sees linked with nature mainly through unconscious powers. The social consciousness of Lessing's later
works is also primarily a consciousness of environment. In
addition to being aware of the threat of atomic power and the
arms industry, it encompasses an anti-technological and anti-
technocratic standpoint. It is through this sort of consciousness that Doris Lessing is able to communicate with the progressive ideas of the late 1970's, which are increasingly committed to environmental problems and to the need of a modified
political strategy to deal with these problems.

During the 1970's a new protest movement has grown -
that of the environmentalists. In various ways they have
criticized different phenomena in capitalist society, but
this criticism has not always been clearly pro-socialist.
For example, I have in front of me a newspaper clipping
containing a newly published "Ecological Manifesto,"
written by ecological activists from eleven different

countries (*Dagens Nyheter*, 6 June, 1979). It urges a
campaign against technocracy and the reign of experts and
demands popular decision-making. In an implicit polemic
against the Communist Manifesto, it is proposed that future
politics must be based on ecological principles alone, not
on political ideology.

The political vagueness of the ecology movement cannot
be ascribed to lack of socialist consciousness or bourgeois
tendencies only. One can equally charge the socialist movement and the more or less socialist countries with ecological
ignorance or indifference, and an uncritical attitude towards
the expansion of the productive forces which technological
development involves. The socialist movement has to a great
extent accepted the growth mechanism which is built into
the capitalist system. This applies primarily to the social
democratic and reformist workers' movements, but also the
communist movement shows similar tendencies - e.g., most
communist parties support atomic power. The domestic economy
of, for instance, the Soviet Union can be seen as an extension of traditional ideas of development within communism.
Socialism's planned economy is more of a necessary pre-
requisite than a guarantee for a society where technological
development is governed by social needs and ecological demands. The support which the large social democratic parties
give to capitalism - the principle that what is good for big
capital is good for society - is an important factor in
explaining the scepticism felt in the environmentalist movement towards traditional party politics and ideas. The issue
of the environment has burst traditional party boundaries
and created new political alliances - a new, still vague,
collective "we" who confront a vaguely defined power
structure.

The picture of society and politics drawn by Doris
Lessing in her later work, especially *The Four-Gated City*,
but also *The Summer before the Dark* and *The Memoirs of a
Survivor* show certain points of contact with the ideas of
the ecological movement. In *The Four-Gated City* society is
ruled by a power structure with fascist tendencies, where

big capital, technical expertise, the Labour Party, the
military and also the church and the media are included.
Against this conglomerate stands a popular opposition, which
consists of various groups of outsiders - youths who have
"dropped out" of society, mad people, especially mad women,
and finally former communists, like Mark Coldridge. The
young people react against consumer culture, individualism,
the careerist mentality; they try to create an alternative
culture, new forms for living together and for social life
in general. The mad women question assumptions about normality and rationality and show the latter's connections
with technocratic "male" mentality. The ex-communist, Mark
Coldridge, opposes ideologically induced attitudes, which
make it impossible for him to understand the global exploitation of people and resources, and technological expansion.
The oppositional groups and what they stand for as traced
by Doris Lessing are interesting from an anti-capitalist,
pro-ecology point of view. The protest she has portrayed is
directed against tendencies towards decay in late capitalist
society; it opposes alienating, undemocratic and life-
damaging institutions and social structures.

Doris Lessing's focussing on women is especially interesting since women have emerged as a new progressive
force in the environmentalist movement; for example, it is
a fact that women, more than men, oppose nuclear energy.
Women's engagement seems to issue from their social and
psychological ties to the reproductive area of society;
that is, to an existence centred around the re-creation
of human life both from generation to generation and from
day to day. The life, work and mentality of women today is
often summarized in the idea of a "female culture." I
have earlier related Doris Lessing to the debate about
female culture and in that context pointed to her ambiguous attitudes towards womanhood. Lessing sees woman as
bearer of a life-preserving potential which cannot seem
to find a satisfying social form. In this her ideas are
marked by a realistic awareness of the deforming influence of female oppression. The oppression of women and

subsequent distortion are also results of women's reproductive function, which is often neglected in the
female culture debate. Women's assertion of life appears
indirectly in *The Four-Gated City* as madness, which contains
elements of social protest, directed towards the normality
and rationalism represented by male-dominated technocratic
institutions.

The group that suffers by its absence in Doris Lessing's
register of social revolt in *The Four-Gated City* is the
working class. Its exclusion can be related to her general
political stance, which is concentrated on racial problems
and women's oppression, and which excludes the working
class. Even more important in this context is the fact that
the working class as a whole has not been a progressive
force in the struggle for the environment. Workers often
defend the capitalist growth mechanism out of fear of
unemployment and reduction in standards. Doris Lessing's
presentation of the integration of the Labour Party into
the repressive state apparatus is not a picture lacking in
veracity.

Up to now I have concentrated upon the social consciousness that Doris Lessing reveals in *The Four-Gated
City*. This contains however indissoluble ties with her
mysticism, which means that it is the result of biological
or metaphysical ideas - depending upon how one interprets the
creative natural powers which are the basis of mysticism.
The discrepancies between social observation and metaphysical or biological explanation constitute a general
problem in Doris Lessing's later work, which I have touched
upon earlier in connection with the female problematic. The
social consciousness in *The Four-Gated City* has more
immediate interest for my discussion of socialism and
ecology than mysticism, but mysticism can also be thought-
provoking, particularly if it is seen as a symptom of
simplifications and shortcomings which are to be found
in Lessing's earlier lines of thinking. Since her early
view of reality is associated with the struggle for
socialism and her mysticism is related to the question of

the survival of the planet, her development must represent
a challenge if one seeks to integrate the intentions of the
ecology movement with the struggle for socialism.

Doris Lessing's attempts to find solutions for what she
sees as crucial problems of her own time have led her from
socialist ideas to concepts of biological or metaphysical
sources of power or energy. From having been a social being,
the human being has become for her a natural creature, an
organism, whose significance lies in its connection with all
other organic life. From having been a rational creature,
whose orientation in reality is guided by a reflective awareness, Lessing's human being has acquired a consciousness directed by a "natural dimension" channelled through irrational
elements and intuition. From having been forward-looking
fighters for social change, her fictional characters have
become introspective and enmeshed in the past, bent upon
inner consciousness and a lost communion with nature or the
state of nature.

Doris Lessing's thinking has passed into its opposite:
from having been what she herself calls progressive, rational
and atheistic,[63] it has become what could be called regressive, irrational and religious. But is is exactly this development which today can raise the question as to what is
progressive and regressive, rational and irrational.
Lessing's return to nature can be seen in relation to
capitalism's technological expansion and to myopic ideas
about progress which are also present within the socialist
movement. Her criticism of rationalism increases in weight
and import at a time when accusations of irrationality are
lodged against socially critical groups, for example against
women who oppose nuclear power and the military establishment. One does not need to be religious or mystical to
assert that Western culture suffers today from a form of
hubris in relation to nature which must be broken for a
truly progressive social development to be possible.

In its basic elements Doris Lessing's mysticism is
however hardly useful for the sort of integrated or synthetic set of ideas I have sought after. In this context

she represents primarily a warning, a "sign of the times," an example of how social and cultural crises tend to engender extreme and fantastic solutions. Her criticism of concepts of rationality results in a condemnation of the reflective and structuring consciousness in general. In her criticism of normality, only the mad are considered sane and wise. Criticism of individualism leads to disintegration of the concept of the individual. Criticism of culture reduces all human and social phenomena to "forces."

Doris Lessing's idea of force is (as I have already indicated) problematic in many ways. Therefore I shall confine myself to considering briefly a few absolutely central objections to it. Through seeing human social life as an expression of energy or of the spirit she deprives herself of the possibilities of understanding the social and cultural phenomena which have created the developments she reacts against. She becomes incapable of understanding the interaction between humanity and nature and between society and nature. Her biological approach is more marked after *The Four-Gated City*, principally in *A Briefing for a Descent into Hell* and *The Memoirs of a Survivor*, where humanity appears as the victim of its own "animal" violence. Her ideas of force also implicate technical, instrumental attitudes which reduce to a certain degree the pungency of her own criticism of that technocratic, rationalist mentality. Finally, the idea of a fundamental force has extremely dubious political implications. It gives rise to the notion that human communality is naturally given and spans all social oppositions. In its concrete form, as in the mystical city in *The Four-Gated City*, this view creates a picture of society as a harmonious social organism, incarnated by a "natural" leadership. This social structure gives unpleasant associations with various undemocratic, even downright fascist states, which clearly illustrates the problem of basing social analysis upon natural mysticism.

Conclusion

Doris Lessing has progressed from being socialistically
oriented and concerned with the relationship between the
individual and society to becoming a cultural critic, concentrating on the connection between nature and culture.
This progression can be traced through Martha's development in *Children of Violence*. This series of novels deals
with violence and oppression but gives varying definitions
of violence and suggests different ways of mastering it.

    Martha Quest through *A Ripple from the Storm* treats
violence mainly as a socially created phenomenon. Violence
in society is primarily represented by the institution of
the family. The family is characterized by bourgeois and
patriarchal norms which give rise to authoritarian, hierarchical relationships between parents and children and
women and men. The family oppresses woman through its
demands on her to adjust to an existence of being solely a
wife and mother. The authoritarian social structure also
occurs in racial relationships, but racial oppression is
less developed than that of the family.

    Mrs. Quest is a product of the authoritarian family
pattern and through her it is reproduced in Martha.
Martha's revolt against the socializing ambitions of her
mother turns their relationship into a complex struggle
for power with sado-masochistic components. To survive this
battle Martha develops the attitude of an uninvolved reflective, "detached observer," which she has gained from
her reading of socially critical literature.

    The dream of the ideal city provides the point of
departure for Martha's outwards-directed quest for identity.
The city is a vision of a new society free from racial and
family oppression. It also represents a new home imbued with

love and harmony instead of conflict and struggle. Within
the city private life and politics are mixed: it contains a
fusion of political and emotional needs, a dream of alternative personal relationships as well as a new ideology.

Martha first attempts to realize the city through
love, then through communism. Love leads to marriage and her
re-experience of the oppressive mechanisms of her parental
family. She becomes tied to marriage and motherhood through
the social and biological demands on her as a woman. Her
sexual needs and her longing for love make her submissive
and compliant in relation to men: in order not to feel lacking as a woman she develops a sexually pleasing and maternally understanding attitude which ties her to her functions
within marriage. Her instinct to reproduce life is socially
manipulated by the myth of motherhood which sees female
revolt against maternity as unnatural. Through the pressures
of married life Martha's relationships with Douglas and
Caroline become affected by the same authoritarian pattern
which was present in her interaction with her mother.

Martha's attempt to "live differently" in a communist
group not only demonstrates once more the problem of family
oppression but also the difficulty of fighting racism.
Through her life with Anton the pervasiveness of the
authoritarian pattern is again illustrated in personal
as well as political life.

Martha's outwards-directed search leads to a dead end
both as regards her female identity and her political one.
She discovers repetition instead of change, oppression
instead of love and equality. Instead of wholeness she
finds constant fragmentation. In her marriage she never
overcomes the opposition between being a woman and a human
being, a "person." She experiences a gap between her
emotional and instinctive needs and her demands for consciousness and detachment. Her political existence manifests the
conflicts between feeling and intellect, theory and practice,
politics and private life. After her experiences of
political and married life, Martha gives up her dreams
for social change and accepts the family as an inevitable
necessity.

In *Landlocked* and *The Four-Gated City* Martha is no longer
concerned with achieving social unity. Instead she strives for
a new unified, visionary consciousness which will replace the
"ordinary," fragmenting mentality that characterizes her
life as a cultural being. Cultural consciousness which is
closely allied with analytical and rational properties of
the mind is described as instrumental in creating violence
in the sense that it separates humanity from nature and from
the unconscious, "natural" dimension of the human psyche.

In the later novels violence emanates from a basic
psycho-physical source of power or energy, neutral in value
but containing both creative and destructive potentials.
These potentials can be employed by human beings. In a
culture pervaded by a fragmented type of consciousness
humanity does not see itself as a unified whole. Then the
negative potential dominates and leads to class divisions,
racial and sexual conflicts, and ultimately to war.

The notion that human life is in the final analysis
ruled by some sort of fundamental power first occurs in
Martha Quest. Through a mystical experience Martha becomes
at one with nature and the elemental forces it represents.
This experience gives her a sense of human life as futile
and unimportant which seems to puncture her dream of a
better society. At the same time she is given a glimpse
of a new, creative approach to life which, however, can
only be achieved through a dissolution of her self and her
world view. There are other experiences of the same kind
which she is said to have had during her childhood, when
she lived a life of harmonious unity with nature. They
remain in her mind in the form of the knowledge that she
is part of a context larger than herself. This insight
becomes a special mode of consciousness, an intuitive
"conscience" which guides her in her relationship with
reality.

Martha's mystical experience is the starting point
for her search inwards. It provides a kind of undercurrent
within the early novels but it does not fully surface
until the later ones. Through her female body and the

intuitive and receptive elements of her female consciousness, Martha re-experiences a closeness to elemental forces. During pregnancy and childbirth she feels nature to be both creative and destructive. Her womanhood appears as an extension of the mystical dimension which she had as a child but lost when she became a cultural being. This part of herself conflicts with her quest outwards: it ties her to the family and it threatens those parts of her identity which she sees as allied to her "true" self, notably the reflective attitude which is her main pro-tection against forces that prevent her self-realization.

In the last two novels Martha is, however, guided by her body and her intuitive consciousness, her "soft dark receptive intelligence." This consciousness is now the central part of her identity. It has as it were become materialized as an inner self, a "watcher" or "monitor." But in order for this new self to develop into its full visionary potential Martha must go through the dissolution of her old self which was demanded in her first mystical experience. She must transcend the boundaries of "ordinary" consciousness and also liberate herself from the social and personal elements which earlier determined her identity.

Martha realizes her inner self through her contacts with Thomas, Jack and the various members of the Coldridge family. Her erotic love-relationship with Thomas puts her in touch with a creative energy which gives her a new image of herself. Her analytical consciousness dissolves and her bodily and irrational forms of perception are developed. This experience she uses consciously with Jack: sexuality becomes an "instrument" through which she can break through the compartmentalized existence of everyday life and reach inner unity. In her relationship with Thomas, Martha also gets a sense of the destructive power at work in human life. Thomas stands for both the life-giving forces of sexuality and the death-bringing forces of war, but at this stage of her development Martha is only capable of acknowledging the creative part of his personality.

Martha's life with the Coldridges is a mixture of
penance and therapy, based on the fact that in *The Four-Gated
City* the family as an institution is described as an in-
escapable necessity from which there is inner, psychological
liberation but not outer, social freedom. Martha pays her
"debts" for her former rebellion against the family by
assuming responsibility for the Coldridges. At the same
time she liberates herself psychologically by reliving and
distancing herself from her former life, her teenage
rebellion, her life as a mother, and her political activity.
Above all she frees herself from her mother and from men.
She tears herself away from her need for love which still
binds her to oppression within society and which hampers
the development of her inner being. Martha makes herself
anonymous and depersonalized: she reaches a cosmic distance
from which human life appears as an unavoidable but absurd
play - here the notion of human life as insignificant and
futile is realized.

Free from her social and personal life, Martha is ready
to meet the basic forces which in *The Four-Gated City* are
manifested as a type of collective unconscious, the "human
mind." Her confrontation with them is helped by Lynda who
through being "mad" has special resources for extra-sensory
experiences. During an "inner journey" Martha meets a
principle of evil, the authoritarian, sado-masochistic
structure as a generalized principle of violence. By admitting that she is part of it and by acknowledging evil as an
ever-present potential within the basic force, Martha
completes her educational process and reaches final unity
and freedom. By realizing her inner self, described as the
essence of life, Martha may be said to have regained the
unity with nature which she once lost.

Martha's search for identity is filtered through two
different forms of consciousness. That which dominates her
search outwards, I have called the social or sociological
consciousness; it regards Martha primarily as a social
being, formed by categories such as sex role, class membership, and family background. The consciousness which

characterizes her quest inwards I have termed nature versus culture since it underscores the "nature" in Martha and sets it in opposition to "culture." What the concepts nature and culture consist of shifts throughout the series (see Ch. IV, Sec. 2). According to this mode of consciousness Martha is essentially conditioned by her biology, her unconscious, and her intuitive and irrational modes of perception.

Both forms of consciousness are materialistic. The biological materialism of the nature-culture approach is, however, unclear in the sense that the concept of nature in the last two novels can signify a spiritual as well as a biological entity. Nevertheless, the basic forces, which inform all of life in these novels, ultimately appear to be biological. While the social materialism is non-deterministic, the biological equivalent is deterministic. The social thinking is associated with change, whereas the biological is cyclic and directed at adjustment to the laws of nature. Fundamentally, the nature-culture mode of consciousness contains an organic and evolutionary view of human and social development. This view is, however, not unequivocal as Martha's expansion of consciousness is presented as partly volitional. In *The Four-Gated City* the nature-culture outlook can be seen as a form of mysticism. The basic forces of nature seem to be a transcendental entity which human beings can partake of and thereby develop an expanded or evolved consciousness characterized by extra-sensory modes of perception. Social consciousness, on the other hand, is connected with socialism and with analytical and rational attitudes of mind.

In *Martha Quest* through *A Ripple from the Storm* the two forms of consciousness conflict with each other. The tension between them is largely resolved in the last two books of the series. These are dominated by a dualism between nature and culture which generates a general biological view of mankind with priorities given to the instinctive and irrational. The social mode of thinking never fully disappears, however. It remains as a surface awareness but no longer constitutes the basic model for explanation. When

the social problematic of the earlier novels is approached
on the basis of the nature-culture outlook, its content
becomes biological-psychological instead of socio-psychological, abstract and generalized instead of concrete and
specific, and is finally reduced to the idea of the basic
force (see Ch. III, Sec. 3).

The social consciousness and that which is based on
the opposition between nature and culture are both informed
by a female perspective. In my study I have put special
emphasis on this perspective since the tension between the
two modes of consciousness is particularly apparent in the
ambiguous image of Martha's female identity presented in
the earlier novels.

What has been called the social female consciousness
appears in Martha's battle against the family. It gives an
image of a deformed, passive, potentially masochistic womanhood which must be overcome in order for Martha to achieve
an authentic identity. The perspective of biological female
consciousness, on the other hand, considers femininity
central to Martha's identity. According to this perspective,
Martha's true and creative being is that which is formed by
her sexuality and her reproductive instinct and whose
consciousness is marked by intuition. This Martha is allied
with nature and unconscious powers; she represents a life-
giving female principle which stands in opposition to
destructive, male-dominated culture.

Although the social female consciousness dominates in
the earlier books of the series, the biological approach
often seems to have more affinity with what is shown to be
Martha's own experience of herself as a woman. When the
biological mode becomes dominant in *Landlocked*, those
aspects of her identity which she had earlier repressed in
order to escape domesticity become paths for her personal
and political development.

Despite the fact that *The Four-Gated City* contains a
polarization between the male and female psyche resembling
that of the earlier novels, female consciousness in that
novel takes on a more abstract philosophical character.

Martha's concrete and personal experience becomes less and
less important for her development towards mysticism. Nevertheless, the mystical dimension, which has earlier been
presented as more available to women than to men, becomes
increasingly central and provides an outlet for Martha's
identity as a woman; in mystical inner life Martha's
sexuality and female modes of perception are creative,
whereas in social life her femininity is constantly distorted. Love and sex which in the non-social relationship
with Thomas leads to new insights, create in the family-like
relationship with Mark the dependent masochistic woman.
Martha's role as mother activates the receptive and intuitive
elements in her psyche, but these are only shown to function
unequivocally positively when they have become part of the
inner life and are transformed to "watching" and "listening,"
i.e. extra-sensory perception. In *The Four-Gated City* the
picture of deformed womanhood occurs as a remnant of the
struggle of the social female consciousness against the
family. This mentality continues, although the family there
is projected as woman's biological and cultural destiny.

The biological female consciousness provides fertile
ground for the inner life's mental growth in several different ways: it creates a foundation for a generally biological
or instinctive way of thinking, which anticipates speculations about energy and violence as a destructive power.
Also, it sees the analytical, reflective consciousness as
splitting and fragmenting, while intuition, instincts, and
the forces of the unconscious are all seen as unifying.
However, this mentality does not dominate until that
socialism which is related to the battle waged by the
social female consciousness against the family is rejected.
When disillusion with socialism occurs in *Children of
Violence* it leads to a crisis in the analytical and rational
consciousness, both the narrator's and Martha's, which then
allows the biological dimension with its special wholeness
and thinking in terms of forces to take over.

The tensions and shifts of consciousness discussed above
can also be related to Doris Lessing's intellectual background.

The treatment of Martha as a social being whose identity
is conditioned by her functions in the family can be related
to Marxist theory. The description of family patterns in the
early novels stresses an authoritarian and repressive
bourgeois family structure, related to the sexual division
of labour and the patriarchal organization of society.

The conflict between nature and culture and the notion
of a biologically defined womanhood, on the other hand, point
to an inspiration from depth psychology. Both Freud and Jung
can be traced in *Children of Violence*, but Lessing's adaptation of the nature-culture conflict is closer to Jung than to
Freud. Like Jung she stresses that the powers of nature and
the unconscious are creative, whereas Freud emphasizes the
sublimation of these powers in human life. In its view of
mankind as ultimately conditioned by instinctive and unconscious forces depth psychology can be a point of departure for the philosophy which dominates in the later novels.

The fully developed mysticism of *The Four-Gated City*
can be related to a variety of thought with idealist and
metaphysical implications; the most directly noticeable
influences seem to stem from Jung, from the psychiatrist
R.D. Laing, and from the contemporary exponent of Islamic
Sufi mysticism, Idries Shah. Martha's development of an
inner life may be viewed as a Jungian "individuation process."
Like Laing, in *The Politics of Experience*, Lessing sees
mental illness as a potential for transcendental experience.
Shah appears to be the most important influence on Lessing's
mysticism as she seems to have acquired from him the notion
of an evolution of the human mind. Both Shah and Lessing
demonstrate an ambiguous view toward the change of the
human consciousness. On the one hand they describe it as
strictly evolutionary, on the other they indicate that it
can be influenced by human effort.

In sections 5 and 6 of Chapter IV, I have attempted to
broaden the analysis of the development of consciousness in
Children of Violence by giving an overview of Doris Lessing's
outlook on women and society. In this discussion I have
included other works by her, mainly *The Summer Before the*

Dark and *The Memoirs of a Survivor*, and I have also considered statements made by her in essays, articles and
interviews.

As regards her view of women, I have tried to demonstrate
that her work displays two types of attitudes which have
points of contact with tendencies within historical feminism.

The first attitude agrees with what is generally meant
by feminism, i.e. a militant attitude, directed against female oppression in the sense of economic, political, and
psychological mechanisms which prevent women from developing
their full potential as human beings. Lessing demonstrates
her critical awareness of the oppression of women through her
portrait of the family. The earlier books in *Children of
Violence* suggest that the family can be struggled against
and surmounted. This type of militancy disappears in
Lessing's later works, from *The Golden Notebook* onwards:
in these she presents a special female nature, determined by
biology, which binds woman to the family or to family-like
monogamous relationships. The family, however, is still
presented as a deforming influence.

At the same time as Lessing's biological ideas result
in a social determinism vis-à-vis the woman's role in the
family, it engenders another type of feminism based on the
assumption of the creativity of female nature. Women are
connected with unified consciousness, whereas men represent
the rationalistic, fragmenting mentality which is linked
with war, technological expansion, and environmental
destruction. This feminism includes an ecological awareness
directed against the technocratic, instrumental mentality
of male-dominated Western culture. For a discussion of
historical analogies to the two types of feminism, see
Chapter IV, Sec. 5.

The latter feminism is never realized socially but
remains a creative potential expressed through mysticism.
It is combined with a detachment from concrete female
experience and from the traditionally female sphere of
personal and emotional life which makes it ambiguous.
The Four-Gated City, *The Summer Before the Dark*, and *The*

Memoirs of a Survivor are characterized by a common structure which presents mysticism as a final means of liberation
from the social and personal dimensions of female life.

The Summer Before the Dark and *The Memoirs of a Survivor*
are also connected with *Children of Violence* through their
image of the mother as exploitive and despotic. The idea of
a destructive mother links together Lessing's early and
later representations of the family; it appears pivotal in
explaining why she presents the family, and finally the
entire area of personal existence, as oppressive and
constricting.

Schematically Doris Lessing's view of society can be
described in the following manner: *Children of Violence*,
I-III, is marked by humanist socialism or communism, *The
Golden Notebook* by humanism, and *Landlocked* and *The Four-
Gated City* and later works by mysticism.

There is a vagueness in Lessing's comments on socialism; she seldom discusses class analysis, but talks in
terms of human rights, equality and solidarity amongst all
people. This vagueness can on the one hand be explained
by the fact that her social concerns - problems of women
and racism - are difficult to analyse purely in terms of
class, and on the other by the fact that most of her
remarks about socialism are distinguished by a sense of
disappointment in the kind of socialism practised in the
Soviet Union.

Nevertheless, there is an idealistic element in
Lessing's socialism which can explain why it could not
survive the political upheavals of the post-war period.
It seems to have been the political mentality of the 50's,
characterized by awareness of atomic power, the cold war,
Stalinism, which compelled Doris Lessing to take the
definite step from social radicalism to mysticism and
thinking in terms of "forces."

Mysticism provides Doris Lessing with a new form of
thinking which functions as a solution to the female as
well as the general social concerns in her work. I find
this solution problematic in a number of ways, partly

because her mysticism contains a progressively more marked division between inner and outer life, and partly because it is ultimately deterministic.

The only solution to the female problematic is the mystical female principle of inner life, but the achievement of this mentality is associated with a depersonalization which renders the individual anonymous, i.e. with what I have called the "death" of the concrete, individual woman. In general human terms mysticism leads to an erosion of Lessing's humanism, to a nullification of the concept of the individual. If the notion of the dissolution of the individual is related to the tendencies towards subjection and assimilation which were a problem in Martha's search for a social identity, mysticism may be interpreted as a logical conclusion of such leanings. Then mysticism becomes flight - an escape from both social and human life, from conflicts, emotional problems, and the demands of consciousness.

But one can also interpret mysticism more positively and stress its utopian dimension, its vision of a creative, life-giving potential within women and its hope for a harmonious unity between mankind and nature. The utopian dimension of Lessing's work has lately become quite relevant for me through the growth of the environmentalist movement and its concerns (see Chapter IV, Sec. 7). Even her utopia, however, seems to me to be undermined by the determinism of her mysticism.

The transition from the outer to the inner dimension occurs fundamentally through evolutionary laws; the outer dimension moves inexorably towards apocalypse, the final annihilation, from which the inner dimension is created. In *The Four Gated-City* the main hope resides in the new children, described as biological mutations, not as products of a culture stamped with a new consciousness. The presentation of a new human being, who like a phoenix rises out of the ashes of civilization, indicates to me a utopia more ridden with doubt about the potential of mankind than belief in it. But it is a logical utopia considering Doris Lessing's evolutionary determinism, which gives rise to

a non-dialectic, static attitude towards mankind's relationship to cultural and social development.

Notes

Introduction

1. "This book is what the Germans call a *Bildungsroman*," Doris Lessing remarks about *Children of Violence* in the "Author's Notes" to the final volume of the series, *The Four-Gated City* (p. 711).

2. *Children of Violence* includes:
    Martha Quest. London: Michael Joseph, 1952.
    A Proper Marriage. London: Michael Joseph, 1954.
    A Ripple from the Storm. London: Michael Joseph, 1958.
    Landlocked. London: MacGibbon & Kee, 1965.
    The Four-Gated City. London: MacGibbon & Kee, 1969.

3. See Paul Schlueter, *The Novels of Doris Lessing* (Carbondale: Southern Illinois Univ. Press, 1973), pp. 3-4. For further information on Lessing's marriages see Claudia Dee Seligman, "The Autobiographical Novels of Doris Lessing," Diss. Tufts Univ. 1975, pp. 36-39, 45-47.

4. Besides *Children of Violence* Doris Lessing has published the following novels:
    The Grass Is Singing. London: Michael Joseph, 1950.
    Retreat to Innocence. London: Michael Joseph, 1956.
    The Golden Notebook. London: Michael Joseph, 1962.
    Briefing for a Descent into Hell. London: Jonathan Cape, 1971.
    The Summer Before the Dark. London: Jonathan Cape, 1973.
    The Memoirs of a Survivor. London: The Octagon Press, 1974.
    Shikasta: Canopus in Argos-Archives. London: Jonathan Cape, 1979.
    For titles and publication dates of Lessing's short stories, plays, poems and other narratives, see Agate Nesaule Krouse, "A Doris Lessing Checklist," *Contemporary Literature*, 14 (1973), pp. 591-593.

5. See the biographical note preceding Lessing's essay "The Small Personal Voice," in *Declaration*, ed. Tom Maschler (London: MacGibbon & Kee, 1957), p. 12. See also Schlueter, p. 4.

6. See C.J. Driver, "Profile 8: Doris Lessing," *The New Review*, 1, No. 8 (1974), pp. 21-22.

7. Idries Shah published *The Sufis* in 1964 (London: W.H. Allen), *The Way of the Sufi* in 1968 (London: Jonathan Cape), and *The Magic Monastery* in 1972 (London: Jonathan Cape). Doris Lessing wrote an enthusiastic review of *The Sufis* when it first came out. See "An Elephant in the Dark," *The Spectator*, 18 Sept. 1964,

p. 373. Subsequently she wrote a number of articles on Shah's books: "An Ancient Way to New Freedom," *Vogue*, July 1971, pp. 98, 125, 130-131; "In the World, Not of It," *Encounter*, August 1972, pp. 61-64; "What Looks Like an Egg and Is an Egg?," *New York Times Book Review*, 7 May 1972, pp. 41-43.

8. See Doris′Lessing, "Doris Lessing at Stony Brook: An Interview by Jonah Raskin," in *A Small Personal Voice*, ed. Paul Schlueter (New York: Alfred A. Knopf, 1974), pp. 65-66, 70; Driver p. 20; Joseph Haas, "Doris Lessing: Chronicler of the Cataclysm," *Chicago Daily News*, 14 June, 1969, pp. 4-5; Lessing, Preface, GN, p. 10.

9. "this is a study of the individual conscience in its relations with the collective." "The Small Personal Voice" in *A Small Personal Voice*, p. 14 (originally published in *Declaration*).

Survey of Research

1. Dorothy Bergquist Wells, "The Unity of Doris Lessing's *Children of Violence*," Diss. Tulane Univ. 1976, pp. 3, 34; cf. pp. 20-22.

2. Ibid. p. 6.

3. Florence Howe, "A Conversation with Doris Lessing (1966)," *Contemporary Literature*, 14 (1973), pp. 431-432.

4. Actually there is yet another thesis which is concerned with formal and ideological changes in Lessing's fiction: Lorelei Cederstrom's "From Marxism to Myth: A Developmental Study of the Novels of Doris Lessing," *DAI*, 38 (1978), p. 7320-A (The Univ. of Manitoba). This work, which is not available through the regular microfilm service, unfortunately reached me too late for consideration.

5. Karen A. Kildahl, "The Political and Apocalyptical Novels of Doris Lessing," Diss. Univ. of Washington 1974, p. 24.

6. Ibid. *DAI*, 35 (1975) p. 4528-A.

7. Diane E. Sherwood Smith, "A Thematic Study of Doris Lessing's *Children of Violence*," Diss. Loyola Univ. of Chicago 1971, p. 6.

8. Ellen Cronan Rose, "Doris Lessing's *Children of Violence* as a Bildungsroman: An Eriksonian Analysis," Diss. Univ. of Massachusetts 1974, pp. 6, 15-20, 25-26.

9. From the *Doris Lessing Newsletter*, 3, No. 1 ('79), p. 3,
    I learn that the first dissertation on Lessing was in
    fact Gottfried Graustein's "Entwicklungstendenzen im
    Schaffen Doris Lessings," Diss. Univ. of Leipzig 1963.
    Since this dissertation is not available through the
    microfilm service and was written as early as 1963, I
    have decided not to take it into consideration.

10. Mary Ann Singleton, *The City and the Veld: The Fiction
    of Doris Lessing* (Lewisburg: Bucknell Univ. Press, 1977),
    pp. 19-20.

11. Tamara K. Mitchell, "The Irrational Element in Doris
    Lessing's Fiction," Diss. Boston Univ. 1978, p. 30.

12. Noeline Elizabeth Alcorn, "Vision and Nightmare: A
    Study of Doris Lessing's Novels," Diss. Univ. of
    California, Irvine 1971, pp. v-vii.

13. Sally Hickerson Johnson, "Form and Philosophy in the
    Novels of Doris Lessing," Diss. Univ. of Connecticut
    1976, Abstract, p. 1.

14. Ibid. p. 7.

15. Ibid. pp. 3-4.

16. Ibid. Abstract, p. 2.

17. Mary Elizabeth Draine, "Stages of Consciousness in
    Doris Lessing's Fiction," Diss. Temple Univ. 1977,
    p. 4.

18. Susan K. Swan Sims, "Repetition and Evolution: An
    Examination of Themes and Structures in the Novels
    of Doris Lessing," Diss. Univ. of Oregon 1978, p. 1.

19. Agate Nesaule Krouse, "The Feminism of Doris Lessing,"
    Diss. Univ. of Wisconsin 1972, pp. 22-23.

20. Donna Joanne Walter, "Twentieth-Century Woman in the
    Early Novels of Doris Lessing," Diss. Univ. of
    Tennessee 1978, pp. 5-6.

21. Ibid. p. iv.

22. Michele Wender Zak, "Feminism and the New Novel," Diss.
    The Ohio State Univ. 1973, p. 6.

Chapter I

1. The changes in the function of the narrator have
    been pointed out by several critics. The most de-
    tailed analysis of the narrator is given by Wells and
    Seligman. Wells ties her discussion of the narrator
    to the general formal development of *Children of
    Violence* and Seligman connects it with what she sees
    as Lessing's changing image of self: according to
    Seligman Lessing maintains an ironic distance to

herself through the narrator in the early novels and
when the narrative perspective changes a more positive,
integrated self-image is created. See Wells, pp. 30-34,
68-69, 185-188; Seligman, pp. 54, 77-82.

2.   Bourgeois demands on women refer to those ideals of
     womanhood that were established in the bourgeois family
     during the 19th century. In this type of family women
     were relegated to the domestic sphere of life, their
     social functions were those of mothers and sexual
     objects. Motherhood especially was emphasized and often
     idealized. These notions about women are discussed by
     Eli Zaretsky in *Capitalism, the Family and Personal
     Life* (London: Pluto Press, 1976), pp. 47-55.

3.   As I have indicated in the Introduction I pay more
     attention to the family than other critics do. Without
     using the family as the basis for their analyses of
     Martha's relationship to the collective certain critics,
     however, point to the crucial impact of the family and
     the mother on the shape of Martha's identity. Brooks,
     for example, states that "Mrs. Lessing views the family,
     headed by a demanding, manipulating middle-aged woman,
     anxious for power, as the special threat to the indi-
     viduality of the growing person." Brooks also sees the
     relationship between parent and child as the principal
     one in *Children of Violence*. Krouse likewise underlines
     the threat of the mother, calling her an "ogre," and
     Carey singles out the conflict between generations as
     an important motif underlying the relationship between
     the individual and the collective. See Ellen W. Brooks,
     "Fragmentation and Integration: A Study of Doris
     Lessing's Fiction," Diss. New York Univ. 1971, p. 419;
     Krouse, p. 190; Alfred Augustine Carey, "Doris Lessing:
     The Search for Reality. A Study of the Major Themes in
     her Novels," Diss. Univ. of Wisconsin 1965, p. 94.

4.   Critics do not note the change in the definition of Mrs.
     Quest's identity but explain her character either in
     social or in psychological terms. In the context of her
     analysis of Lessing's criticism of marriage Krouse
     stresses the perverting influence of domestic life on
     Mrs. Quest. In agreement with her general psychological
     approach Rose, on the other hand, regards Mrs. Quest's
     identity as the result of mother deprivation. Other
     critics usually give psychological explanations based
     on traits in Mrs. Quest's personality, e.g., Brooks who
     sees her as an "energetic, extrovertive" character
     "mismatched" to Mr. Quest. A social explanation which
     I find less convincing is that of the war which is argued
     by Singleton (cf. Sec. 4 of this chapter). See Krouse,
     p. 340; Rose, p. 44; Brooks, p. 422; Singleton, p. 167.

5.   Cf. Brooks who claims that Martha's behaviour during
     the pink eye episode demonstrates an "unconscious wish
     to play the role of victim" (p. 403).

6. My use of the terms sadism and masochism is inspired by
    thinkers such as Erich Fromm and Karen Horney who regard
    sado-masochism as a primarily socio-psychological
    phenomenon.
         Fromm looks upon sado-masochistic strivings as signs
    of an authoritarian bent within the individual which
    issues from a fear of loneliness and independence. This
    fear is an existential problem but it is reinforced by
    various social structures which prevent the individual
    from achieving self-reliance.
         According to Fromm the masochistic leaning is mani-
    fested as an attraction to powerlessness and insignif-
    icance, and as a tendency to court suffering, for
    example in the form of exaggerated self-criticism or
    neurotic illnesses. The sadistic impulse, on the other
    hand, is displayed as a need to gain absolute power over
    others, to exploit them, sometimes to humiliate them. Its
    essence is however not to make people suffer but to
    control them. This need may seem contradictory to the
    masochistic one, but the masochist and the sadist have
    a common purpose, namely to rid themselves of their
    individual selves through the achievement of a symbiotic
    union with another human being. Sadism and masochism are
    connected, they are active and passive manifestations of
    the same psychological pattern. In relationships between
    parents and children there is often a sadistic element
    which is covered by what seems to be the parent's
    "natural" concern for the child. See Erich Fromm,
    The Fear of Freedom (London: Routledge & Kegan Paul,
    1942), pp. 121-154.
         Karen Horney is concerned with masochism in women.
    She defines masochism as the "attempt to gain safety and
    satisfaction in life through inconspicuousness and de-
    pendency," and she argues that a masochistic strategy may
    be developed in women through various cultural phenom-
    ena that encourage women's dependency. See Karen Horney,
    "Feminine Psychology," in *New Ways in Psychoanalysis*
    (New York: W.W. Norton & Co., 1939), p. 113.
         Besides being present in the relationship between
    Martha and her mother sado-masochistic elements are also
    hinted at in the interaction between Donovan and his
    mother and between Mrs. Talbot and her daughter Elaine
    (see MQ, pp. 133-136; PM pp. 95-106). Other critics do
    not use the term sado-masochism in connection with
    parent-child relationships in *Children of Violence*,
    but both Brooks and Krouse underline the strongly antag-
    onistic quality of the relationship between Martha and
    Mrs. Quest. Brooks discusses the power struggle between
    mother and daughter and according to her it contains
    deeply imbedded psychological conflicts. She as well
    as Krouse sees Mrs. Quest's attitude to Martha as
    aggressive, even hateful, and as an encouragement of
    passivity in her daughter. According to Brooks Mrs.
    Quest sees herself as the Jungian "Great Mother" and
    regards Martha as the prototype of the "wicked child."
    Martha in her turn reacts to her mother with "intense

hatred" mixed with "guilt" and "dependency." Brooks
further claims that all parent-child relationships in
Children of Violence are characterized by tension -
their interaction "ranging from parasitic mutual dependency and flirtatious intimacy, through degrees of
loyalty to rejection and antagonism." See Brooks, pp.
419, 422-423, 425; Krouse pp. 340-342.

7.   Cf. Fromm: "The result of his |the sadistic tendency
within the parent| is often a profound fear of love
on the part of the child when he grows up, as 'love'
to him implies being caught and blocked in his own
quest for freedom" (p. 126).

8.   That Martha's development of her intellect is part of
her rebellion against her mother has been noted by
several critics. See Velma Fudge Grant, "The Quest for
Wholeness in Novels by Doris Lessing," Diss. State Univ.
of New Jersey 1974, p. 37; Lynn Sukenick, "Feeling and
Reason in Doris Lessing's Fiction," *Contemporary Literature*, 14 (1973), p. 518.

9.   Since I emphasize Martha's split identity, her insecurity,
and her potentially masochistic passivity I am not far
from Rose's analysis of her in terms of a "schizoid"
personality characterized by "ontological" insecurity
and "oral" passivity. (See Survey of Research, note 8.)
However, Rose sees Martha's personality as the result
of a primary psychological conflict, whereas I see it
as a product of her interaction with society represented
by the family and the mother as socializing agent.

10. My interpretation of Mr. Quest can be supported by Doris
Lessing's essay "My Father." Her portrait of her father
is practically identical with her representation of Mr.
Quest. Because of the correspondence, I think it safe
to say that Mr. Quest is modelled on Lessing's father and
that what she says about her father could be used to
throw light on Mr. Quest. Lessing summarizes her father's
experience of war thus: "I think the best of my father
died in that war, that his spirit was crippled by it."
She exemplifies the crippling of his psyche by contrast-
ing his young man's memories with his war memories:

>   His childhood and young man's memories, kept fluid,
>   were added to, grew, as living memories do. But his
>   war memories were congealed in stories that he told
>   again and again, with the same words and gestures,
>   in stereotyped phrases. They were anonymous, general,
>   as if they had come out of a communal war memoir.

Doris Lessing, "My Father," in *A Small Personal Voice*,
pp. 86-87.
     The destructive influence of war on Mr. Quest is
generally noted by critics, e.g., Singleton, p. 167,
and Wells who also refers to Lessing's essay. See Wells,
pp. 55-56.

11. In *Children of Violence* love and sex appear in two
     different forms of which one is corrupt and manipula-
     tive, and the other authentic and liberating. Mr. Quest
     here represents sex in the latter form. The same is true
     of Martha's sexuality in this chapter. The various
     aspects of Martha's sexuality are discussed in Chapters
     II and III.

12. This "authentic" aspect of Martha's sexuality is only
     realized in LL (see Ch. III, Sec. 2). In the early
     novels it is a liberating potential which is most
     clearly manifested in the "pot-hole" episode in PM
     (pp. 174-176) which is discussed in Chapter II. In MQ
     Martha defies Donovan's socializing ambitions because
     of her sense of the strength of nature latent in her
     body. See MQ, pp. 195-196.

13. In the essay about her father Lessing implicitly con-
     nects her father's appreciation of nature and outdoor
     activities and his sexuality by discussing them in close
     conjunction with each other. Also she summarizes the
     qualities which make up her father's pre-war self with
     the words a "naturally vigorous, sensuous being." See
     "My Father," pp. 85-86.

14. Carey is the only critic who deals with Mr. Quest in
     detail. He argues for a difference between the Quests:
     Mr. Quest is a defeated rebel whereas Mrs. Quest never
     questioned her society. As they come from the same social
     background according to Carey, the difference between
     them proves that Lessing regards character as more im-
     portant than society. See Carey, pp. 101-102.
         Carey's view of the Quests can be explained by the
     fact that his study does not include LL where Mrs.
     Quest's rebellion is most strongly emphasized. Even
     so, her protests are already mentioned in PM and her
     complex relationship to her past is indicated throughout
     the series. Furthermore, the Quests do not have the same
     social background. Mr. Quest's background is not dwelt
     upon, but in PM we are given the information that his
     origin is more humble than Mrs. Quest's. He spent his
     childhood in an "English country cottage" characterized
     by "honest simplicity" (PM, p. 87). His childhood is,
     however, not associated with a specific class background
     but with nature. The characterization of Mr. and Mrs.
     Quest does not point to the superiority of character
     over society; both are described as rebels defeated by
     forces larger than themselves. But Mrs. Quest is seen
     as formed by the social institution of the family
     whereas Mr. Quest's character reflects a conflict
     between life-bringing and death-bringing forces which
     points to a dichotomy between nature and culture. This
     dichotomy will be touched upon in section 5.1 of this
     chapter and will be developed in consecutive chapters.

15. See Smith, p. 21; Brooks, p. 400.

16. According to Singleton nature in Lessing's work repre-
     sents an area of life which is "absolutely removed from
     the social values that effect the health of society"

(p. 57). Similarly she looks upon mystical experiences as a meeting with a *"nada"* dimension of existence which is "entirely inimical to human consciousness (pp. 50-51). Brooks argues that Martha's mystical experience implies a "vision of meaninglessness, of the Existential void" (p. 407). Nevertheless, they both claim that this experience is constructive in that it implies an enlarging of a limited consciousness. How this expansion of consciousness is brought about is not discussed by Brooks and only touched upon by Singleton who argues that it "must" take place: "Somehow man must make room in his imagination for everything that is . . ." (p. 62).

17. This aspect of the city is the one generally emphasized by the critics, e.g. Singleton who sees Martha's city as an image from "traditional myth" (p. 53), Smith who looks upon it as "some kind of collective perfection that excludes racism" (p. 21), and Brooks who regards it as on the one hand a "Utopian society" and on the other as a "Jungian archetype of the self" (p. 400).

18. Rose claims that Martha's mystical experience shows a regressive longing for fusion with forces greater than herself. This she relates to her idea of Martha's lack of "basic trust." See Rose, p. 22.

19. As I have indicated in the Survey of Research there are several critics who are concerned with the relationship between reason and intuition in Lessing's work. As their treatment of this theme is connected with female concerns in Lessing's writing I will refer to them in the context of my discussion of Martha's female identity in the chapters to follow.

20. Martha's reading has been discussed by Marchino and by Schlueter. Marchino investigates Martha's reading as an aspect of the theme of self-knowledge which she claims is central in Lessing's work. She is not concerned with the tension between reflective and intuitive modes of apprehension, however. Schlueter gives a rather descriptive overview of the development of Martha's reading throughout the series. See Lois Anette Marchino, "The Search for Self in the Novels of Doris Lessing," Diss. Univ. of New Mexico 1972, pp. 2, 121-126; Schlueter, pp. 36-43.

21. The narrator's distanced and often ironic attitude towards Martha appears to be based on a rational and sensible approach to reality. The narrator often points out Martha's limited powers of reflection in phrases like: "Perhaps, if she could have expressed what she felt, she would have said . . ." (MQ, p. 13); "She felt, though dimly . . ." (MQ, p. 20).

Chapter II

1. Without relating it to Martha's vision of the city
    several critics strongly emphasize her longing for a
    love relationship with a man. Walter, in fact, makes
    this the central concern of Martha's quest: "The
    importance of the search for monogamous intimacy with
    a man forms the core of Martha's search for identity
    and relationship in the twentieth century." See Walter,
    p. 92; see also Carey, p. 197; Marchino, pp. 99-100;
    Kildahl, p. 31. Martha's relationship to love and men
    in *Children of Violence*, 1-3, is analysed in more
    detail further on in this chapter and is also com-
    mented on in Chapter IV.

2. Critics generally agree that Martha's marriage and
    motherhood should be seen as the result of collective
    pressures. See for example Brooks, p. 450; Krouse,
    pp. 189-191; Carey, p. 170; Wells, p. 81. As I pay
    special attention to Martha's female identity I have
    attempted to make a more thorough and systematic
    analysis of the collective demands on her as a woman
    than is to be found among other critics of *Children
    of Violence*.

3. See note 2, Ch. I.

4. In Martha's marriage to Anton the image of the ideal
    lover again functions as a safety mechanism which
    allows her to be "kind" to Anton (RS, p. 269). This
    mechanism might also explain the seemingly incidental
    occurrence that Mrs. Quest, Mrs. Maynard and Mrs.
    Talbot all cherish memories of dead young lovers
    whose photographs they keep (see PM, pp. 103, 218).

5. Psychoanalytical thinking has concentrated on sexuality
    rather than on reproduction. According to orthodox
    Freudian theory woman's desire for a child is a
    secondary, compensatory phenomenon in that she wants
    a child as a compensation for her lack of a penis.
    This theory has been criticized by, for example, Karen
    Horney and Erik H. Erikson who both suggest that it
    implies a male-centred view of woman's role in re-
    production. Erikson may be said to postulate a repro-
    ductive instinct as he bases his analysis of female
    psychology on the woman's ultimately biological need
    to fill up her "inner space." See Karen Horney, "The
    Flight from Womanhood," and Erik H. Erikson, "Woman-
    hood and the Inner Space," in *Women & Analysis*, ed.
    Jean Strouse (New York: Grossman Publishers, 1974),
    pp. 171-186, 291-319.

6. The description of Martha's reaction to Billy can be
    compared with a passage from GN where a young woman
    in a similar trancelike state is described and where
    sexuality is referred to in an explicit manner. GN,
    p. 88.

7. Critics often note Martha's compliance and passivity
    but usually refrain from trying to determine its cause.
    Zak, however, points to a vaguely social explanation
    when she relates Martha's "conditioned passivity" to an
    "image of womanhood" imbued in women "from birth."
    Wells, on the other hand, comes close to a biological
    view through her statement that Martha's compliance
    demonstrates the "seemingly ancient and irresistible
    instinct of the female to please her sexual partner."
    Walter gives neither a social nor a biological explana-
    tion but one based on Jungian psychology. She sees
    Martha's dependence on men in terms of her being bound
    to the Jungian "animus" or "unconscious soul image of
    man." I suggest a differing psychological interpreta-
    tion of Martha's relationships to men in section 2.6
    of this chapter. See Zak, pp. 289-290; Wells, p. 84;
    Walter, pp. 83-84.
        The issue of society versus biology with regard
    to Martha's womanhood is further discussed in Ch. III,
    where the outlook of the late novels in *Children of
    Violence* is analysed, and in Ch. IV, where an overview
    of Lessing's presentation of women is given.

8. Douglas, for example, is on the one hand described as a
    "sensible, masculine, responsible young man" and on the
    other as a "sulky, litte boy" (PM, p. 337). Here the
    weak aspect of his boyish mentality is stressed; the
    active, adventurous elements of the boyish male role
    are displayed in the Sports Club, for example. The most
    consistently paternal characters are Dr. Stern and Mr.
    Maynard.

9. Carey stresses the mother-centred, childish traits in
    Lessing's male characters. He mentions Douglas, Donovan,
    Adolph, and Dick Turner in *The Grass Is Singing*.
    Martha's father and Anton Hesse might be added as other
    examples. See Carey, p. 179.

10. See the discussion of sado-masochism in note 6, Ch. I.
    Horney argues that a cultural phenomenon which fosters
    masochism in women is dependence on family, husband and
    children for content and significance in life. When the
    masochistic mentality is established it may prevail also
    in the sexual sphere. See Horney, "Feminine Psychology,"
    pp. 112-113.

11. Cf. Smith: "Douglas' patriarchal sense of being
    threatened and the white colonialists' feeling of
    being misunderstood have their roots in the same soil:
    the attitude of one power group toward another" (p. 57).

12. Rose maintains that Martha's longing for motherly love
    combines with social expectations on her as a woman in
    a way which strengthens her passivity and compliance
    towards men. I am in agreement with this, although, as
    I have stressed before, I do not share Rose's basic
    premise. Cf. note 9, Ch. I; see Rose, p. 47.

13. There is general critical agreement that Martha's marriage demonstrates the force of repetition and that the ferris wheel functions as a symbol of this. See, for example, Smith, pp. 36-38; Brooks, p. 439; Krouse, p. 282.

14. Mrs. Van appears in RS. Nevertheless I deal with her in the context of Martha's first marriage as she is the female character that most clearly illustrates the danger of the specific female consciousness which is related to woman's function in marriage.

15. As regards the significance of Mrs. Van as a character the critical appraisals differ. Mostly, Mrs. Van is seen as a negative character meant to represent a fragmented identity rejected by Lessing. See Smith, p. 74; Kildahl, pp. 82-84.
      These critics do not take into account that Mrs. Van's split identity, like Martha's, is presented as necessary for her survival as an authentic human being. This point of view is, however, argued by Sukenick who claims that Lessing treats emotional and irrational forces as traps for her female characters in that they lead them to domesticity and to a loss of self. See Sukenick, pp. 522-523. Still, I differ from Sukenick as I find the treatment of emotions and of the irrational in *Children of Violence* to be more ambiguous than she does. This ambiguity is treated further on in this chapter as well as in subsequent chapters.

16. Critics point to the powerful impact of the pot-hole episode and to its celebration of nature and fertility. According to Selma Burkom, who is the critic that besides Singleton emphasizes nature as a vital force in Lessing's work, Martha's entry into the pot-hole gives an image of an "infinitely fecund nature in which man is an integral part." In Krouse's view it "affirms the triumph of female fecundity." Walter, on the other hand, argues that the pot-hole incident demonstrates that woman even in her "most visibly animal condition" is removed from nature, as this celebration of woman's biological nature is bounded by Martha's use of the automobile and by her awareness of getting dirty. "Lessing does not, then, try to suggest that woman is more deeply rooted to nature than man," Walter claims. I am convinced that she is wrong: although Martha's female identity is ambiguously treated her biological nature is of vital importance. It is the basis of a creative female mentality which is contrasted with a destructive male mentality founded on men's removal from nature. This contrast, which is not discussed by Walter, is a recurring element in PM and more important than Martha's use of the automobile. See Selma Burkom, "A Reconciliation of Opposites: A Study of the Works of Doris Lessing," Diss. Univ. of Minnesota 1970, p. 21; Krouse, pp. 329-330; Walter, pp. 69-70.

17. Sukenick and Kaplan are the critics that are mainly concerned with the tensions between feeling and intellect
and between rationality and irrationality in Lessing's
presentation of women. Sukenick sees rationality and
reflection as the essence of Martha's identity, whereas
Kaplan points to her body, her intuition and her receptivity as central to her sense of self. Personally
I believe that the early novels, although they are
ambiguous in this respect, mainly support Sukenick's
view, while the late ones support Kaplan's. Kaplan
confirms my belief that the representation of Martha's
biological womanhood is relevant to the inwards-directed,
mystical tendency of her quest in the following statement: "The evolution toward a universal consciousness
in Doris Lessing's novels appears to begin with an
approach to reality centered in the physical body and
its relationship with nature. Even though Martha's
rebellion starts initially on the basis of abstract
ideas, yet it is surely through her body - as she later
experiences sexual relationships, pregnancy, and childbirth - that her most profound discoveries are achieved."
The issues touched upon here will be further discussed
in Chapters III and IV. See Sidney Janet Kaplan,
Feminine Consciousness in the Modern British Novel
(Urbana: Univ. of Illinois Press, 1975), pp. 142,
160-161; Sukenick, p. 521.

18. There is general critical agreement that Athen is the
character of the group who is most positively described.
Carey is the critic who has paid most attention to
Lessing's treatment of communists and communism. He
argues that all of her positively rendered communists
are basically humanists. The relationship between
humanism and communism in RS will be discussed in Ch.
IV of this work. See Carey, pp. 63, 82; see also Smith,
p. 71; Alcorn, p. 151.

19. Several critics notice the split in Martha's political
identity but do not analyse it closely. See, for
example, Brooks, pp. 451, 454; Smith, p. 59.

20. Critics often see Martha's marriage to Anton as altruistic, thus for instance Singleton and Kildahl who both
claim that she marries out of "comraderie" in order to
prevent Anton from being deported as an enemy alien. See
Singleton, p. 169; Kildahl, p. 82.
    This threat against Anton is what makes Martha
agree to legalize their relationship, but it does not
explain why they initially established themselves as
a couple. Furthermore, Martha's need for love and
emotional confirmation is also stressed in the context
of her decision to legalize her affair with Anton:
Anton's happiness about a possible marriage influences
her decision as, for the first time, it makes her
realize that he "really cares" for her (RS, p. 189).

21. Critics usually see Anton as representing a criticism
     of bureaucratic, authoritarian and intellectualized
     aspects of communism and communist party activities.
     See Smith, pp. 68-69; Kildahl, p. 82; Carey, pp. 67-70.
          I agree with this but, unlike Carey, I do not
     regard the criticism of Anton as implying a total
     rejection of the group and its philosophy. According
     to Carey, Lessing shows that communism as a political
     system turns to centralism and bureaucracy and even-
     tually to a "stifling of the human spirit." This
     process takes place in the Communist Party of which
     Anton is a typical product. See Carey, pp. 65-70. To
     my mind Carey's picture of Lessing's view of communism
     is more applicable to her works from GN onwards. RS
     does not leave itself open to generalizations of this
     kind. Anton is only one of a group of communists, and
     although he assumes the leadership of the group, Athen,
     Andrew and to begin with Jackie Bolton are also pre-
     sented as influential members. It is highly debatable
     whether Anton is more of a party product than Athen or
     Andrew. Like Anton, Andrew is described as a party
     veteran (PM, p. 374), and like Athen, Anton has been
     involved in underground political activities (PM, pp.
     376-377). Carey ignores the political isolation of the
     group which to a large extent accounts for its
     peculiarities, including Anton's. The ultimate failure
     of the group is shown to stem from the colonial situa-
     tion rather than from defects of communism or individual
     communists. In this context the description of the group
     can be compared with the treatment of the Social Demo-
     cratic Party in RS. The latter also fails despite its
     more "realistic," practical, reformist approach to
     politics. Lessing's attitude towards communism will be
     further discussed in Ch. IV.

22. Wells deals with still another couple in the group,
     Marjorie and Colin. She points out that the sex role
     behaviour of this couple recalls that of Martha and
     Douglas: in marriage Colin becomes increasingly "pro-
     prietary" towards Marjorie and wants to turn her into
     a domestic woman. Thus this couple as well illustrate
     the pervasiveness of bourgeois and patriarchal family
     patterns. See Wells, p. 102.

Chapter III

1.   Regardless of whether critics do or do not emphasize
     thematic changes in LL and FGC, several of them note
     the inward movement in these novels, at least in FGC.
     Wells states that "from the beginning page of *The
     Four-Gated City* the main interest of the novel lies
     in Martha's slow discovery of the unknown laws that
     govern the non-rational areas of the mind." A similar

assessment of Martha's quest in FGC is made by, e.g.
Brooks, who points to her discovery of an "inner world,"
and Marchino, who refers to her "total descent into
self." See Wells, p. 218; Brooks, p. 494, Marchino, p.
166.
    The existence of a visionary apprehension in LL
is also noticed by critics. See, for example, Wells,
p. 172; Kildahl, pp. 87-88; Johnson, pp. 102-104;
Seligman, "The Sufi Quest," *World Literature Written
in English*, 12 (1973), pp. 190-206.

2.   Certain critics have stressed the quality of mysticism
in the relationship between Martha and Thomas. Singleton
and Johnson connect their relationship with Martha's
early mystical experiences and point out that these
elements within the novel series prefigure the development of FGC. Seligman underlines the presence of
alchemical imagery in the description of the love
affair. According to her, this imagery is in keeping
with the "Sufi context" of LL and FGC. I will deal with
Sufism in Ch. IV.
    Johnson and Singleton also emphasize the affilia-
tions between Thomas and natural life. See Johnson, pp.
102-104, 106; Singleton, pp. 64, 196-197; Seligman,
"The Sufi Quest," p. 195.

3.   The importance that violence has in the contact between
Martha and Thomas has been noted by several critics, for
example, Seligman and Smith. Seligman places Thomas
within a Sufi context (see note 2), whereas Smith sees
him as a Lawrentian hero, representing sexuality and
fertility, on the one hand, and on the other as a
character within the tradition of the "problematic
rebel." In the latter role he eventually turns destructive, faced with the incomprehensibility of violence.
See Seligman, "The Sufi Quest," p. 194; Smith, pp.
196-198.

4.   Jung's influence on *Children of Violence* is discussed
in Ch. IV.

5.   "Inner journey" is a term borrowed from the psychiatrist
R.D. Laing whose relevance for *Children of Violence* will
be dealt with in Ch. IV.

6.   Martha's identity as a woman in FGC must be related to
the total ideological development of the novel series
to be understandable. As I have suggested in the Survey
of Research Krouse does not do this and therefore finds
Martha's female role puzzling and at odds with Lessing's
low appraisal of the traditional duties of women. Other
critics who likewise seem somewhat disturbed by Martha's
female role in FGC explain it by relating it to her
discovery of the inner identity. Zak, for example,
states that Martha's life is a "penance" for her de-
sertion of her child and that this idea is articulated
in deterministic terms. Zak, however, reconciles herself
to this determinism by seeing it as a necessary pre-
requisite for a "visionary understanding of the human

condition." According to her it releases the individual from an "egotistical sense of self," and gives him/her a perspective on existence as part of "time" and of a "larger life force." Brooks likewise rejects the idea that Martha's life with the Coldridges is a "surrender" for the "rebel from domesticity" in the claim that the issue of repetition is given a "positive significance" in FGC, which links it to Martha's "real work," the discovery of the inner world. See Krouse, p. 125; Zak, pp. 333-335; Brooks, pp. 492-494.

Personally I believe that in FGC family life is presented mainly as a contrast to inner life and not as a link with it. Further on in this chapter as well as in Chapter IV, I will, however, point to aspects of family life which are related to Martha's mystical identity. I will also develop the issue of determinism further. My position on this question differs from that of other critics; how, I intend to make clear in connection with my discussion of determinism in Ch. IV.

Brooks also sees Martha's life with the Coldridges as an act of service to humanity. She argues that Martha's "debts" refer not only to her daughter, but also to "humanity in general, in return for being spared in the war." This interpretation ignores that FGC explicitly connects Martha's debts with her family relationships. Brooks's generalized, "humanitarian" understanding of Martha's development is in fact shared by the majority of the critics. Most of them simply regard her motherly function as a sign of her responsibility and maturity without relating it to her former rebellion against the family or to the determinism involved with her new female identity. See Brooks, p. 490; Walter, pp. 182-183; Singleton, pp. 204-205.

7. Woman in love is also described as "that poor craving bitch in every woman" (FGC, p. 335). The biological view of women will be further discussed in Ch. IV.

8. LL and FGC also contain complex psychological portraits of Martha's parents, mainly Mrs. Quest (see LL, pp. 74-94; FCG, pp. 277-321). The deepened psychological insight into Mrs. Quest has been most fully discussed by Seligman. Her autobiographical approach makes her see this phenomenon as a sign of Martha's - Lessing's greater tolerance of Mrs. Quest. See Seligman, pp. 90-91.

9. Those critics who see Martha's life with the Coldridge family simply in terms of responsibility and maturity (see note 6 above) may be said to share the exclusively psychological view of Martha.

10. It may be argued that in FGC the connection between the sado-masochistic pattern and the family is repressed, since this link is reestablished in a later work by Lessing, *The Memoirs of a Survivor*, which serves as an interesting comment on the theme of the family in *Children of Violence*. See Ch. IV, Sec. 5.

11. Both Walter and Singleton claim that Martha conquers
    the mentality of the woman in love in her relationship
    with Thomas and that she never again searches for love
    and security after that affair. While it is true that
    Martha's search is not *ultimately* directed towards love
    in FGC, this claim ignores the unresolved character of
    her relationship to men. It makes her development seem
    more harmonious than it is, something which can be
    related to a general critical tendency to see FGC as a
    work in which the themes of *Children of Violence* reach
    a harmonious synthesis (Cf. Survey of Research). See
    Walter, p. 179; Singleton, p. 198.

12. In Ch. IV I will also discuss the possible connection
    between mysticism and a female consciousness. Such a
    connection is made by several critics who will also be
    referred to in that context. One of them Kaplan, I have
    already cited in note 17, Ch. II.

13. Smith points to the parallel between Mark's and Martha's
    projects and confirms my idea that it should be inter-
    preted as pointing away from political solutions in the
    ordinary sense. See Smith, pp. 160-161. In all the
    studies which emphasize Martha's inner quest there is
    implicit agreement that the expansion of consciousness
    constitutes the final political solution of *Children of
    Violence*. Cf. Survey of Research.

14. Several critics observe the recurring city symbolism in
    Children of Violence and use it as a proof of a basic
    unity within the work. See Brooks, p. 532; Smith, p.
    243; Singleton, pp. 186-190.
         Critics also relate the city symbolism to various
    fictional and non-fictional sources. Smith and Singleton
    point to a literary tradition of city symbolism which
    includes writers such as St. Augustine, Dante, Blake,
    Bunyan. They also see Jungian theory and Sufi mysticism
    as shaping influences. Smith argues that if the designs
    of Martha's early and later cities are combined they
    form a "mandala," Jung's symbol for the inner self.
    Singleton stresses the connection between the mythic
    city of FGC and Sufism. See Smith, pp. 225, 239;
    Singleton, pp. 186-187, 198-199.

15. In FGC Martha's inner development is mainly related to
    one manifestation of organic life, the sycamore tree
    outside her window (see FGC, pp. 124, 253, 258-259;
    cf. p. 554). This tree is part of the nature theme of
    Children of Violence. Its significance has been pointed
    out by Draine and Rose, who also link the organic
    thinking of the novel series with the development of
    the "new," expanded consciousness. This I agree with
    and will come back to in Ch. IV. See Draine, pp.
    126-130; Rose, pp. 105-109.

Chapter IV

1. The basic structure of GN which I have outlined is
    emphasized by several critics and by Doris Lessing
    herself. In the Preface to the new edition of GN,
    published in 1972, Lessing describes her novel in the
    following manner:

    > The Notebooks are kept by Anna Wulf. . . . She
    > keeps four, and not one because . . . she has to
    > separate things off from each other, out of fear
    > of chaos, of formlessness - of breakdown. . . .
    > In the inner Golden Notebook, things have come
    > together, the divisions have broken down, there
    > is formlessness with the end of fragmentation -
    > the triumph of the second theme, which is that
    > of unity (p. 7).

    Brooks claims that GN is shaped on two opposing prin-
    ciples, chaos versus form. The principle of chaos
    which Anna tries to control by separating life into
    four different notebooks is represented by her
    experience of an anarchic, destructive spirit which
    she calls "joy in spite" (GN, p. 408). Brooks and
    Singleton both demonstrate that Anna's psychic devel-
    opment entails her learning to handle the destructive
    spirit. This she achieves through mental disintegration
    which leads to a new sense of unity. By giving up her
    ordering intellect and instead relying on intuitive
    and unconscious modes of perception, she is able to
    experience the destructive force as both good and
    evil, both destructive and creative. "The central
    paradox of *The Golden Notebook* is that the same force
    that gives rise to malicious cruelty, war, hopeless
    madness . . . may also be the seedbed of new creation,"
    says Singleton. She further points out that the idea
    of the "union of life and death" in GN predicts FGC,
    in which the "explosion of nuclear weapons . . . causes
    not just grotesque physical mutations but also the mental
    ones that may lead to perfection of the human race." The
    mysticism involved in Anna's experience of a basic force
    is also indicated by Singleton who compares her develop-
    ment towards integration to the process of alchemy. See
    Brooks, pp. 94-95; Singleton, pp. 114-118, 120.

2. For the relationship between the novel and the private
    sphere of life, see Ian Watt, *The Rise of the Novel*
    (London: Peregrine Books, 1963). In his study of the
    English Bildungsroman Buckley points to rebellion
    against the family and conflicts between generations
    as typical characteristics of this type of novel. See
    Jerome Buckley, *Season of Youth* (Cambridge: Harward
    Univ. Press, 1974), pp. 17-18.

3.   Kaplan and Zak both see Martha's mysticism as emerging
     from her female identity. As I have pointed out in note
     17, Ch. II, Kaplan shows that Martha's visionary appre-
     hension is originally connected with her biological
     womanhood. Kaplan's statement that "the evolution toward
     a universal consciousness in Doris Lessing's novels
     appears to begin with an approach to reality centered
     in the physical body and its relationship to nature,"
     may be said to support my notion of the mystical
     potential of the biological female consciousness.
        Zak emphasizes the mystical capacity of the uniquely
     female consciousness demonstrated by Martha and by other
     Lessing heroines. This consciousness creates a feminine
     principle in the novels which manifests itself as a
     search for wholeness. Zak argues that "Anna (and Molly
     and Martha Quest in *The Four-Gated City*) represents
     an *Eros* that embraces even madness, and seeks to make
     whole the divided selves of men. . . . Somehow the
     passivity, sexual and emotional, and the receptiveness
     of these women enables them to attain an ontological
     security that in turn affords a release from self."
        While it is true that Martha's receptivity is
     important to her achievement of an inner identity, Zak
     appears to disregard that it only functions unequivo-
     cally positively within impersonal contexts. Also, her
     idea of a female "eros" does not take into account the
     rejection of the "woman in love" in FGC, a phenomenon
     which also occurs in GN, as Brooks has pointed out.
        A similar simplification of the connections between
     mysticism and womanhood is made by Mitchell who sees
     Martha's role as mother in FGC as a creative function
     linked with the development of her inner identity. "It
     is but one logical and natural step from awareness of
     others' needs to awareness of their thoughts . . .,"
     Mitchell states in explanation of Martha's faculties of
     ESP. Although I agree that Martha's family life allows
     her to cultivate her receptive and intuitive qualities
     and thus becomes instrumental in her development of
     mysticism (cf. Ch. III, Sec. 3.1), I cannot agree with
     Mitchell's implication that Martha's serving function
     is regarded as in itself creative.
        Rapping, on the other hand, sees the mysticism of
     FGC as a kind of escape from an intolerable female con-
     dition. The only "free space" for women is "inner space,"
     she argues. Therefore, women like Lynda, "who will not
     or cannot function as wives, mothers and housekeepers,
     retreat into a private world of dreams and fantasies
     and are labelled clinically insane." Rapping also
     argues that madness grows logically out of the female
     condition in that women serve as "receptacles of all
     the psychic and emotional tension which the male world
     creates but will not acknowledge or deal with." She
     mentions Lynda's relationship with her parents and
     Martha's relationship with the Coldridge children as
     examples of the female function as "receptacle."
     Although Rapping sees this female madness as creative,

as a dimension of protest directed against the rationality of male-dominated Western society (an idea which
I will touch upon further on in this chapter), she still
underlines the deforming quality of Martha's social
identity in FGC and confirms my belief that through
mysticism Martha finds an outlet for her female identity.
      Spacks, like Rapping, maintains that Lessing's
heroines only achieve freedom as women through fantasy.
According to her, they retreat from "intolerable
experience into the wider expanses of conscious or
subconscious reshaping of it." See Elayne Antler
Rapping, "Unfree Women: Feminism in Doris Lessing's
Novels," *Women's Studies*, 3 (1975), pp. 38-39, 42;
Kaplan, p. 142; Zak, p. 318, cf. pp. 290-292; Mitchell,
pp. 106-107; Patricia Meyer Spacks, *The Female Imagination* (New York: Avon Books, 1972), p. 402; Brooks, pp.
193-196.

4.   Since Doris Lessing was a communist, Marxism may be
      assumed to be part of her intellectual background. She
      explicitly discusses the social influence of Marxism
      in the Preface to the second edition of GN; what she
      says there is however influenced by the fact that at
      this period she is disillusioned with Marxism and
      socialism.
            In an interview with Jonah Raskin, Lessing demon-
      strates her familiarity with the in-depth psychology
      of Freud and Jung. She also offers the information that
      she has undergone Jungian psychotherapy. See Preface,
      GN, pp. 14-15; "Doris Lessing at Stony Brook," in
      A Small Personal Voice, pp. 67-68.

5.   These elements in Marxist analysis of the family can
      be traced back to the writings of Marx and Engels,
      for example in the *Communist Manifesto* and in *The
      Origin of the Family*. While Marx and Engels tend to
      concentrate on the economic significance of the family,
      the socio-psychological aspects of the authoritarian
      family structure have been discussed by Wilhelm Reich
      and the members of the Frankfurt School, for example
      Max Horkheimer and Erich Fromm. See Zaretsky, pp. 55,
      90-97; Mark Poster, *Critical Theory of the Family*
      (London: Pluto Press, 1978), pp. 46-55.
            Krouse is the only critic who has noticed the
      Marxist influence in Lessing's treatment of the family
      in *Children of Violence*. She does not mention the
      authoritarian family pattern but argues that Lessing's
      presentation of domestic life and housework as destruc-
      tive to women parallels ideas presented by communist
      writers on women, such as Lenin, Engels and Clara
      Zetkin.
            Walter claims that Lessing's first novel, *The Grass
      Is Singing*, displays a Marxist criticism of the "non-
      productive role to which women are reduced in the . . .
      Rhodesian farming system," but she does not discuss
      Marxism in relation to *Children of Violence*. She
      instead emphasizes a Jungian influence and regards

Martha's development as illustrating the Jungian concept of the "individuation process." This idea I believe
is more applicable to Martha's development in LL and
FGC, which I will show further on in this section.
     Kildahl refers to Marxism to describe Lessing's
thought in the first part of *Children of Violence*, but
she does not illustrate how this influence is manifested. Johnson, finally, argues that Lessing's Marxism
is an expression of a "religious impulse," and that
there is no significant change in her political outlook
from *The Grass Is Singing* to "The Temptation of Jack
Orkney," a short story from her later period. I will
comment on Johnson's ideas when I discuss Lessing's
overall views on society and politics later on in this
chapter. See Krouse, pp. 160-165; Walter, pp. 9, 75;
Kildahl, cf. Survey of Research, Johnsson, p. 7, cf.
Survey of Research.

6.   See Zaretsky, pp. 51-53. For a Marxist outlook on love
     in the bourgeois family, see Engels, *Ursprung der
     Familie* (Hottingen-Zürich, 1884), pp. 40-43.

7.   Jung explains his view of nature and of the unconscious
     as creative powers in "Approaching the Unconscious,"
     in *Man and His Symbols*, ed. Carl G. Jung (London: Pan
     Books, 1978), pp. 91-94.
          Freud's outlook on the opposition between nature
     and culture is, for example, brought out in his ideas
     about the "pleasure principle" and the "reality
     principle." In order for the human being to survive
     in society, the organic instincts of the unconscious,
     which operate according to the pleasure principle,
     i.e., which seek full and instant satisfaction, must
     be controlled by the ego, which embodies the reality
     principle. See Freud, *An Outline of Psycho-Analysis*
     (London: The Hogarth Press, 1973), pp. 54-61.
          Doris Lessing adopts the Jungian view of the
     unconscious in the interview with Jonah Raskin. See
     "Doris Lessing at Stony Brook," in *A Small Personal
     Voice*, pp. 67-68.

8.   Jung sees the unconscious as an independent and active
     creative force beyond the control of the conscious mind.
          Through its properties the unconscious acquires a
     religious function; it gives the human being recourse
     to a transcendental reality. Jung often emphasizes the
     religious function of the unconscious as he regards it
     as crucial for the psychic health of the individual.
     See Jung, "The Relations between the Ego and the
     Unconscious," and "Psychology and Religion," in *The
     Basic Writings of C.G. Jung*, ed. Violet Staub de Laszlo
     (New York: Random House, 1959), pp. 105-118, 469-530.
          For Freud's view of women, see his essay "Some
     Psychical Consequences of the Anatomical Distinctions
     between the Sexes," in *Women & Analysis*, ed. Jean
     Strouse (New York: Grossman Publishers, 1974), pp.
     17-26.

In relation to GN, Krouse states that Lessing's ideas about womanhood are Freudian. See Krouse, pp. 397-399.

9. For the metaphysical implications of Jung's theories, see note 8.

10. Brooks has demonstrated a thorough-going and deep Jungian impact on GN. See Brooks, pp. 216-266.

11. As I have indicated in the Survey of Research, Magie analyses Doris Lessing's mysticism in the light of romanticism, whereas Burkom sees romanticism as a general influence on Lessing's work. Generally, however, critics concentrate on Jung, Laing and Idries Shah. Jung's influence is most extensively treated by Brooks, that of Idries Shah by Singleton, Seligman, and Hardin, and that of Laing by Vlastos. Specific references to most of these critics and to others will be given below.

12. See Jung, "The Relations between the Ego and the Unconscious," in *The Basic Writings of C.G. Jung*, pp. 136-182. A Jungian interpretation of Martha's development is suggested by, e.g., Brooks, Singleton, and Walter. Both Singleton and Walter apply the Jungian concept of individuation to Martha's total development in *Children of Violence*. One reason why they can do this is that they only emphasize her inner, mystical, guardian or voice as vital for her development and disregard the conflict between rational and irrational ways of perceiving reality which is crucial for Martha's development in the earlier novels. See Brooks, p. 528; Singleton, pp. 131-132; Walter, pp. 75ff.

13. See Jung, "The Relations between the Ego and the Unconscious," in *The Basic Writings of C.G. Jung*, pp. 113-157.

14. See FGC, pp. 229, 329, 363; LL, pp. 23-24, 229-231.
    Lessing adheres to the Jungian notion about the function of dreams in the following statement: "The unconscious artist who resides in our depths is a very economical individual. With a few symbols a dream can define the whole of one's life, and warn us of the future, too." See "Doris Lessing at Stony Brook," in *A Small Personal Voice*, p. 67. See also Brooks, pp. 258-262; Singleton, p. 68.

15. See Jung, "Approaching the Unconscious," in *Man and His Symbols*, pp. 72-75, 83-84, 90-94.

16. See R.D. Laing, *The Politics of Experience* (New York: Pantheon Books, 1967), pp. 10-12, 86-90, 101, 116.

17. Although Laing is the best-known exponent of the theory of mental illness as a potentially healing process and Lessing knows of him and seems clearly indebted to him in her treatment of schizophrenia in LL and FGC and also in Briefing, she appears to be somewhat unwilling to acknowledge the importance of his theories

to her. During her lecture series at the New School for
Social Research (Sept. 27, 1972), Lessing refers to Laing
as a "peg" and as a "key authority figure" whom educated
people need in order to accept nonconventional thinking.
In this context she also refers to a certain Bert Kaplan
whom she considers "every bit as revolutionary as Laing."
(Lessing's comments on Laing are quoted in Nancy Shields
Hardin, "Doris Lessing and the Sufi Way," *Contemporary
Literature*, 14 (1973), pp. 571-572, 575. Hardin also re-
fers to Bert Kaplan's work *The Inner World of Mental
Illness* (New York: Harper and Row, 1964).

Despite her deprecating comments on Laing, Lessing's
work can definitely be fruitfully analysed within a
Laingian context. This has been demonstrated by several
critics of whom Marion Vlastos has given the most
extensive analysis with regard to FGC. Besides the
general Laingian characteristics of FGC, which I have
already pointed out, she stresses that Lessing's presentation of the psychiatric establishment (represented
by Lynda's and Martha's psychiatrist, ironically named
Dr. Lamb), parallels Laing's criticism of official
psychiatry. (I have touched on this issue in Ch. III,
Sec. 3.2, where I argue that in FGC psychiatry is regarded as one of the institutions that upholds social
violence through promoting the "ordinary," fragmenting
consciousness.)

Vlastos has also pointed to a Laingian influence on
Briefing. In this novel, the main character, Charles
Watkins, makes an inner journey that can be compared
with that of the sculptor Jesse Watkins, which Laing
has recorded in *The Politics of Experience*. Vlastos
underlines that it hardly seems coincidental that Charles
and Jesse have the same surname. See Marion Vlastos,
"Doris Lessing and R.D. Laing: Psychopolitics and
Prophecy," *PMLA*, 91 (1976), pp. 248-253.

As indicated above, the general Laingian impact on
Lessing is often noted among critics. See, for example,
Brooks, p. 519; Smith, pp. 183-189; Singleton, pp.
83-84.

18. See Laing, *The Politics of Experience*, pp. 59-60,
77-79. The description of Lynda's family background
reads very much like the case studies of families with
schizophrenic children recorded by Laing and his
colleague A. Esterson in *Sanity, Madness and the
Family* (London: Pelican Books, 1970). Brooks (pp.
421-422), and Kildahl (p. 90), both cite Laing as an
influence on Lessing's outlook on the family in FGC.

19. The passage from Shah cited in FGC is to be found in
Shah's work *The Sufis*, p. 54. This passage Doris Lessing
cites already in her first article on Shah, "An Elephant
in the Dark," and she returns to his evolutionary concept
in her other articles on Sufism, for example in "An
Ancient Way to New Freedom" and "In the World, Not
of It." Lessing also documents her belief in the evolution of consciousness in a personal letter to Marchino

quoted by the latter on pp. 203-204 of her dissertation.
The Sufi influence on Lessing's evolutionary belief is
generally acknowledged by critics. See for example Smith,
pp. 139-140; Singleton, pp. 121-122; Nancy Shields
Hardin, "Doris Lessing and the Sufi Way," pp. 567-570.

20. See Shah, *The Sufis*, pp. 58, 131; see also pp. 15, 46.
According to Shah the Sufi struggle against "pattern-
thinking" comes out particularly well in the so-called
Nasrudin jokes (see *The Sufis*, pp. 56-97). Lessing quotes
two such jokes in LL (pp. 11, 241), and in the article
"What Looks Like an Egg and Is an Egg?" (pp. 41-42), she
comments on the ability of these jokes to recondition
given ways of thinking. Lessing's use of the Nasrudin
stories has been pointed out by Hardin in "Doris Lessing
and the Sufi Way," pp. 568-569, and in "The Sufi Teaching
Story and Doris Lessing," *Twentieth Century Literature*,
23 (1977), pp. 314-326.

21. See Shah, *The Way of the Sufi*, pp. 113-114. See also
Seligman, "The Sufi Quest," p. 200.

22. Shah, *The Sufis*, pp. 1-10.

23. For the Sufi concept of the teacher, see Shah, *The Sufis*,
pp. 345-355. For the concept of love, see *The Sufis*, pp.
X-XI, XIII and pp. 29, 317, 325. See also *The Way of the
Sufi*, p. 231. For a detailed analysis of the relationship between Thomas and Martha from a Sufi point of
view, see Seligman, "The Sufi Quest," pp. 193-199.

24. See Lessing, Preface, GN, pp. 8, 9, 11.

25. Through its representation of female experience and female consciousness Lessing's work may serve as a "forum"
for women. This term is used by Cheri Register to
describe one of the functions of feminist literature.
The forum function is the basic function of feminist art
Register claims, as literature must "express female
experience authentically" before it can fulfill other
consciousness-raising purposes. See Cheri Register,
"American Feminist Literary Criticism: A Bibliographical Introduction," in *Feminist Literary Criticism:
Explorations in Theory*, ed. Josephine Donovan (The
Univ. Press of Kentucky, 1975), p. 19.

26. Like me Krouse allies Doris Lessing with the new feminist
movement. Krouse points out that Lessing is not interested in the legal aspects of marriage as were the old
feminists. Rather, like the new feminists, she emphasizes
social and psychological pressures experienced by women
in the nuclear family. See Krouse, pp. 180-181.
For a work which represents the view of the family
within the new feminist movement, see Sheila Rowbotham,
Woman's Consciousness, Man's World (London: Pelican
Books, 1973), pp. 47-126.

27. See Josephine Hendin, "Doris Lessing: The Phoenix 'Midst
Her Fires," *Harper's*, June 1973, pp. 84-85.

28. In the interview with Josephine Hendin referred to in
    note 27 above, Doris Lessing talks about the awareness
    of the over-riding importance of biology in human life
    which comes with growing old. This she does in a way
    which applies to Kate's experiences in Summer, although
    these experiences as they are in fact described in the
    novel contain important social implications. Most critics
    do not notice the biological foundation of Summer, but
    regard it as a work about the social roles of women. See
    for example, Brigitte Wichmann, "From Sex-Role Identi-
    fication toward Androgyny," Diss. Purdue Univ. 1978,
    pp. 90-96; Alice Bradley Markow, "The Pathology of
    Feminine Failure in the Fiction of Doris Lessing,"
    Critique, 16 (1975), pp. 96-97.
       Krouse, however, has noted that in GN Lessing pre-
    sents women as ultimately determined by sexuality. Like
    me, Krouse suggests that Lessing's concept of female
    nature is Freudian. See note 8 above.

29. Krouse has demonstrated other anti-feminist consequences
    of Lessing's biological views of women. In relation to
    GN she states: "a woman is a sexually active creature
    who relates to men; spinsters, old maids, lesbians and
    consistent manhaters are something else." This view of
    womanhood is sexist rather than feminist, according to
    Krouse. See Krouse, p. 381.

30. Sims is the critic who is closest to my interpretation
    of Summer. She claims that for Kate personally change is
    possible, but the "sense of history repeating itself is
    reinforced at the end of the novel as Maureen . . .
    prepares to begin her cycle by making the same choices
    Kate had made twenty-five years ago."
       Another interpretation of the ending of Summer is
    that it is informed by realism. Seligman argues that
    Lessing suggests that "for now marriage is a system
    within which most people still operate." Kate never
    doubts that she will return to her family, according
    to Seligman, and Maureen "gives herself over to the
    state of marriage in a final acquiescence to the whole
    thing." The argument of realism is applicable to Kate
    whose whole life is determined by her marriage, but it
    is less convincing with regard to Maureen who does not
    share Kate's experiences. To my mind, Seligman's own
    description of Maureen's fatalistic attitude to marriage
    supports my interpretation rather than her own. The
    sense of determinism in Summer could have been alleviat-
    ed if Lessing had presented us with a scene in which
    Kate relates to her family on the basis of her new-found
    inner consciousness. This issue is touched upon by
    Johnson, who suggests that the meaning of Kate's choice
    to return to the family is left unclear as we never see
    how her change influences her attitude to her former
    life.
       Markow (and Wichmann, who bases her analysis on
    Markow's), both think that Kate's return to her family
    indicates a change in Lessing's negative view of the

the family. They argue that Kate's achievement of
spiritual health demonstrates that the family does not
necessarily destroy woman's sense of identity. "Lessing
leaves her enroute home, apparently intending to indicate that marriage does not destroy - unless one
permits it . . .," says Markow. Personally, I do not
believe that the fact that Kate realizes her inner
identity and then returns to her family makes the
picture of the family given in Summer appear less
destructive. Markow's suggestion that the issue of
the family is one of attitude is too complex to be
dealt with here; however, it seems to me that Summer
presents all of Kate's experiences as inevitable, and
not as a matter of choice or attitude. Her marriage
is inevitable, and her crisis in middle age likewise.
Her only choice lies in her positive, active response
to the inner, self-healing process represented by the
dream sequence.

    See Sims, p. 4; Seligman, pp. 183-184; Johnson,
pp. 173, 175; Markow, p. 98; Wichmann, p. 94.

31.   Se Simone de Beauvoir, *The Second Sex* (London: Penguin
Books, 1972). The basic points in Simone de Beauvoir's
theory are given in the Introduction, pp. 13-29.

    Resemblances between Simone de Beauvoir and Doris
Lessing have been noted by Walter and Karl. Walter
points to parallels with regard to details, but she
never discusses the relevance of de Beauvoir's basic
theory to Lessing's rendering of Martha's development.
Karl proposes that the early volumes of *Children of
Violence* may be regarded as a fictional working out of
whole chapters of *The Second Sex*, but he does not
illustrate how this is done. See Walter, pp. 17-21;
Frederick Karl, "Doris Lessing in the Sixties: The
New Anatomy of Melancholy," *Contemporary Literature*,
13 (1972), p. 25.

32.   As suggested in note 3 above, Rapping interprets the
society of FGC in male-female terms. According to
Rapping, the world of religion, mysticism and madness
is a "feminine world," which opposes a male society informed by a death-bringing, rationalistic, technological mentality. Rigney, as well, underlines the
existence of a destructive male power in FGC and points
to Dr. Lamb as one of its representatives. See Rapping,
pp. 42-43; Barbara Hall Rigney, "Madness and Sexual
Politics in the Feminist Novel," Diss. Ohio State Univ.
1977, pp. 9-10, 98, 117-119.

33.   See Virginia Woolf, *Three Guineas* (London: Penguin
Books, 1977). See also Herbert Marder, *Feminism and
Art: A Study of Virginia Woolf* (Chicago: The Univ. of
Chicago Press, 1968), pp. 2-3.

34.   See Elin Wägner, *Väckarklocka* (Stockholm: Bonniers,
1978). First issued in 1941.

35. See Ronny Ambjörnsson, *Samhällsmodern: Ellen Keys kvinno-
     uppfattning till och med 1896* (Göteborgs univ. Institu-
     tionen för idé- och lärdomshistoria, 1974), pp. 47-50,
     250-256. In Ambjörnsson's summary in English, pp.
     257-281, "Samhällsmodern" is translated as the "social
     mother."

36. The concept of a "female culture" was first formulated
     by the Norwegian psychologist Berit Ås. She was not
     primarily concerned with the ideological content of
     female culture but wanted to prove its existence and
     its value as an area of study and as a platform for
     feminist struggle. She did, however, propose that the
     ideology of female culture "stems from women's participa-
     tion in unpaid production," and she pointed to such
     values as "cleanliness" and "conserving" to indicate
     typically female behaviour. See Berit Ås, "On female
     culture: an attempt to formulate a theory of women's
     solidarity and action," *Acta Sociologica. Journal of
     the Scandinavian Sociological Association*, Vol. 18,
     No. 2-3, pp. 142-161. The female characteristics
     associated with the concept of a female culture and
     their social and political impact are discussed by
     Louise Waldén in "När det osynliga blir synligt för-
     ändras världen. Om kvinnokulturens materiella bas."
     (When the Invisible Is Made Visible the World Will Be
     Changed. On the Material Basis of a Female Culture),
     Vi mänskor, 29, No 4 (1977), pp. 10-13.

37. See Ambjörnsson, pp. 20-57, 250-255, 257-266, 279-281.
     In her work on the Victorian woman Françoise Basch
     states that from the 1830's to the 1870's the English
     feminist movement did not question the bourgeois notion
     of the woman in the family. See Basch, *La Femme
     Victorienne: Roman et Societé, 1837-1867.* (Service de
     Réproduction des Thèses: Université de Lille, 1972),
     pp. 32-35.

38. In note 3 above, where I discuss the connections between
     female consciousness and the mysticism of FGC, I have
     shown that several critics emphasize that Lessing's
     women only realize their female identities indirectly
     through mysticism or madness. To these critical inter-
     pretations one can add that of Sukenick who strongly
     underlines Lessing's thorough-going scepticism towards
     emotional and personal experiences of life. Sukenick
     argues that Lessing's concern with the irrational
     element should not be seen as a cultivation of emotional
     and personal states of mind but as a political interest
     and as a means of "circumvent|ing| the personal, an area
     of experience about which she has always been ambiva-
     lent." See Sukenick, pp. 531-532.

39. See Hendin, p. 84.

40. This issue is touched upon by Sukenick who argues that
     Lessing has "little vindictiveness toward men" and
     stresses "woman's vulnerability" rather than man's
     "culpability." This attitude Sukenick relates to

Lessing's fear of the female psyche, especially its
tendencies toward emotional dependence and hysteria.
This scepticism toward female emotions can in Martha's
case be connected with her "matrophobia," according to
Sukenick.

Writing about GN, Morgan in a similar way claims
that Lessing's heroines have no real solidarity toward
other women and instead sympathize with men against
their own interests. This attitude Morgan ascribes to
Lessing's influence from a cultural climate which
ridicules feminism rather than searching for its roots
within Lessing's own vision.

See Sukenick, pp. 519, 523; Ellen Morgan, "Alienation of the Woman Writer in *The Golden Notebook*,"
Contemporary Literature, 14 (1973), pp. 471-480.

41. In addition to the references given in note 5,
    Introduction, see Howe, p. 425.

42. See Howe, p. 425.

43. See Haas, p. 5; cf. Preface, GN, pp. 14-15.

44. Doris Lessing explicitly refers to the issue of Stalin-
    ism in LL (pp. 248-249), GN (pp. 293, 257-259), and in
    her essay "The Small Personal Voice," which I will deal
    with further on in this section. Like many other British
    communist intellectuals, she denounced the Soviet
    intervention in Hungary in 1956 and criticized the
    British Communist Party leadership for its defence of
    the Soviet aggression. See Neal Wood, *Communism and
    British Intellectuals* (London: Victor Gollancz, 1959),
    pp. 196-208.

45. See, for example, Smith, pp. 8-9; Alcorn, pp. 4-44;
    Johnson, pp. 2-4.

46. "The Small Personal Voice," in *A Small Personal Voice*,
    pp. 11-12.

47. Cf. note 44 above.

48. "The Small Personal Voice," p. 17.

49. Ibid., pp. 18-19.

50. Ibid., p. 14.

51. The critics referred to in note 45 above exemplify the
    tendency to level out Doris Lessing's ideological devel-
    opment through an exclusive concern with her humanism.
    In Smith's case this leads to a simplified analysis of
    Children of Violence, which I have pointed out in the
    Survey of Research. Johnson's attitude is brought out
    in her claim that there is no relevant change in
    Lessing's political outlook from her first novel to
    the short story "The Temptation of Jack Orkney" (1972).
    Throughout Lessing has been concerned with individual
    responsibility, according to Johnson. In my opinion
    this statement is too generalized and disregards
    important shifts in Lessing's outlook on the individual.

For example, her views about individual responsibility
are ambiguous in her later work, an issue which I will
deal with subsequently.

Other critics who likewise decide that Lessing has
never been a communist but instead consistently embraces
humanism are Carey and Burkom. As already indicated in
note 21, Ch. II, Carey uses Lessing's description of
Anton Hesse to demonstrate her ideological orientation.
Burkom agrees with Carey and largely bases her analysis
on his. Most of the Lessing critics at some point make
pronouncements about her humanism - I will return to
other aspects of this critical discussion shortly.

See Smith, pp. 8-18; Johnson, p. 42; Carey, pp.
65-70; Burkom, pp. 78-79.

52.   The English socialist and feminist, Sheila Rowbotham,
may serve as an example of a woman who in her work
repeatedly stresses the need for the Left to include
the private sphere of life in its political theory
and practice. In *Women, Resistance and Revolution*
(London: Pelican Books, 1972) she makes the case that
if a revolutionary movement is to fully involve women
the "scope of production must be seen in a wider sense
and cover also the production undertaken by women in the
family and the production of self through sexuality"
(p. 246).

For information on Reich and Fromm, see the
reference given in note 5 above.

53.   See "Doris Lessing at Stony Brook," in *A Small Personal
Voice*, pp. 65-66.

In the statement referred to here Lessing indicates
her experience of an "all-pervasive violence." Such a
mood is also present in the comments on *Children of
Violence* that she makes after she had finished the first
three volumes. In 1963 she describes *Children of
Violence* in the following manner:

> The idea is to write about people like myself . . .
> who are born out of wars and who have lived through
> them. . . . I want to explain what it is like to be
> a human being in a century when you open your eyes
> on war and on human beings disliking other human
> beings.

See "Interview with Doris Lessing by Roy Newquist," in
A Small Personal Voice, p. 57.

54.   Cf. Johnson who claims that Lessing's Marxism expresses
a "religious impulse" (p. 7).

55.   See "Doris Lessing at Stony Brook," in *A Small Personal
Voice*, pp. 65-66, 70-72.

56.   "The Small Personal Voice," p. 7.

57.   See the postscript to *Going Home*, written in 1967, pp.
316-317. See also the interview with Jonah Raskin where
Lessing expresses her strong concern with "the preservation of liberties" (*A Small Personal Voice*, p. 73).

58. "Doris Lessing at Stony Brook," in *A Small Personal Voice*, p. 84.

59. See, for example, Hendin, p. 84.

60. As suggested in note 51 above, Lessing's humanism is a major concern much discussed among her critics. Most critics point to her humanist aspirations in "The Small Personal Voice," and claim that this pathos informs all of her work. Brook's assertion that Lessing constantly expresses a faith in the human being is typical. This faith is most clearly dramatized through the "utopian dreams and high aspirations" of the characters in her later works, according to Brooks. Martha's special visionary abilities serve as a "key to the future," which demonstrates her consistent pursuance of a humanitarian goal. Similar views are expressed by Smith, and by Marchino. Another variant of this argument is the stress on wholeness as a key to Lessing's humanism. This stance is taken by Burkom, who sees the "new" children as embodiments of this wholeness, and by Grant.

   Certain critics, however, question or qualify the humanism of Lessing's later works. Johnson demonstrates a dualism in Lessing's work, which qualifies the notion of her faith in mankind. Johnson shows that Lessing divides humanity into "us" and "them": the new children of FGC are contrasted with the evil officials; Charles Watkins of Briefing has a split personality - the social side of him is evil, and the inner side is good; and in Memoirs the "survivors" are contrasted with the rest of humanity. Johnson sees this dualism as a central thorough-going tension in Lessing's work, which stems from the conflict between her utopian beliefs and her awareness of political realities. All of Johnson's examples are, however, taken from Lessing's later period, where the split between inner and outer reality is a dominant feature.

   Wells also questions Lessing's faith in humanity. She suggests that the idea of the new children implies that Lessing's "deep and persistent humanism" fails her at the end of FGC. Here, Wells claims, "she gives up her hope that the human race will be able to survive through the efforts of intelligent and concerned human beings such as Martha." Without being explicit about it, Wells here approaches the issue of Lessing's ambiguous treatment of the value of the critical and reflective consciousness in FGC. Wells's view of the new children also brings up the question of the evolutionary, deterministic tendency in Lessing's later books. Both these questions are discussed by Draine. She makes the case that from FGC onwards, Lessing retreats into an irrational system of belief which involves the obliteration of the reflective consciousness and the invocation of apocalypse. Draine does not refer to Lessing's humanism when she makes these comments, but her observations are relevant in this context.

See Brooks, pp. 47, 496-497; Smith, p. 283; Marchino, pp. 8, 204; Burkom, p. 132; Grant, pp. 10, 108; Johnson, pp. 7-8, 126-128, 145-147, 205, 230-233; Wells p. 252; Draine, pp. 260-264.

61. As I have indicated in the Survey of Research, Draine and Sims are concerned with Lessing's determinism. Draine is most relevant for my discussion here, since she claims that Lessing's characters can become conscious of and act upon the evolutionary force in a way which leads the human race forwards in its development. Sims stresses the cultivation of the interior life as a solution to the cyclic pattern she observes, and she seems less concerned with the social and political impact of Lessing's determinism.

As should be clear from my analysis, I find it highly debatable that Lessing's characters can *act* upon the evolutionary force in any way that is significant to the welfare of society. Draine herself also does admit that basically Lessing's evolutionary idea is deterministic. Draine sees all of Lessing's work as deterministic; according to her, the evolutionary concept replaces a Marxist notion that is equally deterministic. This I disagree with. As pointed out in section 2 of this chapter, I consider the materialist consciousness that dominates *Children of Violence*, I-III, to be non-deterministic, as it gives rise to a social criticism which contains the promise of collective and individual change. In this context I differ not only from Draine but also from other critics. Vlastos, for example, maintains that Lessing's earlier works are stamped by "historical determinism." As I have suggested in my discussion of Lessing's humanism in note 60 above, critics generally see the evolution of consciousness as an instrument through which the individual can influence his or her own life and that of society in a positive direction.

See Draine, pp. 253-254, see also *DAI*, 38, No. 4 (1977), p. 2138-A; Vlastos, p. 245.

62. Doris Lessing, The Situation of Modern Man," public lecture at Göteborg, 9 Nov. 1970.

63. See Driver, p. 21.

Bibliography

Works by Doris Lessing

Novels:

The Grass Is Singing. London: Michael Joseph, 1950.

Martha Quest. |*Children of Violence*, Vol. I.| London: Michael Joseph, 1952.

A Proper Marriage. |*Children of Violence*, Vol. II.| London: Michael Joseph, 1954.

Retreat to Innocence. London: Michael Joseph, 1956.

A Ripple from the Storm. |*Children of Violence*, Vol. III.| London: Michael Joseph, 1958.

The Golden Notebook. London: Michael Joseph, 1962.

Landlocked. |*Children of Violence*, Vol. IV.| London: MacGibbon & Kee, 1965.

The Four-Gated City. |*Children of Violence*, Vol. V.| London: MacGibbon & Kee, 1969.

Briefing for a Descent into Hell. London: Jonathan Cape, 1971.

The Summer Before the Dark. London: Jonathan Cape, 1973.

The Memoirs of a Survivor. London: The Octagon Press, 1974.

Shikasta: Canopus in Argos-Archives. London: Jonathan Cape, 1979.

Autobiographical narrative:

Going Home. Rev. ed. London: Panther Books, 1968.

Articles, essays, interviews:

"The Small Personal Voice." In *Declaration.* Ed. Tom Maschler. London: MacGibbon & Kee, 1957, pp. 12-27.

"An Elephant in the Dark." *The Spectator*, 18 Sept. 1964, p. 373.

"An Ancient Way to New Freedom." *Vouge*, July 1971, pp. 98, 125, 130-131.

"What Looks Like an Egg and Is an Egg?" *New York Times Book Review*, 7 May 1972, pp. 6, 41-43.

"In the World, Not of It." *Encounter*, August 1972, pp. 61-64.

Preface. *The Golden Notebook*. London: Panther Books, 1973,
                    pp. 7-22.

A Small Personal Voice: Essays, Reviews, Interviews. Ed. Paul
                    Schlueter. New York: Alfred A. Knopf,
                    1974.

Unprinted material:

"The Situation of Modern Man." Lecture at Göteborg, 9 Nov.
                    1970.

Secondary Works

Alcorn, Noeline Elizabeth. "Vision and Nightmare: A Study of
                    Doris Lessing's Novels." Diss. Univ.
                    of California, Irvine 1971.

Ambjörnsson, Ronny. *Samhällsmodern: Ellen Keys kvinnouppfatt-
                    ning till och med 1896*. Diss. Göteborgs
                    universitet. Institutionen för idé- och
                    lärdomshistoria, 1974.

Basch, Françoise. *Le Femme Victorienne: Roman et Societé
                    1837-1867*. Diss. Service de Réproduction
                    des Thèses: Université de Lille, 1972.

Beauvoir, Simone de. *The Second Sex*. London: Penguin Books,
                    1972.

Brewster, Dorothy. *Doris Lessing*. New York: Twayne Publishers,
                    1965.

Brooks, Ellen W. "Fragmentation and Integration: A Study of
                    Doris Lessing's Fiction." Diss. New York
                    Univ. 1971.

Buckley, Jerome. *Season of Youth*. Cambridge: Harward Univ.
                    Press, 1974.

Burkom, Selma. "A Reconciliation of Opposites: A study of
                    the Works of Doris Lessing." Diss. Univ. of
                    Minnesota 1970.

Carey, Alfred Augustine. "Doris Lessing: The Search for
                    Reality. A Study of the Major
                    Themes in her Novels." Diss. Univ.
                    of Wisconsin 1965.

Cederstrom, Lorelei. "From Marxism to Myth: A Developmental
                    Study of the Novels of Doris Lessing."
                    DAI, 38 (1978), p. 7320-A. (The Univ.
                    of Manitoba.)

Doris Lessing: Critical Studies. Ed. Annis Pratt, and L.S.
                           Dembo. Madison: The Univ.
                           of Wisconsin Press, 1974.

Draine, Mary Elizabeth. "Stages of Consciousness in Doris
                           Lessing's Fiction." Diss. Temple Univ.
                           1977.

─────────   *DAI*, 38 (1977), p. 2138-A.

Driver, C.J. "Profile 8: Doris Lessing." *The New Review*, 1,
           No. 8 (1974), pp. 17-23.

Engels, Friedrich. *Ursprung der Familie, des Privateigenthums
                   und des Staats.* Hottingen-Zürich, 1884.

Erikson, Erik H. "Womanhood and the Inner Space." *Women &
                 Analysis.* Ed. Jean Strouse. New York:
                 Grossman Publishers, 1974, pp. 291-319.

Freud, Sigmund. *An Outline of Psychoanalysis.* London: The
                 Hogarth Press, 1973.

─────────   "Some Psychological Consequences of the
                 Anatomical Distinctions Between the Sexes."
                 In *Women & Analysis.* Ed. Jean Strouse. New
                 York: Grossman Publishers, 1974, pp. 17-26.

Fromm, Erich. *The Fear of Freedom.* London: Routledge & Kegan
             Paul, 1942.

Grant, Velma Fudge. "The Quest for Wholeness in Novels by
                    Doris Lessing." Diss. State Univ. of
                    New Jersey 1974.

Graustein, Gottfried. "Entwicklungstendenzen im Schaffen
                      Doris Lessings." Diss. Univ. of
                      Leipzig 1963.

Haas, Joseph. "Doris Lessing: Chronicler of the Cataclysm."
             Chicago Daily News, 14 June 1969, pp. 4-5.

Halliday, Patricia Ann Young. "The Pursuit of Wholeness in the
                              Works of Doris Lessing: Dualities,
                              Multiplicities, and the Resolu-
                              tion of Patterns in Illumination."
                              Diss. Univ. of Minnesota 1973.

Hardin, Nancy Shields. "Doris Lessing and the Sufi Way."
                       Contemporary Literature, 14 (1973),
                       pp. 565-581.

─────────   "The Sufi Teaching Story and Doris
                       Lessing." *Twentieth Century Literature*,
                       23 (1977), pp. 314-326.

Hendin, Josephine. "Doris Lessing: The Phoenix 'Midst Her
                   Fires." *Harper's*, June 1973, pp. 82-86.

Horney, Karen. "Feminine Psychology." In *New Ways in Psycho-
               analysis.* New York: W.W. Norton & Co., 1939,
               pp. 101-119.

─────────   "The Flight from Womanhood." In *Women &
               Analysis.* Ed. Jean Strouse. New York: Gross-
               man Publishers, 1974, pp. 171-186.

Howe, Florence. "A Conversation with Doris Lessing (1966)."
          Contemporary Literature, 14 (1973), pp. 418-436.

Johnson, Sally Hickerson. "Form and Philosophy in the Novels
          of Doris Lessing." Diss. Univ. of
          Connecticut 1976.

Jung, Carl G. "Approaching the Unconscious." In *Man and His
          Symbols*. Ed. Carl G. Jung. London: Pan Books,
          1978, pp. 1-94.

————   "Psychology and Religion."

————   "The Relations between the Ego and the Un-
          conscious." Both in *The Basic Writings of
          C.J. Jung*. Ed. Violet Staub de Laszlo. New
          York: Random House, 1959, pp. 469-530;
          105-182.

Kaplan, Bert. *The Inner World of Mental Illness*. New York:
          Harper and Row, 1964.

Kaplan, Sidney Janet. *Feminine Consciousness in the Modern
          British Novel*. Urbana: Univ. of
          Illinois Press, 1975.

Karl, Frederick R. "Doris Lessing in the Sixties: The New
          Anatomy of Melancholy." *Contemporary
          Literature*, 13 (1972), pp. 15-33.

Kildahl, Karen A. "The Political and Apocalyptical Novels of
          Doris Lessing: A Critical Study of *Children
          of Violence, The Golden Notebook, Briefing
          for a Descent into Hell*." Diss. Univ. of
          Washington 1974.

————   *DAI*, 35 (1975), p. 4528-A.

Krouse, Agate Nesaule. "A Doris Lessing Checklist." *Con-
          temporary Literature*, 14 (1973),
          pp. 591-593.

————   "The Feminism of Doris Lessing." Diss.
          Univ. of Wisconsin 1972.

Laing, R.D. *The Politics of Experience*. New York: Pantheon
          Books, 1967.

Laing, R.D., and Esterson, A. *Sanity, Madness and the Family*.
          London: Pelican Books, 1970.

Magie, Michael L. "Doris Lessing and Romanticism." *College
          English*, 38 (1977), pp. 531-552.

Marchino, Lois Anette. "The Search for Self in the Novels of
          Doris Lessing." Diss. Univ. of New
          Mexico 1972.

Marder, Herbert. *Feminism and Art: A Study of Virginia Woolf*.
          Chicago: The Univ. of Chicago Press, 1968.

Markow, Alice Bradley. "The Pathology of Feminine Failure in
          the Fiction of Doris Lessing." *Critique*,
          '16 (1975), pp. 88-100.

Mitchell, Tamara K. "The Irrational Element in Doris Lessing's Fiction." Diss. Boston Univ. 1978.

Morgan, Ellen. "Alienation of the Woman Writer in *The Golden Notebook*." *Contemporary Literature*, 14 (1973), pp. 471-480.

Poster, Mark. *Critical Theory of the Family*. London: Pluto Press, 1978.

Rapping, Elayne Antler. "Unfree Women: Feminism in Doris Lessing's Novels." *Women's Studies*, 3 (1975), pp. 29-44.

Register, Cheri. "American Feminist Literary Criticism: A Bibliographical Introduction." *In Feminist Literary Criticism: Explorations in Theory*. Ed. Josephine Donovan. The Univ. Press of Kentucky, 1975, pp. 1-28.

Rigney, Barbara Hall. "Madness and Sexual Politics in the Feminist Novel: Studies of Charlotte Brontë, Virginia Woolf and Doris Lessing." Diss. Ohio State Univ. 1977.

Rose, Ellen Cronan. "Doris Lessing's *Children of Violence* as a Bildungsroman: An Eriksonian Analysis." Diss. University of Massachusetts, 1974.

Rowbotham, Sheila. *Woman's Consciousness, Man's World*. London: Pelican Books, 1973.

————— *Women, Resistance and Revolution*. London: Pelican Books, 1974.

Schlueter, Paul. *The Novels of Doris Lessing*. Carbondale: Southern Illinois Univ. Press, 1973.

————— "A Study of the Major Novels of Doris Lessing." Diss. Southern Illinois Univ. 1968.

Seligman, Claudia Dee. "The Autobiographical Novels of Doris Lessing." Diss. Tufts Univ. 1976.

————— Ed. *Doris Lessing Newsletter*, 3, No. 1 ('79), p. 3.

————— "The Sufi Quest." *World Literature Written in English*, 12 (1973), pp. 190-206.

Shah, Idries. *The Magic Monastery*. London: Jonathan Cape, 1972.

————— *The Sufis*. London: W.H. Allen, 1964.

————— *The Way of the Sufi*. London: Jonathan Cape, 1968.

Sims, Susan K. Swan. "Repetition and Evolution: An Examination of Themes and Structures in the Novels of Doris Lessing." Diss. Univ. of Oregon 1978.

Singleton, Mary Ann. *The City and the Veld: The Fiction of Doris Lessing*. Lewisburg: Bucknell Univ. Press, 1977.

———————— "The City and the Veld: A Study of the Fiction of Doris Lessing." Diss. Univ. of Oregon 1973. (In Dissertation Abstracts Singleton is listed under *Naumer*, Mary Ann Singleton).

Smith, Diane E. Sherwood. "A Thematic Study of Doris Lessing's *Children of Violence*. Diss. Loyola Univ. of Chicago 1971.

Spacks, Patricia Meyer. *The Female Imagination*. New York: Avon Books, 1972.

Sukenick, Lynn. "Feeling and Reason in Doris Lessing's Fiction." *Contemporary Literature*, 14 (1973), pp. 515-535.

———————— "Sense and Sensibility in Women's Fiction: Studies in the Novels of George Eliot, Virginia Woolf, Anaïs Nin, and Doris Lessing." Diss. City Univ. of New York 1974.

Vlastos, Marion, "Doris Lessing and R.D. Laing: Psycho-politics and Prophecy." *PMLA*, 91 (1976), pp. 245-258.

Waldén, Louise. "När det osynliga blir synligt förändras världen: Om kvinnokulturens materiella bas." *Vi mänskor*, 29, No. 4 (1977), pp. 10-13.

Walter, Donna Joanne. "Twentieth-Century Woman in the Early Novels of Doris Lessing." Diss. Univ. of Tennessee 1978.

Watt, Ian. *The Rise of the Novel*. London: Peregrine Books, 1963.

Wells, Dorothy Bergquist. "The Unity of Doris Lessing's *Children of Violence*." Diss. Tulane Univ. 1976.

Wichmann, Brigitte. "From Sex-Role Identification toward Androgyny: A Study of Major Works of Simone de Beauvoir, Doris Lessing, and Christa Wolf." Diss. Purdue Univ. 1978.

Wood, Neal. *Communism and British Intellectuals*. London: Victor Gollancz, 1959.

Woolf, Virginia, *Three Guineas*. London: Penguin Books, 1977.

Wägner, Elin. *Väckarklocka*. Stockholm, Bonniers, 1978.

Zak, Michele Wender. "Feminism and the New Novel." Diss. The Ohio State Univ. 1973.

Zaretsky, Eli. *Capitalism, the Family, and Personal Life*. London: Pluto Press, 1976.

Ås, Berit. "On female culture: an attempt to formulate a theory of women's solidarity and action." *Acta Sociologica. Journal of the Scandinavian Sociological Association*, Vol. 18, No. 2-3, pp. 142-161.